The Early Elizabethan Succession Question
1558–1568

The Early Elizabethan Succession Question
1558–1568

Mortimer Levine

1966
STANFORD UNIVERSITY PRESS
STANFORD CALIFORNIA

Stanford University Press
Stanford, California
© 1966 by the Board of Trustees of the
Leland Stanford Junior University
Printed in the United States of America
L.C. 66-17563

To the memory
of
Conyers Read

Preface

This book is a revision of a dissertation submitted in 1954 for the degree of Doctor of Philosophy at the University of Pennsylvania. Though happily shorter in length, it is more than the usual revision for publication. Books and articles that have appeared since 1954, and further research of my own, have raised new questions and suggested new approaches. The result is a work of somewhat expanded scope and, I hope, of more mature scholarship.

I must acknowledge my gratitude to those who have helped me prepare this work: to the staffs of the Public Record Office, the British Museum, the Bodleian Library, the Cambridge University Library, the Library of the Institute of Historical Research, the Princeton University Library, the University of Pennsylvania Library, and the West Virginia University Library for numerous services; to West Virginia University for a research grant in 1963; to Dean C. M. Frasure and Professor W. T. Doherty of West Virginia University for a reduced teaching load in 1965; to Provost J. F. Golay of West Virginia University for deeply appreciated encouragement; to Librarian R. F. Munn of West Virginia University for listening that certainly went beyond the call of duty; to Professor R. L. Johnson of Hunter College for reading an earlier and partial draft of this work; to Professor Holden Furber of the University of Pennsylvania for his critical reading of my dissertation and for reading the whole of this book in manuscript; and to Jacob Levine, my father, for a careful job of proofreading.

I am indebted in many ways to Sir John Neale, sometime Astor Professor of English History in the University of London. Sir John's comprehensive bibliography of manuscripts at the British Museum that deal with the succession was made available to me by Professor Conyers Read prior to my departure for England in 1952. During my stay in England Sir John extended several kindnesses to me. He permitted me to attend his famous seminar at the Institute of Historical Research; he allowed me to examine pertinent chapters in his then unpublished first volume on Elizabeth and her Parliaments; he discussed many matters with me, and offered valuable advice and suggestions. It was Sir John who first made me aware of the significance of *Gorboduc* to my subject. What I owe to his works should be apparent in my chapters on the Parliaments of 1563 and 1566. I am, of course, most grateful for his kind permission to use his first volume on Elizabeth's Parliaments, and to quote liberally from his authoritative versions of two of the Queen's speeches made in the Parliament of 1566.

I owe my largest debt to Conyers Read, late Professor of English History in the University of Pennsylvania. My decision to make Tudor history my field of specialization was primarily inspired by his lecture courses; it was in his seminar that my interests were directed toward the subject of this book. Letters from Professor Read and the use of his name opened many doors to me while I was in England. From his retirement to his death, his residence at Villanova was always open to me for scholarly purposes of every sort. Professor Read was particularly helpful to me in matters concerning Sir William Cecil, and acquainted me with pertinent material from his biography of that great Tudor statesman before its publication. His influence has doubtless prevented me from going too far astray in considering the unsupported conclusions often made about Cecil's succession activities and preferences. But really my many debts to Professor Read are impossible to record in a preface. As a small payment I have dedicated this book to his memory.

M. L.

Contents

Introduction

This work admittedly and unashamedly deals with an abortive history. That the early Elizabethan succession question eventually became no question was largely due to accident: the long life of a queen, the death of one lady, and the folly and ill luck of another. Men of the first decade of the reign of Elizabeth I, who could not foresee the accidents that would make possible the easy solution of 1603, had to live with and face the question of succession. It hung over them like no other issue. It was above all a question of whether the next wearer of the crown should come from the line of Stuart or that of Suffolk. This was a vital question in an age when the monarch still ruled as well as reigned, and when men were still haunted by the memory of the Wars of the Roses. It was far from being simply a legal problem; such issues as Catholic or Protestant, war or peace, anarchy or security, were also involved. Moreover, the succession question played a role in the diplomacy of the period; it shared responsibility for developments in Scotland; it helped divide English domestic politics; it had significant manifestations in parliamentary history. In short, it embraced a good deal more than may be apparent at first glance. Therefore, we deal with a history that, although abortive, is important to what is still the historian's basic task, the attempt to recreate the past as it actually was.

Until now no full study of the most important period of the succession question, 1558 to 1568, has been published. Perhaps because of this, textbooks and general works usually tend either to ignore it or to assume that Mary Queen of Scots was without doubt Elizabeth's heir presumptive, and that the only opposition to her claim was religious or political. Of course, certain aspects of the story have been capably handled by eminent historians. The parliamentary field has been rather thoroughly covered by Sir John Neale. Much of the story of Mary Stuart and the succession has been investigated by Father Pollen. Professor Pollard has made a penetrating, though recently challenged, analysis of the authenticity of the will of Henry VIII. Other significant aspects of the succession question, however, have not been dealt with satisfactorily. Books on the Suffolks have been, for the most part, popular accounts by somewhat biased commentators. No real attempt has been made to solve the problem of the legitimacy of the Suffolk claimants. Nor has the question of the eligibility of an alien to ascend the throne been considered adequately. The succession activities of John Hales and the storm created by them have not been discussed as fully as they deserve to be. And the succession tracts of the period have not received sufficient attention. It is my hope to remedy these defects, to add something to the contributions already made, and to put together as coherent an account as possible.

PART I

The Conditions of the Question

1. *The Succession Situation at the Accession of Elizabeth I*

When the first Elizabeth ascended the English throne in November 1558, the question of succession in one way or another had plagued the Tudor monarchy since its birth on Bosworth Field. Bosworth may have terminated the Wars of the Roses, but neither it nor the subsequent marriage of Henry VII and Elizabeth of York put the succession question to rest. The conspiracies and executions of Henry's reign testify to this. Even Henry VIII, England's most indisputably lawful sovereign since Richard II, was not free from worry about the succession. The complicated business of Henry's first three marriages can largely be explained in terms of his desire for a son, a desire born out of fear that England might hesitate to accept a daughter as his successor. Even the birth of Prince Edward did not satisfy Henry that the problem was safely solved, as can be seen from his Third Succession Act and his last will. The brief reign of Edward VI, as is well known, concluded with the Duke of Northumberland's futile attempt to set aside Mary and Elizabeth in favor of the Suffolk claimant, Lady Jane Grey. Mary I's reign was troubled by plots, real and alleged, to replace the Catholic and half-Spanish Queen with Elizabeth. This nearly caused Mary to hasten the extinction of the Tudor line by sending her half sister to the block. In November 1558 the past boded ill for the future.

Elizabeth's accession promised to aggravate the succession question. Though welcome enough at home as a fully English Tudor, Anne Boleyn's daughter was a bastard in the eyes of

Catholic Europe. And Mary Queen of Scots, the daughter-in-law of Henry II of France, had the next hereditary claim to the English crown. Even before the Parliament of 1559 restored "Protestantism," Henry had begun activities in Rome aimed at having Paul IV declare Elizabeth illegitimate and Mary Stuart to be Mary I's rightful successor.[1] By the time the religious legislation was completed, England and France had concluded their war at Cateau-Cambrésis, but Henry followed up the peace by inducing the Scottish Queen to make an open display of her pretensions to Elizabeth's throne by assuming the title and arms of England.[2] This signified that the Stuart claim was already asserted: asserted not for the succession to Elizabeth but for her very crown.

The picture, however, was not as dark as it may appear. Mary Stuart's claim was more than unpopular in England during the time she was Queen Dauphiness or Queen of France (April 1558 to December 1560). Likewise it was odious to Philip II of Spain, Europe's greatest Catholic prince, who wrote about how convenient it would be if Mary should pass away.[3] Moreover, the Frenchman's bark was worse than his bite after Cateau-Cambrésis. Nevertheless, the situation was serious and subject to change.[4] England's position was insecure. Two facts loomed large on the horizon: Elizabeth was the last remaining Tudor, and Mary was next in line according to blood.

The obvious way out of this predicament was for Elizabeth to marry and have issue. This seemed no problem. The Queen of England was the greatest matrimonial prize in Christendom. She could choose a consort from numerous candidates, foreign and domestic. Perhaps the most advantageous selection would be the readily obtainable Archduke Charles.[5] This Hapsburg-Tudor match would assure Elizabeth of Philip II's backing in the event of any future Stuart threat, but would not necessarily commit England to anything more than the loss of the Queen's virginity.* And nothing could more ensure the loyalty of England to Elizabeth than a son.

---

* *Burghley Papers*, I, 444. Charles might be expected to accept England's religious status quo. Klarwill, p. 29. Complete data on works cited in the footnotes are given in the Bibliography, pp. 231–38.

But the Queen had told the Parliament of 1559 of her preference to live and die a virgin.[6] Though her words could not have
been taken too seriously at the time, rumors were soon circulating that she would never marry because she was incapable of
bearing children.[7] It is unlikely that there was any foundation
for this idea other than the imaginations of those who spread
it about, but it is possible that Elizabeth herself had fears that
it was true, given the tragic experiences of her sister.[8] At any
rate, the Queen's flitting from suitor to suitor was cause for worry. Past performances indicated that it was not wise to gamble
on either the life expectancy or the procreativity of a child of
Henry VIII.

In this atmosphere it was only natural that many people
would turn their attention to the succession and to the idea
of establishing a satisfactory alternative to the Queen of Scots.
There was no lack of potential claimants to choose from, but
most of their claims were too distant to merit serious consideration.[9] A selection could not be justified on the mere basis of
remote descent from Edward III. Therefore, we need only discuss a few likely candidates before turning to Lady Catherine
Grey, Mary Stuart's main rival.

One of these was Henry Hastings, Earl of Huntingdon, a
scion of the White Rose. Sir William Cecil once told Bishop
Quadra, the credulous Spanish ambassador, that Huntingdon
was the real heir of England because Henry VII had usurped
the realm from the House of York.[10] Secretary Cecil doubtless
knew better. Huntingdon's Yorkist title was clearly inferior to
that of any Tudor, Stuart, or Suffolk who descended from Elizabeth of York.* Nonetheless, the Earl was an important claimant for several reasons, his sex not the least of them. In 1560
Quadra reported: "The cry is that they do not want any more
women rulers."[11] Huntingdon's patronage of the Puritans won
him adherents among those inclined to the religious "left."[12]
Another source of the Earl's strength was his influence and popularity in his native Leicestershire.[13] But probably the greatest

* See Appendix, charts I and V. This would not be true if Elizabeth of York
had been illegitimate. The charge against her is discussed and rejected in
Levine, "Richard III."

factor was the support he received at Court from his brother-in-law, Lord Robert Dudley.*[14]

Huntingdon's prospects seem to have reached their high point about the time of the Parliament of 1563. On its eve Quadra wrote that Elizabeth was determined to declare the Earl her successor, no matter what the opposition.[15] This would have been about the last thing to enter her mind, but there evidently was some truth in Quadra's later estimate that many of the Commons favored Huntingdon in 1563.[16] It seems probable, however, that these were Dudley's followers rather than Huntingdon's. After 1563 the Earl's importance as a claimant apparently declined. Dudley was too much an opportunist to be a steadfast supporter. His interests doubtless were transferred elsewhere in 1564, when Elizabeth created him Earl of Leicester, evidently hoping to make him acceptable to the Queen of Scots as a husband.† Eventually the "heretics," as Quadra called them, appear to have concluded that it would be best to unite behind one claimant, who was not Huntingdon but Lady Catherine Grey. It is unlikely that he had any real strength in the Parliament of 1566, by which time we can probably dismiss him as a serious contender.

Two other candidates who cannot be ignored were Lady Margaret Lennox and her son, Lord Darnley. Their claims, like Mary Stuart's, came from their descent from Henry VII via his daughter Margaret. Though the Scottish Queen had the superior hereditary right, it was possible to argue that the Lennox title was the better one on the ground that both mother and son were born in England. It could be objected here, however, that the Englishry of their descent was broken because Lady Margaret's parents were not under allegiance to the King of England at the time of her birth.[17] And the will of Henry VIII, which favored the Suffolk line, presented the same obstacle to the Lennox Stuarts as it did to Mary Stuart. Moreover, there

---

* Since 1553 Huntingdon had been married to Lord Robert's sister, the former Lady Catherine Dudley.

† Steuart, pp. 91–92. This is not meant to imply that Dudley wanted to marry Mary. He probably supported the Darnley match in the hope that it would lead to his marrying Elizabeth. Read, *Cecil*, pp. 315, 488.

was another matter that could be brought up against them: Lady Margaret's legitimacy was questionable.*

The Lennox claim had great appeal among Catholics, especially during the period when the Queen of Scots was also Queen of France.[18] After Mary's return to Scotland in August 1561, she began to be viewed more favorably by many English Catholics, but the Lennox Stuarts still held their own with other English Catholics who did not trust Mary's orthodoxy.[19] This difference of preference was also reflected in the policies of foreign Catholics. In 1562 Quadra apparently tried to get Philip II to promote a rebellion in Darnley's behalf; in the next year Quadra spent his last days working to bring about a match between Mary and Don Carlos, Philip's demented son.[20] The French, although not abandoning Mary, were perhaps thinking seriously of Margaret as an alternative, and were reported hoping to persuade Darnley to marry in France.[21] This confused situation came to an end in July 1565, when Mary married Darnley. The merger of the Stuart claims really amounted to an absorption of the Lennox one. Little was heard of it after that.

One more candidate who may deserve mention was Lady Margaret Strange, wife of Henry Stanley, Lord Strange, son of the Earl of Derby. This Lady Margaret represented the junior branch of the Suffolk line; hence her hereditary title was inferior to those of her cousins of the senior branch, Ladies Catherine and Mary Grey. As early as 1557, however, it was reported that Lady Margaret had alleged that the Ladies Grey were excluded from the succession because their elder sister, Lady Jane, had corrupted their blood by her treason. Consequently, she could claim to be next in line by the will of Henry VIII and "as the nearest in blood . . . legitimately of English birth."[22] This case was based on an unacceptable premise: that the common-law rule against inheritance by persons of attainted blood ap-

---

* Her father, Archibald Douglas, Earl of Angus, obtained a divorce from Margaret Tudor on the ground of a precontract. Because of this, Lady Margaret was not allowed to inherit from her father and was openly reputed a bastard in Scotland. *CSP, For.*, ser. iii, V, 14–15, and VI, 223–24; *Burghley Papers,* I, 381.

plied to the succession. The precedents of the preceding hundred years stood against it;* so would the opinions of Elizabethan writers of various religious and political complexions.[23]

Lady Margaret Strange probably never had much backing for her rather weak claims. She may have derived some support from having married into one of the more important Catholic families. The Earl of Derby was perhaps the most powerful figure in Lancashire.[24] But this was not enough to make his daughter-in-law an attractive candidate to Catholics. They had obviously better choices among the Stuarts. And Lady Margaret's Stanley connections would hardly impress Protestants who otherwise might have been interested in her as a Suffolk. Nevertheless, she evidently had some followers in the Parliament of 1563.[25] This support does not appear to have much outlived the Parliament. In 1565 Philip II wrote, "Some claim is put forward by Lord and Lady Lestrange, although I am given to understand that their party is much reduced in consequence of the poor esteem in which they are held."[26] There is no evidence of Lady Strange having any following in the Parliament of 1566, by which time we may consider her out of the running also, if indeed she ever really were in it.

We are now ready to turn our attention to Lady Catherine Grey, the Scottish Queen's chief competitor for the succession. Amid the confusion at the beginning of the reign, it was only to be expected that men would back claimants helter-skelter. It was at this time that Huntingdon, the Lennox Stuarts, and Lady Strange enjoyed their greatest popularity as succession prospects. But as the situation began to take shape more clearly and to be better understood, men tended to abandon these minor candidates and unite behind one or the other of the major ones, Mary Queen of Scots and Lady Catherine Grey. We meet some evidence of this in the Parliaments of 1563 and 1566. It really becomes manifest in the contemporary literature on

---

* Henry VI's attainder under Edward IV; Edward's probable attainder during Henry's "readeption"; Richard III's accession despite the attainder of his elder brother, George, Duke of Clarence; Henry VII's attainder under Richard. *Rotuli Parliamentorum*, V, 478, and VI, 193–94, 246–47; Fabyan, p. 660.

the succession, which was largely a debate over the respective rights of Mary and Catherine. The former obviously had the best Stuart claim; the latter clearly had the best Suffolk one. It was perhaps inevitable that the succession question would become almost entirely an issue between the Queen of Scots and Lady Jane Grey's sister. Considerations of justice, law, logic, and expediency all pointed to such a conclusion.

Now a case for Catherine Grey could not be presented along the lines usually followed in matters of succession. Mary Stuart undeniably had the better hereditary right. She was the granddaughter of Henry VII's elder daughter, Margaret Tudor, Queen of Scotland; Catherine Grey was a granddaughter of his younger daughter, Mary Tudor, Queen of France and Duchess of Suffolk. Nor could the purity of Mary Stuart's descent from Henry VII be disputed; indeed, she was his only living descendant whose lineage could not be challenged with a charge of bastardy by alleging a doubtful marriage.* The adherents of the Suffolk claim would not show to their best advantage if they brought up questions of blood.

But other arguments more favorable to Catherine Grey were available. One argument was that the common-law rule against an alien's inheriting ordinary property could be extended to the royal dignity. Mary Stuart was born in Scotland of a Scottish father and a French mother; Catherine Grey, like Elizabeth Tudor, was "mere English." This had patriotic as well as legal appeal. And there was the strong case that could be made from Henry VIII's will, which had appointed the line of his younger sister to the succession after his own children and their issue. It was mainly on these points, of Mary's foreign birth and Henry's testament, that Catherine's advocates staked her claim.

Perhaps Catherine alone among all the possible candidates for the succession had a really conceivable chance of winning out against Mary. The failure of her sister Jane in 1553 had shown that attempting to effect an obviously illegal limitation of the crown was futile, but there were significant distinctions

---

* The charge against Elizabeth is well-known. For the case against the Lennox Stuarts, see p. 9n. The legitimacy of the Suffolk descent is the subject of Chapter 8.

between the choices Mary Tudor or Jane Grey, and Mary Stuart or Catherine Grey. Mary Tudor was a daughter of King Henry VIII of famous memory; Jane Grey was merely a great-granddaughter of his father. Though Mary Stuart was of the senior line, both she and Catherine Grey were great-granddaughters of Henry VII. Such a difference in degree made the lack of the Tudor name seem like a difference in kind. Moreover, Mary Tudor had priority over Jane Grey according to the will of Henry VIII; the same testament preferred Catherine Grey to Mary Stuart, if indeed it did not exclude the Queen of Scots altogether. The difference here was manifest. Equally clear was the fact that Catherine Grey was more English than Mary Tudor, and Mary Stuart less English. Most Englishmen of the first decade of the reign of Elizabeth I, like those of 1553, probably thought that the question of a just title was more important than such questions as Catholic or Protestant, foreign or domestic, and Stuart or Grey. But there was a reasonable doubt whether Mary Queen of Scots or Lady Catherine Grey had the better claim. This left room for expediency to enter the situation. Men could surrender to the more convenient illusion with a clear conscience.

2. A Spanish Plot and a Clandestine Marriage

The first efforts in behalf of Catherine Grey probably came from a surprising source. The idea that Philip II, Mary I's consort, would support the succession of Jane Grey's sister seems absurd, until one considers the state of England at the beginning of Elizabeth's reign. At that time nothing would have been less to Spain's interest than to see Mary Stuart gain the English crown and doubtless make England a French satellite. Philip, not without some justification, feared the worst, and looked for an alternative to Mary in the event that something happened to Elizabeth.

In March 1559 the Count of Feria, Quadra's predecessor, regarded himself as a confidant of Catherine. He reported to Philip that she was "dissatisfied and offended" with Elizabeth, who did not want her as a successor and treated her poorly. Feria also informed his master that Catherine had promised that she would neither change her religion—she apparently had been a Catholic under Mary—nor marry Lord Henry Herbert, to whom she had once been engaged.[1] These promises opened the way for Spanish support of her claim. As a Catholic she would be a desirable alternative to Mary Stuart in the succession. If she did not marry Lord Herbert, a Hapsburg husband might be provided for her. The sister of Jane Grey might be the means for a future return to the days of Philip and Mary. Feria's report may well have inspired the weird scheme that was soon imputed to the Spaniards.

Our only source for the Spanish plot to abduct Catherine is Robert Hogan, an Englishman who claimed to be a party to it. His connections lend credence to his story. In Mary's reign Hogan had entered the service of Spain and participated in the Duke of Alva's attack on Rome. Both Philip and Alva regarded him highly.[2] After Elizabeth's accession he apparently offered his services to England as a spy against Spain. His loyalty to Elizabeth was later vouched for by Sir Thomas Gresham.[3] Sir Thomas Chaloner, the English ambassador to Spain, expressed no doubts about the veracity of Hogan's story in reporting it to Elizabeth from Flushing in August 1559.[4] Lacking evidence to the contrary and knowing from other sources of Spanish interest in Catherine, we may regard Hogan's account of the Spanish plot in a letter to Cecil as believable.

Hogan wrote that the "practice" was "more than three or four several times talked of with the full determination of what should be done therein." The idea arose out of fear that Henry II of France would take advantage of England's weakness to conquer her in behalf of the Queen of Scots. Philip II's Council decided that the best way to "geg" Henry was for Philip to have a title to the English throne,

for the attaining whereunto, if it might by any means be brought to pass, to practice the conveying out the realm the L[ady] K[atherine,] who is supposed to be the next heir unto the Crown of England, and, as it might fall out so, to provide in marriage for her, either the Prince his son [Don Carlos], or else some other of smaller personage, as occasion should serve.

It was expected that Catherine would readily consent to be abducted because she was not loved by her mother, Lady Frances Brandon, or her uncle, Lord John Grey of Pyrgo,* and was despised by Elizabeth. Lady Frances, Lord John's wife, Feria's wife, Lady Hungerford, Lady Montague, and the Earl of Arundel were named as contacts who might advise Catherine of the plan. Hogan, among others, was chosen by the Duke of Alva to be sent to England to serve Quadra in the matter.

---

* This is unlikely. Lady Frances spent her last days working in the interest of Catherine's desired marriage with the Earl of Hertford. *HM* 6286, pp. 46, 66–69, 78–79. Lord John treated his niece kindly when she was later placed in his custody. Ellis, ser. ii, II, 273–83.

It was thought good also that some ships should be sent unto England, which should lay within the Thames to attend only upon the Ambassador for this matter. It was thought that if she was so stolen away it would not be suspected otherwise than that some within the realm had done it, thinking to marry her, and not to convey her out of the realm for any marriage.

How far the execution of this plot progressed cannot be discerned from Hogan's letter. He did not know if any of the proposed contacts or Catherine herself had ever been made aware of the scheme. Nor does he tell if he or the ships actually went to England. He was sure that the plot would have been carried out if Henry II had not died (10 July 1559), but was uncertain whether the Spaniards had changed plans after that. It was his opinion that Philip feared Francis II less than he feared Henry. At any rate, Hogan heard no more about the plot after Henry's death.[5]

Nonetheless, Spanish interest in Catherine continued. In November 1559 Quadra wrote that a match between her and Archduke Charles would be in order if Elizabeth were to meet with a disaster (marry Lord Robert Dudley?).[6] In March 1560 it was reported from Brussels that "there is practicing for a marriage to be made betwixt the Prince of Spain and the Lady Catherine Grey, which is not of the best liked for diverse respects, and by some hindered."[7] This last indicates that there were cooler heads than Feria and Quadra among Philip's advisers. It seems likely that they eventually prevailed with the Prudent King to put the schemes of the fanatics to rest. By the end of 1560 the Spaniards probably thought of Catherine only as a card that might be played if future developments made it necessary. In October Quadra had reported to Philip that the English heretics feared "that if the Queen were to die without issue your Majesty would get the kingdom into your family by means of Lady Catherine."[8]

The fears of the heretics were not to be long-lived. On 12 August 1561 Cecil sent the Earl of Sussex news that would change the entire situation: "The tenth of this [month] at Ipswich was a great mishap discovered. The Lady Catherine is certainly known to be big with child, as she saith by the Earl of Hertford, who is in France. She is committed to the Tower. He is

sent for. She saith that she was married to him secretly before
Christmas last."[9] Edward Seymour, Earl of Hertford, was a son
of the Protestant Protector Somerset of Edward VI's reign—
the same son that Somerset intended to match with Lady Jane
Grey.[10] This meant that Catherine now had thrown off the mask
she had put on for Feria's benefit, and had committed herself
to the religion and the mate of her choice. Whatever Spanish
support she had must have come to an abrupt end when Quadra reported her imprisonment and its cause to his superiors.[11]
Catherine was now obviously the best succession candidate
available to the Protestants, though all of them did not see this
right away.

If Catherine's "great mishap" relieved an anxiety of the heretics, it did the reverse for their Queen. Elizabeth was quick to
assume that a conspiracy was involved. On 17 August she made
her feelings apparent in a letter of instructions to Sir Edward
Warner, Lieutenant of the Tower:

You shall . . . examine the Lady Catherine very straightly how many
hath been privy to the love betwixt the Earl of Hertford and her from
the beginning; and let her certainly understand that she shall have no
manner of favor except she will show the truth, not only what ladies
or gentlewomen of this Court were thereto privy, but also what lords
and gentlemen: for it doth now appear that sundry personages have
dealt therein. . . . It is certain that there hath been great practices and
purposes.[12]

Warner was unable to get Catherine to implicate anyone of consequence, but Elizabeth's suspicions were not allayed.[13]

One cannot blame the Queen for believing that there was
more behind the marriage than met the eye. She had reason to
regard Catherine's nearness to the crown as dangerous. She was
cognizant of the former machinations of the Spaniards.[14] Perhaps she remembered something about the Seymours' being interested in Jane Grey during her brother's reign.* The present
Edward Seymour was hardly the man his father was, but more
formidable figures could have been leading him on. His marriage with Catherine took place shortly after the mysterious

---

* Not only had Somerset been interested in mating Jane with his son, but
Lord Thomas Seymour had assumed her guardianship for dubious purposes.
Burghley Papers, I, 76, 80, 83, 94, 106.

death of Amy Robsart, Lord Robert Dudley's wife.* It was suspected that her death was not an accident, but a murder conceived to open the way for Elizabeth to marry Dudley. This
made plausible the conjecture that Dudley's enemies devised
the Grey-Seymour match as an insurance measure in case the
Queen abandoned caution and wed her Master of the Horse.
Then the sister of Jane Grey and the son of the "good" Duke of
Somerset might be set up against the sister of Mary Tudor and
the son of the "wicked" Duke of Northumberland. Such was the
indignation against Dudley that England might well have accepted the former combination over the latter.[15] Consequently,
it was only natural for Elizabeth to fear that the business of
Catherine and Hertford did not originate as an ordinary love
affair.

But was it a plot? According to Cecil investigation revealed
nothing of the sort: "Nobody can appear privy to the marriage,
nor to the love, but maids, or women going for maidens. The
Queen's Majesty thinketh, and so do others with her, that some
greater drift was in this; but for my part I can find none such."[16]
If there was "greater drift" in the matter, Secretary Cecil probably had the best means to discover it. It is possible, however,
that it was to his interest to belittle the affair; he may have been
involved. The only description of a plot that names names and
implicates people comes from the correspondence of Quadra.
Though this is not too reliable a source, it is reasonable to suppose that if there were a plot behind the marriage of Catherine
and Hertford, it would have followed the lines indicated by
Quadra.

His first account was in a letter of August 1561:

They were married secretly, although, according to suspicion, not
without knowledge and advice of some noblemen, and especially of
the Earl of Arundel, who they say attempted to marry my Lady Jane,
sister of . . . Hertford (who died a while ago), and favors the succession
of my Lady Catherine, in order to make king his would-be brother-in-
law, who is a young man of little enough substance, although very
heretical.[17]

---

* She died on 8 September 1560. Catherine and Hertford testified that they
were married sometime between Allhallows and Christmas 1560. *HM* 6286,
pp. 41, 48–49.

A letter of 6 September named the Earl of Bedford and John Jewel, Bishop of Salisbury, as Arundel's accomplices: "Cecil does not verify it in examining the Earl [Hertford], some think because of finding himself with some fault in this business. I only think that he has not wished to intervene because of having been the servant of the Duke of Somerset, the father of the Earl."[18] A week later Quadra changed his mind about Cecil when he sent Philip II his conclusions about the supposed plot:

> What I understand by it all is that both Lady Catherine's marriage, and the bringing over of the King of Sweden,* were arranged a year ago, after the death of Robert's wife, and that Cecil (who was then in great disgrace with the Queen and at enmity with Robert) was at the bottom of it, in the fear that, in accord with common belief, the Queen would marry Robert and restore religion to obtain your Majesty's favor. Since Cecil has returned to the good graces of the Queen, and has satisfied himself that there will be no change of religion, he has gradually and cautiously separated himself from these negotiations, and is now endeavoring to hush up and amend the past.[19]

Something can be said for Quadra's story. Jealousy could have brought the twelfth Earl of Arundel into such a scheme. Frustrated in his own suit for Elizabeth's hand, he must have been infuriated at the prospect of seeing one of the upstart Dudleys win the coveted prize.[20] The Earl of Bedford, a prominent Puritan, and Bishop Jewel, the author of the first significant defense of the Anglican Church, could have become parties to the affair for religious reasons.[21] If the Queen were to marry Dudley, a restoration of Catholicism would not be unlikely, since Spanish support probably would have been needed to meet opposition at home. And Cecil could have been "at the bottom of it" for fear of the political consequences of such a match. Cecil would have been the last one to want to see Lord Robert become "King Robert" and England become a virtual province of Spain. Moreover, the timing of the marriage of Catherine and Hertford, close at the heels of the death of Amy Robsart, does lend itself to suspicion.

One need not accept any of these points, however. The Cath-

---

* Eric XIV came to England in 1561 to woo Elizabeth. No plot was required to bring that determined suitor to England.

olic Arundel, who was later involved in conspiracies for Mary Stuart, seems out of place in an otherwise Protestant group of "plotters." Bedford and Jewel—in Elizabeth's reign at least—do not make likely figures as conspirators. Bedford proved a loyal and useful servant of the Queen.* Jewel's comment on the affair of Catherine and Hertford in a letter to a Protestant friend abroad hardly sounds like that of one of its instigators:

This affair has much disturbed the minds of many persons; for if this marriage is a legal one, the son now born will be brought up with the hope of succeeding to the crown.† O how wretched are we, who cannot tell under what sovereign we are to live! God will, I trust, long preserve Elizabeth to us in life and safety, and that will satisfy us.²²

And the testimony of the young couple themselves seems to absolve Cecil. On 17 February 1562 Hertford confessed that "before contract or marriage between him and ... Catherine it was said unto him by Mr. Secretary Cecil that it was said that there was good will between him and ... Catherine, and he made answer that there was no such thing." On the day before Catherine testified that after she wed Hertford, Cecil advised her "to take good heed how she proceeded in familiarity with the ... Earl without making the Queen's Majesty privy thereunto."²³ Though these testimonies indicate that Cecil had his suspicions about Catherine and Hertford, they do not reveal him as one who knew what was going on. Moreover, his advice to inform Elizabeth about the affair would hardly be expected from one seeking to carry out a conspiracy.

Nor does the date of the marriage necessarily mean that a plot was involved. The couple told their examiners that their wedding took place between 1 November and 25 December 1560. It is suggestive that this was not too long after Amy Robsart's death on 8 September, but it is also significant that Lady Frances Brandon died on 20 November 1559.²⁴ This may indicate that Catherine and Hertford climaxed a courtship of long standing with matrimony when they did because that was when

---

* He was a Privy Councilor, held high administrative posts, and was entrusted with important diplomatic missions.
† A son named Edward was born in the Tower on 21 September 1561. Machyn, *Diary*, p. 267.

the customary year of mourning for the bride's mother expired.[25] Accordingly, the propinquity of their marriage date to that of the death of Dudley's wife may have been purely coincidental.

Indeed, evidence gathered in investigations conducted by Archbishop Parker and others shows that the romance began long before Quadra's alleged conspirators could have had any motive for instigating a risky clandestine marriage. Both of the lovers testified that their affair began in Mary I's reign, when Catherine was living at Hanworth, the Middlesex residence of Hertford's mother, the Duchess of Somerset. Catherine added that the "love did again renew betwixt them" in the first year of Elizabeth's reign.[26] Their mothers evidently knew of the affair. Hertford stated that the Duchess often admonished him to abstain from Catherine's company. The romance was viewed more favorably by Lady Frances Brandon, who, Hertford claimed, "called him most commonly son."[27] Adrian Stokes, Lady Frances's second husband, testified that she thought the Earl to be "a very fit husband" for her daughter. Stokes also said that Lady Frances had him draft a letter to the Queen asking her consent to a marriage between Catherine and Hertford.[28] Catherine testified that her mother became too sick to copy Stokes's draft. She named Richard Bertie, Thomas Strikeley, and one Gilgett, a servant of Hertford, as privy to the letter. She also said that after Lady Frances's death, the idea of petitioning Elizabeth was dropped; yet "the love did continue, or rather increase," with sundry meetings and talks between the Earl and herself "without making any creature living of their counsel saving the Lady Jane Seymour and one Glynne," a servant of Lady Jane.[29] Eventually, according to Catherine and Hertford, an oral contract to marry was made at Westminster, Lady Jane being the only witness.[30]

The main objection that can be raised against the veracity of this account of a long-developing and innocent love affair is that there were no witnesses other than the parties and people close to them, but that need not mean fabrication. That the testimonies of Catherine, Hertford, and Stokes fit together so well speaks strongly for the truth of their accounts, since they were not allowed any contact with each other after the discovery of

Catherine's pregnancy. That knowledge of the affair was confined to family circles is not strange. Secrecy was essential because the projected union was one the Queen was not likely to approve of, even if Lady Frances Brandon had lived long enough to approach her in its behalf. Elizabeth almost had to be suspicious of an alliance between the Greys and the Seymours, no matter what the circumstances. Nevertheless, a match between the parties was obviously suitable: both were the children of Dukes; if only Catherine was of the blood royal, Hertford was a cousin of Edward VI. No conspiracy of the sort described by Quadra was necessary to bring them together.

Though such a plot could have been devised to take advantage of an ordinary romance of long standing, nowhere in the recorded testimonies are the men named by Quadra mentioned except for the innocuous inquiries and advice of Cecil. This can be taken to mean that those examined were covering up for Cecil and his collaborators. But we must remember that the Queen had made it clear in her instructions to the Lieutenant of the Tower that Catherine could expect no mercy unless she named all those involved. Hertford's position was more dangerous if he did not reveal all. Quadra pointed out that although the law of Henry VIII that made it treason to marry a person of royal blood without the royal license had been repealed in Mary's reign, the Earl still was not without peril.[31] Indeed, it was heard on the Continent that both Catherine and Hertford were in danger of losing their lives.[32] Finding themselves in such a serious predicament, it seems likely that the couple would have implicated others if there were others to implicate. Though we can hardly blame Elizabeth for being "certain that there hath been great practices and purposes," we are far from having sufficient evidence to prove their existence.

Another important question is whether Catherine and the Earl made a true marriage. The Queen appointed a Commission of Inquiry headed by Archbishop Parker to decide this issue. Its verdict was that the cohabitation between Catherine and Hertford was unlawful.[33] I think we must question its finding.

In this connection it is instructive to quote a letter from Elizabeth to Sir Edward Warner:

The Archbishop of Canterbury, with others, have commission to examine, inquire, and judge of the infamous conversation and pretended marriage betwixt the Lady Catherine Grey and the Earl of Hertford. Our pleasure is that, when the commissioners shall send to have either of the parties to appear before them in that cause you shall yourself lead either of them by water, as prisoners in your custody, to Lambeth; and, when they have answered in place of judgment, to suffer neither of them to have any conference with any person, but whilst any of them shall remain there out of the place of judgment, to remain in your custody as your prisoners, and to return them in like manner to their places. For our will is to have justice.[34]

The royal will was to have justice! Justice is a laudable objective, but one ought to look twice when its seeker is a daughter of Henry VIII. Tudor justice sometimes was injustice hiding behind legal processes. In this case a group of men, presumably learned in the laws of matrimony, were appointed to judge a question of matrimony, but their Queen wrote that they had "commission to examine, inquire, and judge of the infamous conversation and pretended marriage" between Catherine and Hertford. This seems to imply that Elizabeth had prejudged the case, and that her commissioners knew in advance what verdict was expected of them. If so, they would have been an extraordinarily dauntless group to reach a decision that did not produce the required "justice."

Moreover, when either party was called for examination Warner was to go along to see that there was no conference with anyone outside the place of judgment. The word "either" indicates that they were never brought to or from their examinations together. This is confirmed by the Commission's records, which show that they were always examined separately.[35] And in the Tower they were "kept in prison, so severed that the one had no conference with the other."[36] In fact, they had had no contact with each other since the discovery of Catherine's pregnancy, when Hertford was in France. Thus they had no opportunity to get together to concoct their stories when they were sure that such stories would be needed.* Besides, throughout their examinations they had no lawyers to advise them. Only

---

* After sentence was pronounced against their marriage, Warner relaxed the severity of their confinement. The result was the birth of Thomas, a second son, on 10 February 1563. Machyn, *Diary*, p. 300. This suggests the possi-

afterwards were they allowed to engage Dr. Aubrey and Dr. Jones as their counselors.[37] Therefore, substantial agreement between Catherine and Hertford about the details of their marriage would lend their testimonies a strong presumption of truth.

While the Commission's investigations were going on, Peter Osborne reported to Sir Thomas Chaloner in Spain, "Here be there no great circumstances but the examinations of my Lady Catherine's marriage and my Lord of Hertford's. . . . I know not but I hear they can bring forth no witnesses of the marriage nor the priest that married them, but allege the Lady Jane Seymour brought the priest and they two were the only witnesses."[38] Here was the weak point in the couple's account of their marriage. Lady Jane Seymour and the priest who officiated were the only witnesses, and Catherine and Hertford could not produce them. Jane was dead* and the priest had vanished. One might assume from this that there was no priest and that Jane's name had been brought up because dead women tell no tales. Such assumptions could relieve the qualms of conscience that the men assigned to "judge" the "pretended marriage" perhaps experienced, but they were not necessarily so.

If there never had been a marriage, it would indeed have been convenient to call upon a corpse as a witness. But if there really had been a wedding, Jane Seymour would have been an obvious witness. She was the groom's sister; she and the bride were both maids of honor to the Queen, and probably had been friends for years.[39] The marriage had to be accomplished in secrecy, but even for a clandestine ceremony, it was useful to have a third party who could assist by accompanying the bride to and fro, securing a priest, acting as a witness, and taking care of other matters that might come up. Who was more suitable for such a role than Jane? Her death may well have cost Catherine and Hertford the one person they always expected to have available to confirm their marriage.

Nor must we accept the inability to produce the priest as

---

bility that Warner also allowed contact between them before the sentence, but it is most doubtful that he would have taken such a risk. Prior to Hertford's departure for France, Catherine's pregnancy was only suspected. *HM* 6286, pp. 50–51, 82, 91–93.
* She died on 20 March 1561. Machyn, *Diary*, p. 253.

proof of his nonexistence. True, in their earliest examinations
both Catherine and the Earl said that they would not know the
priest if they were brought face to face with him; yet later both
claimed that they would know him if they were to see him
again.[40] These statements were at odds but not inexplicable.
Dr. Aubrey and Dr. Jones pointed out that only the later testimonies were binding in law, since they were the ones made
under oath.[41] Ignoring this technicality, it is possible to explain
the contradiction on the ground of uncertainty. The only time
that the couple were supposed to have seen the priest was over
a year before their first examinations, and then only for the few
minutes required for the wedding. Neither could be sure of
identifying him if the opportunity arose, but after several
months or reflection they may have convinced themselves that
they could. There would be nothing so very astonishing about
that. Accordingly, it does not seem too important that they said
different things on different occasions.

It is more significant how much they agreed when they described the priest in their later testimonies. Catherine remembered him as "a well-complexioned man with an auburn beard,
in a long gown with budge, the collar thereof turned down."
Hertford described him as of "mean stature, fair complexion
with an auburn beard, and of middle age; and was appareled
with a plain long gown of black cloth faced, as he remembreth,
with budge and a falling collar . . . , the same such a one as the
ministers used when they came out of Germany."[42] Considering
that the couple had no chance to get together to fabricate a story
after failing to describe the priest in their earliest examinations,
their substantial agreement can hardly be regarded as accidental. They easily could have differed as to the priest's costume.
At the time English clergymen dressed pretty much as they
pleased. It was only several years after that Elizabeth took steps
to make her bishops enforce the rules for uniformity in vest-
ments.[43] And their agreement about the priest's physical aspect,
it goes without saying, stands as a rather convincing argument
for his reality.

Moreover, Hertford's testimony suggests a hypothesis to explain why the priest could not be found. The statement that his

garb was the same as that worn by ministers "when they came out of Germany" makes it likely he was a Marian exile. All clergymen among the exiles did not return to England on receiving news of Elizabeth's accession. Many had studies to complete or obligations to fulfill abroad before they could leave for home. Some had to wait until they could raise funds for transportation. Anyway, exiles were still trickling back to England in 1560. Most of them doubtless passed through London. These latecomers often lacked an English ordination or a preferment to go to. They might stay in London until Bishop Grindal, who had an inordinate zeal for stocking the Church of England with Puritans, could arrange these matters for them, and then they would disappear into the country.[44] One of these transient clerics may well have been the priest who married Catherine and Hertford. As such he could perform the risky ceremony and vanish. To produce him over a year later would have been nearly impossible.

As for the marriage itself, again Catherine and the Earl concurred to a noteworthy degree in recalling details. They agreed that the priest followed the words and order set forth in the Book of Common Prayer; they were in essential agreement about where each person present stood in Hertford's bedroom, where the nuptials took place.[45] Catherine produced a complicated wedding ring for her examiners; the Earl described it for his rather accurately.* If no witnesses of the solemnization were available, Christopher Barnaby and William Powell, servants of Hertford, were able to testify that they saw Catherine and Lady Jane Seymour enter the Earl's house on the morning of the marriage.[46] All this was hardly prejudicial to the case for matrimony.

The most serious contradiction that the inquisitors were able

---

* Catherine's ring was "of five pieces with these verses written in it:
>   As circles five, by art compact, show but one ring in sight,
>   So trust uniteth faithful minds, with knot of secret might,
>   Whose force to break (but greedy death) no wight possesseth power,
>   As time and sequels well shall prove. My ring can say no more."

Hertford said it was "a ring of gold ... of four or five links, written upon every link with certain English metre of his own making containing matter of good will." *HM* 6286, pp. 81, 86.

to elicit was over banns. Catherine said that the priest asked no banns; Hertford claimed that he asked them thrice.[47] Their lawyers tried to explain this variance by pointing out that Catherine also testified that the priest "charged them both if they knew any impediment of either of their parties they should stay from proceeding any further." This, according to Aubrey and Jones, meant that she had in fact confessed that banns were asked; she merely did not understand what banns were or how they were wont to be asked.[48] The argument seems farfetched. Catherine's testimony about the priest's charge sounds like it refers to the wedding ceremony. One does not ordinarily regard the clergyman's charge to the parties at the beginning of the solemnization as banns. At any rate, the lawyers have failed to reconcile Catherine's account with Hertford's statement that banns were asked three times.

This contrariety amid so much agreement over events of the past may be viewed as favorable rather than damaging. It is unlikely that it would have occurred if the parties had been able to get in touch with each other to contrive their stories. Then the Earl or some intermediary surely would have straightened Catherine out on what to say about banns. Hence this contradiction may stand as evidence against the possibility of fabrication.

It is now possible to put together the story of the marriage as it emerges from the testimonies: testimonies that seem quite credible. Six or seven weeks before the nuptials, Catherine and Hertford made an oral contract to marry, Lady Jane Seymour being the sole witness.[49] The solemnization took place in the Earl's bedroom during the proper canonical hours, late in the morning.[50] A priest officiated at the wedding, which was witnessed by Lady Jane. The priest may have asked banns thrice. He conducted the ceremony out of the Book of Common Prayer. Hertford produced a ring with which he wed Catherine.

This was not a model marriage. A more formal betrothal in the presence of the priest would have been more orthodox.[51] Even if the priest asked banns three times on the day of the nuptials, this did not meet the specification of the Prayer Book of 1559 that banns be "asked three several Sundays or holydays, in service time." A church certainly would have been a more appropriate place for the solemnization than the groom's bedroom. At least one more witness besides the priest and Lady Jane would have been desirable.* Someone should have given away the bride as prescribed in the Prayer Book. And the couple should have received Communion on their wedding day as required by the Prayer Book.†

Nonetheless, these defects in themselves did not make it necessary to void the marriage. In an article on the Tudor marriage service a modern Anglican writer comments: "The essential part of marriage is the consent given by the bride and bridegroom in the presence of witnesses. Other ceremonies may be instructive and desirable, but they are not necessary."[52] Thus if we allow Jane Seymour and the priest as being in fact present at the ceremony—and the weight of our evidence seems to indicate that we should—we must accept the marriage according to the fundamental doctrine of the canon law that *consensus facit nuptias*. When Catherine and Hertford took their marriage vows in the presence of Jane and the priest, they had exchanged consent *per verba de praesenti* before two witnesses. This constituted valid matrimony according to the laws of England until 1753.[53]

Therefore, the Commission of Inquiry could have accepted the couple's story and their marriage. Then Catherine and Hertford should have been ordered to have their marriage properly solemnized in a church as provided in an Act of 1549:

When any cause or contract of marriage is pretended to have been made, it shall be lawful to examine the said cause, and having the said contract sufficiently and lawfully proved . . . , to give sentence for matrimony, commanding solemnization, cohabitation, consummation, and tractation as becometh man and wife to have.[54]

---

* "Our marriages be esteemed perfect by the law of England, when they be solemnized in the church or chapel, in the presence of the priest and other witnesses." Sir Thomas Smith, p. 126.
† Catherine testified that no one gave her in marriage, and Catherine and Hertford both said that the priest did not minister the Communion. *HM* 6286, pp. 86, 88, 90. There is no indication that they received Communion elsewhere.

This would have been the merciful and godly thing to do, since Catherine and Hertford had begun living as man and wife after the original marriage, and offspring had resulted. One suspects that it would have been done if the case had involved ordinary people. The very nobility of the parties, Aubrey and Jones wrote in concluding their argument, should have made for a decision giving them the benefit of the doubt: for even "if the contrary presumptions were either stronger or equal, as they be not, yet the law doth more incline to confirm than overthrow the matrimony."[55]

Public opinion evidently was also prone to accept the marriage. Sir John Mason, no friend of the couple or their cause, described the popular temper in a letter to Cecil:

There be abroad, both in the city and in sundry other places in the realm, broad speeches of the case of the Lady Catherine and the Earl of Hertford. Some of ignorance make such talks thereof as liketh them, not letting [scrupling] to say that they be man and wife. And why should man and wife be let [hindered] from coming together? These speeches and others are very common.[56]

It must have been a rather novel experience for Tudor England to see people of high birth insisting they were married instead of trying to find some dubious excuse for dissolving holy wedlock. This alone would have inspired the sympathy of the ordinary man. The fact that a son had already been born only increased the feeling for Catherine and Hertford. Most people were probably disposed to presume his legitimacy. Not only was this the just thing to do in a case of doubt, but males in the line of succession to the crown were, after all, a scarce commodity.

Nevertheless, the premier prelate of the realm and his fellows on the Commission of Inquiry found against the marriage. They probably would not have dared to do otherwise, no matter what their private opinions were. If they had, the Queen would have had real cause to fear that there was more behind the marriage of Catherine and Hertford than met the eye. The very fact that a son had been born must have increased her determination to see the marriage declared void. If the baby Edward Seymour, later known as Lord Beauchamp, was thus legally bastardized, his chances for the succession would be diminished considerably. Just what Elizabeth's true preferences for the succession were is a debatable question, but it seems clear that she had no wish to be followed on the throne by a Suffolk. There probably is no foundation for the often repeated story that at the mention of Beauchamp's name, the Queen rose from her deathbed to exclaim: "I will have no rascal's son in my seat but one worthy to be a king."[57] Yet nothing seems more expressive of her sentiments on the matter. Therefore, the Commission's verdict almost had to be what it was, and Elizabeth would see to it that it would stand.

3. A Scottish Mission and a Senecan Tragedy

During the period when Lady Catherine Grey's clandestine marriage was occupying the center of the stage, two other events of significance to the succession story took place. About a month after the discovery of Catherine's pregnancy, a Scottish statesman conferred with Elizabeth I; approximately two weeks before the Commission of Inquiry was assigned its task, an English play written after the style of Seneca was performed by the gentlemen of the Inner Temple before the Queen. These happenings were important in themselves; they were also harbingers of things to come. The meetings of Maitland of Lethington with Elizabeth indicated—or appeared to indicate—that the Queen of Scots was now ready to give up her previously announced, immediate claim to the English crown in exchange for a present recognition as next in line; they were also preceded and followed by the first statements of the case for Mary Stuart's succession. The tragedy of *Gorboduc* by Thomas Norton and Thomas Sackville was—or could be interpreted as—the first Elizabethan succession tract; it was also by implication the earliest presentation of the arguments for Catherine Grey's succession.

Advance notice of the proposal to be made by Maitland reached England in a letter of 6 August 1561 from Lord James Stuart, Mary's bastard half brother, to Elizabeth via Cecil. Lord James suggested that Elizabeth should guarantee Mary the next place in the succession, after her own issue, in return for Mary's agreement not to press her already asserted claim to the throne. He saw this as a cure-all compromise. Mary would be satisfied; Elizabeth would be secure; England and Scotland would be "united in perpetual friendship." Such wishful thinking was only natural at this stage of the game. Even statesmen like Lord James and Maitland did not yet fully appreciate the problems and the Queens involved.

Lord James also saw fit to defend Mary's title to the succession. He pointed out that her claim was superior to those of her rivals, according to the "law of all nations," by reason of the priority of her descent from Henry VII. He apparently was aware of the obstacles that the common-law rule against inheritance by aliens and Henry VIII's will presented to Mary, but he did not directly attack the applicability of the law or the validity of the will. Instead, like a later James Stuart, he chose to argue that the "succession of realms comes by God's appointment . . . , and no provision of man can alter what He has determined."[1]

Mary returned to Scotland from France on 19 August. Thirteen days later she sent Maitland on his mission to Elizabeth. He was to inform her that Mary had agreed to accept the compromise suggested by Lord James. Maitland had three meetings with Elizabeth, and failed to obtain her consent to having Mary made her heir presumptive. Nonetheless, the meetings are instructive, owing to the light they shed on Elizabeth's attitude toward the succession. If she ever came close to speaking her mind on the subject, these were the occasions.

The Queen made it clear where her preference lay between Mary and her rivals. She reminded Maitland that "in time of most offence and when she [Mary], by bearing my arms and acclaiming the title of my crown, had given me just cause to be most angry with her, yet could I never find it in my heart to hate her, imputing rather the fault to others than to herself."* It is suggestive to compare this with Elizabeth's refusal to forgive Catherine Grey for a far lesser offence than claiming

---

* This is confirmed by Elizabeth's proclamation of 24 March 1560, where she placed the blame for the "injurious pretences" made by Mary on the "principals of the House of Guise." *CSM*, I, 197.

her crown while she was very much alive. Even more revealing is her statement:

> If her [Mary's] right be good she may be sure I will never hurt her, and I here protest to you . . . I for my part know none better nor that myself would prefer to her, or yet, to be plain with you, that case occurring might debar her from it. You know them all [the other claimants]. Alas! What power or force have any of them, poor souls?[2]

Elizabeth let Maitland know, however, that her liking for Mary did not mean that she had the right to force—she probably would have had to use force—an English Parliament to proclaim the Scottish Queen as next in line:

> I have always abhorred to draw in question the title of the crown, so many disputes have been already touching it in the mouths of men. . . . Whosover it [her successor] be, so long as I live I shall be Queen of England; when I am dead they shall succeed that have most right. If the Queen your Sovereign be that person, I shall never hurt her; if any other has better right, it is not reasonable to require me to do a manifest injury. If there be any law against her (as I protest to you I know none for I am not curious to inquire of that purpose) . . . , I was sworn when I was married to the realm not to alter the laws of it.[3]

This was not so detrimental to Mary as she and her friends may have supposed. Elizabeth did not want to do anything that would provoke debates over the title of the crown. Of course, she had selfish reasons for saying this. No young woman, especially one whose brother and sister had passed away after brief reigns, could find it entertaining to have her subjects engaged in a great dispute over what was to happen when she was dead, but it is possible that she also may have been thinking about Mary. Debate over the succession was more likely to be harmful to Mary's cause than not. She had an obvious hereditary claim, but against her stood a rule concerning alien inheritance that few people were aware of, and a will that had to go back to the twelfth century to find a possible precedent.* Moreover, the cases of her competitors needed the publicity that would come of a discussion of the succession in Parliament.

---

* Richard I's apparent designation of his brother John as his successor rather than his nephew Arthur, who had a better claim according to the rule of representative primogeniture.

Maitland could not have been pleased over Elizabeth's inti-
mation that she did not know if his Queen had the best right
to the succession, but this may have been a deception in Mary's
interest. What seems most significant is Elizabeth's statement
that she was not curious to find out if there was any law against
Mary's succession. When we discuss the will of Henry VIII we
shall meet evidence that Elizabeth believed her father's testament to be genuine. If this was so, she could hardly be expected
to make a limitation of the crown that would contradict it. Elizabeth regarded Henry as a great ruler, one worthy of emulation.
She was not disposed to alter his acts without compelling cause,
even those that touched her own legitimacy;* she surely was not
inclined to do so for Mary, who had not always been a loving
cousin.

Therefore, Elizabeth's lack of curiosity may well have been to
Mary's advantage. When one asks a question of law, one should
expect an answer based on law. If, as Elizabeth may have expected it would, the law of England proved to be against Mary's
claim, the Queen of England could not properly change it. Even
if she wanted to, Parliament could not be expected to go along
with her without a fight. Mary would have done better not
to ask the question at all, not until Elizabeth was dead. That
would have been the right time for Mary to have a test of
strength with her rivals. Perhaps Elizabeth was hinting at this
when she referred to the lack of "power or force" of the other
claimants. The wisest policy for Mary would have been to let
sleeping dogs lie.

The one statement in the passage under consideration that
was rather clearly aimed at Mary was that about Elizabeth's being Queen of England as long as she lived. She had previously
told Maitland, "As for the title of my crown, for my time I think
she [Mary] will not attain it, nor make impediment to my issue
if any shall come of my body: for so long as I live there shall be
no other Queen in England but I."[4] Such expressions of con-
fidence were not what Maitland was looking for. He seems to
have been negotiating from the premise that it was Elizabeth

* Elizabeth never sought to invalidate the provisions of 28 Henry VIII, c. 7,
which bastardized her.

who had the most to gain out of Mary's offer to relinquish her present claim in exchange for a guarantee about the future. He implied this to Elizabeth in a somewhat impolitic manner:

It is true that although your Highness takes yourself to be lawful, yet are you not always so taken abroad in the world. First, all that follow in religion the Kirk of Rome, your Highness knows, think the King your father's marriage with your mother unlawful, and consequently the issue of the marriage siclike. The Queen my Sovereign's subjects must, and all others who are for any reason affectionate to her will, think favorably of her title.[5]

It is difficult to believe that Elizabeth saw herself as needing Mary's "charity." She was England's anointed Queen; she was Henry VIII's daughter. This probably settled the matter for most Englishmen, Protestant or Catholic, and that was the most important consideration. As for Mary's Scottish subjects, their mere opinions were of small consequence. What constituted a potential threat was Catholic Europe, where Elizabeth was regarded as a bastard and Mary as the rightful Queen of England. But there were really two Catholic Europes, the Hapsburg and the Valois, and their interests tended to hold each other in check. Neither the Catholic King of Spain nor the Catholic King of France could permit the other to win a hegemony over the British Isles by means of the Queen of Scots. Therefore, the situation did not require Elizabeth to be impressed overly by Maitland's bargain.

Indeed, she doubtless regarded it as a bad one. The proof of this does not necessarily depend on what Elizabeth meant when she twice referred to a Mary Stuart named to the succession as her "winding sheet":

This desire is without any example, to require me in my own life to set my winding sheet before my eye, the like was never required of no [sic] prince.

Think you that I could love my own winding sheet? Princes cannot like their own children, those that should succeed unto them. . . . How then shall I, think you, like my cousin being declared my heir apparent?[6]

Some historians take this to mean that Elizabeth feared that the appointment of Mary to the succession would constitute an invitation for her own assassination; Father Pollen and T. F. Henderson maintain that she was simply saying that she could not love Mary if Mary was actually named to follow her on the throne after her death.[7] The latter view seems the more likely, both because of Elizabeth's words in her second statement and because the possibility of assassination was always there, whether Mary was formally appointed to the succession or not. Elizabeth Tudor has been accused of many things, but she cannot properly be charged with cowardice. She was above refusing a proposition beneficial to her realm merely because it might slightly increase a threat to herself that she could not eliminate under any circumstances.

This, however, does not necessarily verify Henderson's conclusion that Elizabeth's refusal to accept Maitland's proposal "was influenced neither by weak dread of assassination nor by high consideration for the welfare of England, but by a mere adamantine self-regard."[8] There were more substantial reasons for fearing the consequences of naming the Queen of Scots next in line. Elizabeth pointed out an important one to Maitland:

> I know the inconsistency of the people of England, how they ever mislike the present government and have their eyes fixed upon that person that is next to succeed. . . . No prince's revenues be so great that they are able to satisfy the insatiable cupidity of men. And if we, either for not giving to men at their discretion or yet for any other cause, should miscontent any our subjects, it is to be feared that if they knew a certain successor of our crown they would have recourse thither; and what danger it would be, she being a puissant princess and so near our neighbor, you may judge. So that in assuring her of the succession we might put our present state in doubt.

When Maitland sought to relieve this anxiety by promising Mary's guarantee that Englishmen would have no recourse to her, Elizabeth wisely answered, "It is hard to bind princes by any security where hope is offered of a kingdom."[9]

Another danger Elizabeth perhaps had in mind, but found it undiplomatic to bring up, was the fact that Mary was now unmarried. In arguing that Elizabeth would be getting the better of the bargain, Henderson writes, "For Elizabeth, it can hardly be said that she was asked to risk more than Mary. By recognizing Elizabeth's title Mary would, in a manner, tie her own hands. Yet should Mary marry Don Carlos, England would be greatly at the mercy of Scotland and Spain."[10] But this threat might have been greater if the settlement offered by the Scots had been accepted. If their Queen had actually been appointed to the English succession, the King of Spain might have been more receptive to the idea of marrying her to his son than he soon proved to be.* Though Mary probably would have had to agree not to marry without Elizabeth's approval in exchange for being named next in line, Mary, led on by the temptations of empire, could easily have broken her promise, whereas Elizabeth would have made an all but irrevocable commitment. The succession, as Sir John Neale points out, "was not a gift which Elizabeth could lightly make and later withdraw if Mary embarked on a hostile policy. It was a right. Once declared, it could never be rescinded with any show of justice or hope of real effect."[11] This seems to provide a more satisfactory explanation of Elizabeth's refusal to recognize Mary's title than does dismissing it as "a mere admantine self-regard."

Though Maitland's mission failed to achieve its objective, he returned to Scotland convinced that it was Mary whom Elizabeth preferred to have succeed her so long as she had no issue of her own.[12] Hence he did not think that he had received a final no. The negotiation was not dropped. To further it, Maitland wrote a letter to Cecil in October in which he presented a case for the justice of Mary's claim.

His main argument is brief enough to quote in full:

If either by an Act of Parliament or later will of King Henry VIII anything hath been derogatory to the Queen my mistress' interest, I pray you consider what injury hath been done to us and how just cause we have to ask redress of it. It doth appear by the contract of marriage, and it is true, that Queen Margaret was married to King James IV, my Sovereign's grandfather, as eldest lawful daughter to King Henry VII; and by your own histories it doth appear that he meant not by the same marriage to debar her, nor the issue of her body, from the succession of his crown perpetually, but rather the plain contrary.[13]

---

* See Philip's hedging letter of June 1563 informing Quadra that he accepted the proposal to negotiate for the match, and his terse note of August 1564 telling Guzman de Silva to consider the negotiations at an end. *CSP, Span., Eliz.,* I, 332–33, 372. They hardly indicate a real desire for Mary as a daughter-in-law.

It should be noticed that Maitland was not yet ready to deny the authenticity of Henry VIII's will directly. It will be important to remember this when we later discuss that testament, because we cannot dismiss as insignificant the fact that the attack on its genuineness did not begin until it became expedient to make it. All Maitland now wanted was for the will to be overthrown, since it did not treat Mary fairly. If Elizabeth was troubled by the idea of violating her father's will, he offered what might be called the will of Henry VII, her grandfather, to relieve her scruples. The presumed legal justification for Henry VIII's setting aside the hereditary rights of the Stuarts was the common-law rule against the inheritance of ordinary property by aliens. If Henry VIII thought that this rule could be applied to the royal succession, Maitland argued that Henry VII viewed the matter differently.

Maitland found proof of this in Henry VII's refusal to regard Margaret Tudor's marriage to James IV as an obstacle to the succession of her descendants. He referred Cecil to England's histories for evidence backing his case. Here he must have had in mind Polydore Vergil's *Anglica Historia*.[14] There Vergil told of an occasion when certain of Henry's councilors expressed the fear that a marriage between his elder daughter and the King of Scotland might someday expose England to the indignity of having a Scot claim her crown. Henry did not see this possibility as harmful to England; rather, he indicated that England, as the greater realm, would dominate Scotland if chance gave them the same ruler.[15]

This case was open to several objections. Vergil's narrative could have been based on hearsay; it even could have been purely a product of the chronicler's imagination. Henry VII's alleged statement sounds as if he was thinking in terms of expediency rather than law. Nor would his ideas about the applicability of the common-law rule against alien inheritance to the royal succession settle the matter. Moreover, the will of Henry VIII could stand without the common-law doctrine. Henry VIII had statutory authority to designate the succession by will;[16] he did not have to offer—or even have—any legal justification for his wishes.

Though Maitland did not present too good a case for Mary's

claim, he was more on the right track than Lord James Stuart had been. He touched upon English history and law, instead of wholly relying on the notion of a hereditary divine right. He apparently realized that generalizations about a "law of all nations" and "God's appointment" were not enough to convince Englishmen that their own laws were inapplicable. The only practical approach was to attack the validity of those laws. If Maitland failed at the time to do this adequately, a start had at least been made that could later be elaborated on by Maitland himself and by the Stuart tract writers. This was considerably more than could be said about the case for a Suffolk succession.

Indeed, the supporters of the Suffolk claim must have been painfully aware of the head start the opposition was getting. If they did not know of Maitland's letter, they were undoubtedly cognizant of his meetings with Elizabeth. Perhaps they also heard of the rumor that had been circulating on the Continent in August that Elizabeth and Mary had already concluded an agreement whereby the former would acknowledge the latter to be *"princesa y légitima heredera de Inglaterra."*[17] There was enough in the atmosphere to suggest what the Scots were up to. The friends of the Suffolk line doubtless realized that a countermove was in order.

Now they could not, as their rivals had done, open negotiations with Elizabeth. Their principal claimant was not a puissant princess; Catherine Grey was a prisoner in the Tower awaiting judgment. Hence a more indirect approach was needed if they were to present their views. There is no way of proving that the doings of the Scots were the inspiration of *Gorboduc,* but the peculiar applicability of its last act to the contemporary scene was hardly coincidental and may well have been the product of apprehensions over them. At any rate, the performance of *Gorboduc* at Whitehall on 18 January 1562 gave notice to Elizabeth, if she required any such notice, that all of her subjects would not meekly be parties to a declaration in favor of a Stuart succession.[18]

Since the days of Sir Philip Sidney, *Gorboduc* has been acknowledged as a landmark in the history of literature. It was the first regular drama in blank verse in the English language, and the first attempt by Englishmen to write in their native tongue a tragedy in the style and form of Seneca. However, our interest is in its political rather than its literary significance. Though scholars in the field of English literature have recognized for over a century that *Gorboduc* was something of a succession tract as well as a play, this has almost completely escaped the attention of historians.[19] An exception is Sir John Neale, who has written that the fifth act of *Gorboduc* was "no more than a tract for the times on the subject of the succession, containing a palpable attack on Mary's title."[20]

The coauthors of *Gorboduc* were indeed men quite capable of contemplating such an attack. Thomas Norton deserves a prominent place in the annals of the succession politics of Elizabeth's reign. As a young man he had been patronized by the Protector Somerset, and was tutor to his children.[21] This would be reason enough for him to be interested in the cause of his former benefactor's daughter-in-law. He also must have been led in the anti-Stuart direction by his Puritan religious proclivities and his consequent hatred of anything connected with the Church of Rome.* Norton was to be much in evidence in the succession storms of the coming Parliaments. He probably was the man most responsible for the petition of the Commons in 1563 for the limitation of the succession.[22] In 1571 Norton tried to tack onto a main government measure a bill that would have had the effect of depriving Mary Stuart and her son of their claims to the throne.[23] A year later he led the attack on the Queen of Scots and the Duke of Norfolk in the House of Commons.[24] Norton doubtless had more immediate matters in mind than a succession problem in the mythical Britain of long ago when he collaborated on *Gorboduc*.

Much the same can be said, though in a lesser degree, of Thomas Sackville. Sackville, a third cousin of Elizabeth,† came of an important family whose wealth was grounded in Church land.[25] Though he was not a Puritan like Norton, there can be no doubt of his anti-Catholicism.‡ He served with Norton in

---

* Included among Norton's works are an English translation of Calvin's *Institutes* and three polemics against papal bulls. Cooper, I, 488.

† Both were great-grandchildren of Sir William Boleyn.

‡ Sackville was later an ally of no less an enemy of the Puritans than Archbishop Whitgift. Pollard, *Political History*, p. 460.

the Parliaments of 1563 and 1566, but we do not know if he took part in their succession debates.[26] Sackville's association with Norton probably began in the late 1550's at the Inner Temple, where the latter was a member and the former a familiar figure.[27] A common bent for poetry and politics must have drawn them together. If Sackville was not to be as vociferous as Norton about the succession, that does not preclude the likelihood that he was also deeply concerned over the question. Indeed, he is commonly credited with the actual writing of the polemical fifth act of *Gorboduc*.[28]

The story of *Gorboduc* is adequately summarized in the argument prefaced to the play:

Gorboduc, King of Britain, divided his realm in his lifetime to his sons, Ferrex and Porrex. The sons fell to division and dissension. The younger killed the elder. The mother, that more dearly loved the elder, for revenge killed the younger. The people, moved by the cruelty of the fact, rose in rebellion and slew both father and mother. The nobility assembled, and most terribly destroyed the rebels. And afterwards for want of issue of the Prince, whereby the succession of the crown became uncertain, they fell to civil war, in which both they and many of their issue were slain, and the land for a long time almost desolate and miserably wasted.[29]

Gorboduc was essentially a medieval play, the innovations in its composition notwithstanding. It was indeed a gruesome tale, yet one that must have been entertaining to the pre-Shakespearian audience. As was customary, there was a simple moral to the story of *Gorboduc*: if a monarch died without leaving a certain successor, the inevitable results were civil war and anarchy. Men only two or three generations removed from the time of the Wars of the Roses, no matter which claimant they favored, would not be inclined to doubt the truth of this hypothesis. If this was as far as Sackville and Norton were going to go, *Gorboduc* might be dismissed as a comparatively innocuous play. In the final act, however, the authors, in elaborating on the woeful state of Britain after the murders of her ruler and his sons, turned *Gorboduc* into a definitely partisan tract on the contemporary succession question, "a palpable attack on Mary's title."

The name of the villain of this act was suggestive. The man who sought to take advantage of the situation by invading the unfortunate realm was Fergus, Duke of Albany. Albany was manifestly a Scottish title; it was usually held by a Stuart, who often proved to be an enemy of England.* Sackville and Norton probably intended that their audience identify Fergus, Duke of Albany, with Mary Stuart. For example, consider the following words of Fergus:

> Shall I, that am the Duke of Albany,
> Descended from that line of noble blood,
> Which hath so long flourished in worthy fame
> Of valiant hearts, such as in noble breasts
> Of right should rest above the baser sort,
> Refuse to venture life to win a crown?
>
> . . .
>
> Forthwith, therefore, will I in post depart
> To Albany, and raise in armor there
> All power I can: and here my secret friends,
> By secret practice shall solicit still,
> To seek to win to me the people's hearts.[30]

It must not have taken much imagination for many Englishmen to picture Mary uttering such words when the appropriate occasion arose.

Consider further the appeal of Arostus, a counselor of the late King Gorboduc, to the nobility to resist the Duke of Albany:

> And with that heart wherewith ye now prepare
> Thus to withstand the proud invading foe,
> With that same heart, my lords, keep out also
> Unnatural thralldom of stranger's reign;
> Ne [nor] suffer you, against the rules of kind,†
> Your mother land to serve a foreign prince.[31]

To an Englishman of 1562 this was clearly aimed at the Queen of Scots. Though it may have reminded lawyers of the common-

---

* Robert Stuart, Duke of Albany (ca. 1345–1420), initiated several wars and plundering expeditions against England. John Stuart, Duke of Albany (ca. 1481–1536), was a famous enemy of Henry VIII. In 1559 Henry Dudley told Sir Nicholas Throckmorton that the "Lord d'Albany," brother to Matthew Stuart, Earl of Lennox, had a hand in Henry II's having Mary assume the title and arms of England. Forbes, I, 146.

† "Kind" is apparently used here in its archaic meaning of nature or kindred.

law objection to the inheritance of the crown by an alien, it did
not directly present this argument. Instead it called the rule of
a foreigner "unnatural" and against the "rules of kind." This
had a larger appeal to the average Englishman than a debatable
and somewhat obscure point of law. The recent experience of
the reign of Philip and Mary left ugly memories of the rule
of strangers. Moreover, the English probably still hated the
Frenchman more than the Spaniard. As for the Scot, he was
regarded with contempt. And Mary Stuart was half French and
half Scottish.

Sackville and Norton offered their solution to the contemporary problem earlier in the same speech of Arostus:

> . . . first by common counsel of you all
> In parliament, the regal diadem
> Be set in certain place of governance;
> In which your parliament, and in your choice,
> Prefer the right, my lords, without respect
> Of strength or friends, or whatsoever cause
> That may set forward any other's part.
> For right will last, and wrong cannot endure.
> Right mean I his or hers, upon whose name
> The people rest by mean of native line,
> Or by the virtue of some former law,
> Already made their title to advance.
> Such one, my lords, let be your chosen king,
> Such one so born within your native land;
> Such one prefer, and in no wise admit
> The heavy yoke of foreign governance:
> Let foreign title yield to public wealth.[32]

This was the heart of the succession tract of *Gorboduc.* Let us,
as the authors undoubtedly wanted their audience to do, consider the passage in the terms of their own England.

It first stated that the succession was a matter to be settled in
Parliament. This, as we shall see later on, was a notion that contemporaries would not be disposed to challenge. It was further
pointed out that Parliament would do best to base its choice on
the "right." The fact that Mary Stuart was a puissant princess
who had many friends in England and abroad ought not to influence its decision. If justice was not on her side, a declaration

in her favor could not be expected to provide a lasting solution: "For right will last, and wrong cannot endure." This too was a doctrine that most Englishmen of 1562 would accept. The triumph of Mary Tudor over Jane Grey, and the power and schemes of the Duke of Northumberland, still served as a vivid illustration of it.

But what was the "right"? The pointed answer of the play is significant enough to bear repetition:

> Right mean I his or *hers,* upon whose name
> The people rest by mean of *native line,*
> Or by the virtue of some *former law,*
> Already made their title to advance. [Italics mine.]

Considering the peculiar preponderance of female claimants in 1562, the inclusion of "hers" may be taken as deliberate. That the woman whom the authors had in mind was Catherine Grey becomes apparent from the next line. She was the senior candidate of an unobjectionably "native line"; her strongest claim came from the will of Henry VIII, which was authorized by "former law." Catherine was the one to be preferred over Mary. The Scottish Queen was to be excluded for reasons of expediency as well as justice: "Let foreign titles yield to public wealth." This was the first written statement of the case for Catherine's succession. The authors of *Gorboduc* only dared to state it briefly and by implication, but the pen of a less discreet writer would soon reassert it more elaborately and more directly.

Sackville and Norton concluded their drama with a speech by Eubulus, secretary to the late King Gorboduc. He shrewdly observed that the proposition presented by Arostus would have had far better prospects for success while Gorboduc was alive than in the anarchy that followed his death:

> No, no: then parliament should have been holden,
> And certain heirs appointed to the crown,
> To stay the title of established right,
> And in the people plant obedience,
> While yet the prince did live, whose name and power
> By lawful summons and authority
> Might make a parliament to be of force,
> And might have set the state in quiet stay.[33]

These lines must have been meant as an appeal to Elizabeth. They implored her to have the succession settled in Parliament now, while she was still alive. Only then could the peaceful and immediate triumph of justice be assured and civil war averted. This was to be the basic argument of the petitions of the next Parliament.

Just how the Queen reacted to *Gorboduc* is not known. The applicability of its last act to the contemporary scene could hardly have escaped her suspicious ears. She could not have liked its anti-Stuart and pro-Suffolk implications. Nor could she have been receptive to the idea that an immediate settlement of the succession in Parliament was urgent. Nevertheless, Sackville and Norton do not seem to have lost Elizabeth's favor because of their play.[34] Perhaps she enjoyed the sanguinary tragedy too much to be angry with its authors. Then again, she may have underestimated the strength of the anti-Stuart cause. In any case, *Gorboduc* was a warning of things to come. If the Queen did not fully appreciate this in January 1562, it would not be long before she would learn differently.

4. *The Parliament of 1563*

In August 1602 Elizabeth said to William Lambarde, the antiquary, "I am Richard II. Know ye not that?"[1] The old Queen
then must have been thinking of the performances of Shakespeare's *Richard II*, presented in connection with the recently
crushed Essex Rising. She would have come closer to the truth
if she had spoken the same words in 1562. When Richard II
met his tragic end in 1399, he left no certain successor. Though
Henry IV was already King, the better title probably belonged
to Edmund, Earl of March.* The ultimate outcome was the
Wars of the Roses. If Elizabeth had died in 1602, James VI of
Scotland doubtless would have succeeded her as easily as he did
the next year. But if she had died in 1562, civil war would have
been a likely result. At that time she was indeed a sort of
Richard II.

That such an analogy is legitimate is shown by what happened when Elizabeth became ill with smallpox in October
1562. The Privy Council met to try to decide what to do about
the succession in case the worst occurred, but no agreement
could be reached. According to Quadra, the Protestant majority
of the Council was unable to decide whether to put forward
Catherine Grey or the Earl of Huntingdon, and the Catholic
minority sought to delay any decision until the realm's leading
jurists, most of whom were Catholics, could be called to examine

* See Appendix, charts I and II.

the rights of the claimants. He did not know if the Catholic party, which "would have on its side a majority of the country," would be able to decide between the Scottish Queen and Lady Margaret Lennox, but delay would give Philip II time "to take steps in the matter."[2] Though Quadra's information may not be entirely accurate, it is doubtless true enough to suggest that Elizabeth's death at the time probably would have produced civil war, and perhaps even an invasion.

Moreover, in the very October of the Queen's illness a hare-brained scheme was discovered. Arthur Pole, a nephew of the late Cardinal, pretended that he had a better Yorkist claim to the crown than Huntingdon.* It was his idea to turn over his "rights" to Mary Stuart in exchange for her promise to create him Duke of Clarence and to marry one of his brothers once he had won the English throne for her. Pole planned to accomplish this small matter by going to France and offering his services to the Guises. He had approached the French and Spanish ambassadors to enlist their support, but neither would have anything to do with him. The would-be Duke of Clarence, his two brothers, and his brother-in-law were seized as they were embarking for France and were lodged in the Tower.[3]

Pole's affair obviously was not a serious threat to Elizabeth's security, but there were men in high places who found his folly useful. It could be made a source of embarrassment to the English Catholics; it could provide a diplomatic weapon against Quadra. Accordingly, Pole and his cohorts were given more attention than they deserved. This probably created a popular impression that a dangerous plot had been put down. At any rate, the news of Pole's doings, coming about the same time as that of the Queen's illness, must have increased the determination of the men soon to be called to Parliament that their first order of business must be the settlement of the succession.

Elizabeth did not relish the prospect of facing the almost certain ordeal of a succession Parliament, but since she had to replenish her treasury after the expenditures incurred in the recent military adventures in France and Scotland, she could

* That this was not so can be seen from the Appendix, chart V.

hardly avoid it.[4] Early in November writs were sent out calling
for the election of a Parliament to meet in January.[5] The resulting House of Commons promised a stormy session, in that it
contained only 27 Catholics.[6] Quadra believed this was the
product of a deliberate government effort to return only Protestants, but no trace of official intervention in the general election has been found.[7] If the Lower House was predominantly
Protestant and was not packed, the Queen would have no easy
task preventing it from demanding that the succession be settled
against the Queen of Scots.

Moreover, if we may believe Quadra, shortly after the writs
went out certain gentlemen held meetings "on the excuse of
dining together" but really to discuss the succession. Quadra is
not clear about what their preferences about candidates were.
On 22 November he wrote that the "most moderate of them"
inclined to Lord Darnley and "those of a contrary opinion" to
Huntingdon. A week later he reported a meeting at the Earl of
Arundel's attended by the Duke of Norfolk and others. He
understood they favored Catherine Grey. He heard that Elizabeth "wept with rage" when she heard of this meeting, and had
a heated exchange of words with Arundel about it.[8]

Though Quadra is our only source for these meetings, the
urgency with which the succession was viewed at the time makes
it quite possible that they did take place. Their very occurrence
would be significant. An exchange of views beforehand has
obvious value as preparation for a parliamentary fight. Moreover, the meetings were supposed to have taken place in November, whereas the elections were not held until December.[9]
This indicates that the commoners who attended were probably
gentlemen of consequence who knew in advance that they would
have seats in the coming Parliament. That such men were joining great nobles like Norfolk and Arundel in bringing up the
succession boded ill for the Queen. If they could not agree on a
candidate, it was of some import that Mary Stuart was not mentioned as being discussed. If such meetings were the precursors
of the Parliament, Elizabeth did have cause to weep with rage.
She did not want the succession brought up at all; she certainly
did not want to have anything said or done that might offend

the Queen of Scots and furnish her with an excuse for taking hostile steps.

No sooner did the Parliament of 1563 get under way than the Commons began dealing with the succession. After a few days of speechmaking a committee was assigned to draw up a petition concerning the Queen's marriage and the succession. The resulting petition was read to the House on 26 January "by Mr. Norton, one of the committees." Elizabeth heard it two days later.[10]

Nothing better illustrates the temper of the Commons than this petition. Almost at the beginning they reminded Elizabeth that she had summoned Parliament soon after recovering from her illness, from which they drew the seemingly logical conclusion that she had called them "principally for the establishing of some certain limitation" of the crown.[11] The naive majority of the Commons must have believed this was why they were at Westminster, but the committee that drew up their petition and that met with the Privy Council probably realized a succession settlement was the last thing the Queen wanted.*

The authorship of the petition is of interest. That it was read to the House by Thomas Norton may be significant. This somewhat risky privilege might well be assigned to the author. This is made more likely by the way in which the petition goes on to thank Elizabeth for supposedly having taken into consideration the dangers of an unsettled succession in summoning Parliament:

[The Commons] cannot ... but acknowledge how your Majesty hath most graciously considered the great dangers and the unspeakable miseries of civil wars; the perilous intermeddlings of foreign princes with seditious, ambitious, and factious subjects at home; the waste of noble houses; the slaughter of people, subversion of towns, intermission of all things pertaining to the maintenance of the realm, unsurity of all men's possessions, lives, and estates; [and the] daily interchanging of attainders and treasons. All these mischiefs and infinite others are most likely and evident if your Majesty should be taken from us without a known heir.[12]

---

* *JHC,* I, 63. On 14 January Cecil had indicated his fear that Elizabeth's "unwillingness" to have her successor known would "stay the matter." Wright, I, 121.

These words are sufficiently reminiscent of *Gorboduc* to suggest that Norton either wrote the petition or was at least the dominant spirit behind it. And if the Commons were following the lead of such a Protestant insurgent in dealing with the succession, the Queen of Scots must have been their principal target.

This is confirmed a little later on when the petition brings up matters that no doubt had been prominent in the debates leading up to it:

We have been admonished of the great malice of your foreign enemies, which even in your lifetime have sought to transfer the dignity and right of your crown to a stranger; we have noted their daily most dangerous practices against your life and your reign; we have heard of some subjects of this land most unnaturally confedered with your enemies to attempt the destruction of your Majesty and us. . . . We fear a faction of heretics within your realm, malicious Papists, lest they . . . not only hope for the woeful day of your death, but also lie in wait to advance some title under which they may renew their late unspeakable cruelty to the destruction of the goods, possessions, and bodies, and thralldom of the souls and consciences of your faithful and Christian subjects: we see nothing to resist their desire but your only life. Their unkindness and cruelty we have tasted; we fear much to what attempt the hope of such opportunity . . . will move them; we find how necessary it is for your preservation that there be more set and known between your Majesty's life and their desire.[13]

The reference to the former French machinations in behalf of Mary is obvious. The remark about a confederation of subjects and enemies doubtless alluded to the "plot" of the Pole brothers to put Mary on the throne. It could hardly have been accidental that these matters were brought up just before the Commons indicated their fear that "malicious Papists" were lying in wait for an opportunity to advance some title under which they could bring about a return to the Marian persecutions. The mainly Protestant House must have considered this title to be that of the Catholic Queen of Scots.

While on this subject, it seems appropriate to bring up a speech of Sir Ralph Sadler that probably belongs to the Parliament under consideration.[14] In it we get a more open display of the strong sentiments against Mary that were in all likelihood shared by most M.P.'s:

I have heard some speak here touching the title of the Queen of Scots to the Imperial Crown of this realm, wherein it seemeth that she hath some fautors and favorers. . . . I cannot say who hath the best and most just title to succeed the Queen's Majesty . . . , but being a more natural Englishman, I do find in myself a great misliking to be subject to a foreign prince, a prince of a strange nation; and methinks we should not be so unnatural as to seek or desire a stranger to reign over us rather than a prince of our own nation. And for the Queen of Scots, though she were indeed next heir in blood to the Queen's Majesty, yet being a stranger by the laws of the realm, as I understand, she cannot inherit in England, which is a good argument to me that the nature of Englishmen hath always so much detested the regiment of strangers that they have made laws to bar all titles which any stranger may claim of inheritance within the realm.

Even if Parliament did agree to recognize Mary's right to the succession, Sadler passionately concluded, "our common people and the stones in the streets would rebel against it."[15] It should be noted that Sadler's protest was directed against Mary as an alien, not as a Catholic. In this respect it was, I think, representative of the deepest prejudices of the Commons and their England.

To get back to the petition, its requests came at the end. The House first humbly begged the Queen to marry.[16] The Commons sincerely desired Elizabeth to wed and have progeny, but their request was little more than a formality. A mere promise in this regard would not furnish them with the immediate security that they had come to Westminster in quest of. That they had come to see a present settlement of the succession established had already been made manifest in the petition. This they made its last matter of business.

Here they pledged themselves to uphold the limitation of the crown made in Henry VIII's Third Succession Act (1543), and then made a pointed request for clarification:

Your Majesty is the last expressly named within the body of the same Act: and for that your subjects cannot judge, nor do know anything of, the form or validity of any further limitation set in certainty for want of heir of your body . . . it may please your Majesty by publication of certainty already provided, if any such be, or else by limitation of some certainty, if none be, to provide a most gracious remedy in this great necessity.[17]

The Act in question had authorized Henry VIII to appoint the succession after his own children and their issue by his last will. What the petition really said was: if there was a genuine will of Henry VIII, the Queen in Parliament should confirm it and make public its succession provisions; if there was no such testament, the Queen in Parliament should proceed with the declaration of a further limitation of the crown. This was probably the most important passage in the petition.

The House knew that the next heir to the crown according to Henry's will was Catherine Grey, but it is doubtful that any M.P. had ever seen the original will—only constats and copies were available. This made it open to question whether there was an authentic original. The Commons now asked the Queen to have this uncertainty cleared up. If Henry's will was valid, they would accept Catherine as next in line; if not, a new limitation of the crown was in order.

Considering the probable divisions of preference over claimants, it is difficult to say whether the House would have chosen Catherine if a new succession were to be declared. The significant thing is the implication that the Commons felt obligated to recognize Catherine's title if Henry's will proved genuine. This reflected a belief that the determinant in the succession question had to be law and not expediency. And that law had to be English law; vague notions such as the "law of all nations" and "God's appointment" would not do. Therefore, when the petition indirectly asked about the validity of the will of Henry VIII, it brought up what the House probably regarded as the crux of the succession question.

Elizabeth received the petition with thanks, but said she would defer her answer until she had time to consider fully the weighty matters involved.[18] Her strategy clearly was to delay her reply until the Commons granted the subsidy and completed the other business required of them. Since they were not yet prepared to try the radical course of withholding supplies, she eventually was to have her way.[19] Meanwhile the center of the stage shifted to the House of Lords. Here we need not be concerned about a succession petition. The Lords did present one to the Queen, but it is unimpressive compared with its counter-

part in the Lower House.[20] There were other succession activities in the Lords of more interest and perhaps of greater import.

The first of these was reported by Quadra on 28 March: "I
hear that it has been proposed to the Lords in Parliament to
reduce the succession to the crown to four lines or families in
the kingdom, leaving to the Queen the nomination of the one
that has to succeed her out of these four."[21] The significant
phrase here was "in the kingdom": this would exclude the Scottish Queen. Though not specified, the "four lines or families"
probably would be represented by the four obvious claimants:
Lady Catherine Grey, Lady Margaret Lennox, Lady Margaret
Strange, and the Earl of Huntingdon. This could be considered
a compromise proposal. Parliament would achieve its real end
by barring Mary Stuart; Elizabeth would have a limited right
to appoint the succession. Though Quadra is our sole source for
the proposal, it seems quite possible that such a plan was suggested as an alternative to an outright settlement of the succession.

If it was, however, it is unlikely that the proposal was, as
Quadra wrote in a letter of 3 April, "made in behalf of the
Queen." It was hardly to Elizabeth's interest, being too one-
sided. The Parliament men would gain their main objective by
eliminating the one candidate whom the Queen perhaps preferred as her successor; then they would pass her the burden of
making a choice among the claimants on which they probably
would have found it difficult to agree themselves. It might have
been different if they had offered her an unlimited right to appoint the succession by will, but this was the kind of proposition
that would provoke the Queen of Scots into taking the very ac-
tions it was Elizabeth's policy to prevent. Indeed, in the letter
of 3 April Quadra also reported that Maitland of Lethington,
then in London, was threatening to make hostile alliances, perhaps in reaction to the alleged proposal, among other irritants.[22]
Therefore, if the proposal was really advanced, the Queen on
whose behalf it was supposed to have been made probably saw
to it that it was dropped.*

* Neale, *Parliaments*, p. 112, holds that if the proposal was made, it originated from the Queen as "an astute move" to force Parliament "to face the

In the same letter of the third Quadra described a new proposition that came up in the House of Lords:

I understand that they have agreed to pass an act providing that in case the Queen dies no office, either judicial or in the household, shall become vacant, and twenty-four councilors are appointed to administer the government. Besides this, Parliament is notified that they must meet within thirty days (after the demise), and that not only are peers and bishops, who are fixed members, to be summoned, but also the same deputies from the towns that have sat in the preceding Parliament.[23]

Six days later another agent of Spain made essentially the same report, and added that the purpose of summoning Parliament would be to name Elizabeth's successor.[24] In this case our Spanish sources are substantially corroborated in a paper drafted by Cecil and endorsed "A clause to have been inserted in an Act meant for the succession but not passed."*

The proposition probably came from a partisan group. It certainly was aimed at Mary; she could not expect to fare well if the succession were to be determined by Parliament after Elizabeth's controlling hand was no more. Its authors may even have had a further objective than Mary's exclusion. Quadra pictured a plot in which Cecil contemplated having the several English claimants made members of the Council. This would bring them to London, away from their sources of strength, at Elizabeth's death. Then, London "being so much in favor of the Earl of Hertford on the ground of religion, the crown might be suddenly given to Lady Catherine, his wife, and the rest of them all taken prisoners and put safe under lock and key." Quadra understood that the proposal was rejected for fear that such a plot was behind it.[25]

Be that as it may, the proposal raised difficulties that would have constituted sufficient ground to drop it. For one thing, the constitutional notion involved was novel: an interregnum of

---

practical difficulties involved in any decisive action: an apple of discord tossed among the factions." This is a possible interpretation, but, with great respect for Sir John, I prefer the one given above.

* *PRO, SP, Dom., Eliz.,* XXVIII, 20. The only important exception is that it contains no limitation of the councilors to twenty-four.

conciliar government concluded by the naming of a monarch by
a monarchless Parliament. An interregnum proper was strange
to Tudor England. There had always been a king or queen,
albeit sometimes a usurper, in whose name England was ruled.
According to custom, moreover, Elizabeth's Council and Parliament would die with her. It was doubtful that the Queen in
Parliament could legislate life into her Council and last Parliament that would continue after her demise.* Even if this could
be done, it was questionable that power could be given to a
monarchless Parliament to bestow the crown. Henry VIII in
Parliament had thrice changed the succession, but no Parliament had ever appointed a monarch on its own.†

Secondly, the feasibility of the proposal was equally doubtful.
An interregnum of a month or more would almost have to produce menaces. It would afford an opportunity for factions to
form behind the several claimants and prepare for civil war.
It would also be a time when the Queen of Scots, anticipating
an unfavorable verdict from Parliament, would doubtless seek
French and/or Spanish aid, and otherwise make ready for armed
intervention. Nor was it certain that either rebellion or invasion
would serenely await the decision of Parliament. The prospects
of an interregnum were worse than those of Elizabeth's dying
with nothing arranged. In that event the leading political figures might at least seize the initiative by proclaiming one of the
pretenders, who could then face eventualities with a sort of *fait
accompli*. A proposal that promised to be impracticable as well
as unconstitutional would be worse than no solution at all.

Nonetheless, the fact that the Lords considered it is of some
significance. The alleged plan, whereby Parliament would limit
the succession to four lines, from which the Queen would take
her choice, probably went as far as the Lords were willing to go
in the way of a compromise. If this proposition was really of-

---

* Henry VIII, with statutory authority, provided in his will that his own
councilors should govern during his son's minority, but the councilors found
it necessary to seek a new commission from Edward VI before they could
"comply" with the terms of the will. Pollard, *Political History*, p. 6.

† The views that Henry IV and Richard III had parliamentary titles are no
longer tenable. Lapsley, pp. 423–49, 557–606; Gairdner, p. 87.

fered and refused, the Lords may well have become convinced that the present session was not going to see a succession settlement; some of them perhaps even began to suspect that Elizabeth was never going to permit one during her lifetime. Consequently, the idea of a parliamentary settlement after an interregnum was probably suggested as an alternative. If it proved unsatisfactory on reflection, the Lords had at least made an attempt to find a much-needed new approach. They were closer to the right track than their fellows in the Commons.

The doings of the Lords and Commons reveal little of their preferences about where the succession should rest. Indications that majorities in both Houses were opposed to Mary Stuart's claim are merely negative. Hints of moves that may have been made in behalf of Catherine Grey, namely, the implied request of the Commons for information about the validity of Henry VIII's will and the supposed scheme behind the proposal in the Lords for an interregnum, hardly constitute evidence. Nothing suggests that either House was prepared to advocate the recognition of a specific title. In fact, only two witnesses say anything about the inclinations of the Lords and Commons with respect to the choice of a successor.

The first is Lord John Grey of Pyrgo, Catherine's uncle. When asked by his examiners in April 1564 whether he had ever conferred with anyone about the succession, Grey said, "Many communed thereupon in the Parliament, some in favor of the Scottish Queen, some of the Lady Margaret Lennox, some of the Lady Catherine, some of the Lady Margaret Strange, some of the Earl of Huntingdon."[26] This is not too informative. It reveals that all of the obvious claimants had some backers in the Parliament, but it fails to indicate how much support each of them had. It may be significant here that in 1564 Grey was testifying about certain activities of John Hales that we shall take up in the next chapter. It was one of those occasions when Elizabeth smelled conspiracy. Therefore, Lord John may have deliberately avoided touching on the strength of his niece's cause in the Parliament of 1563 to minimize the seriousness of the later situation. Be that as it may, we do not learn much from our only English source.

The second witness is the inevitable Quadra. In a letter of 7 February 1563 he wrote:

I refer to the fact, now known publicly, that the nobles are divided on the subject of succession, as the enemies of Lord Robert see that she (the Queen) would really condescend to appoint Lord Huntingdon her successor, and that this would be opening the door to the marriage with Robert and put the kingdom in his hands, they have most of them met with the Earl of Arundel and the majority are inclined to assist Lady Catherine.

As for the Commons, they were perplexed by the variety of antagonistic claims that confronted them; they blushed to side with such "poor creatures" as the claimants were. "Many have therefore joined the Earl of Arundel more for the sake of company than for any wish to favor Lady Catherine and her husband and, by the same rule, many follow Lord Robert and the Earl of Huntingdon rather out of fear than affection."[27]

Quadra's appraisal of the situation in the Lords depended on the assumption that Elizabeth was willing to recognize Huntingdon's claim in order to have an excuse to marry Dudley: a match between the Queen and the brother-in-law of her heir presumptive could be justified as solidifying the new succession. Though we may be reasonably sure that Elizabeth had no intention of selling the succession for love, in 1563 many nobles probably were afraid that she did. Indeed, Catherine's friends may have been spreading such a story to win the support of the peers, most of whom would be jealous of Dudley's advancement. Now if the main source of Catherine's strength in the Lords was a fear that was in all likelihood unfounded, her cause there must not have been really too formidable. It would take far deeper convictions to present to the Queen the united front that she might not have been able to resist.

Quadra's statements about the Commons probably were substantially correct. The average M.P. must have been somewhat bewildered by the several conflicting claims. He lacked detailed treatises on the succession to help him get acquainted with the facts and arguments for and against each of them. And the claimants themselves, save the Queen of Scots, were not an impressive lot; they certainly lacked the power and prestige of the pretenders who made the political life of the fifteenth century so uneasy. Hence most of the M.P.'s naturally would have found it easier to follow the lead of others than to make up their own minds, but we need not accept Quadra's view that they were only following great nobles. The Lower House had men capable of taking the lead on the succession: we have already met Thomas Norton; we shall meet more like him in due season. At any rate, the really significant element in the situation was the apparent inability of the Commons to unite behind a single claimant.

The evidence permits some fairly safe conclusions about the succession preferences of the men who sat in the Parliament of 1563. There can be little doubt that all of the leading claimants had some support. It seems a good guess that Catherine had the largest party and Huntingdon the second. Mary probably had more secret friends, especially in the Lords, than is apparent.[*] Two points stand out, however. In the first place, it seems certain that no pretender had anything like the backing of a majority of both Houses. Elizabeth might have found it difficult to deny Parliament's request to settle the succession if it could have agreed on a candidate, but a divided Parliament was like putty in her hands. Secondly, the Queen of Scots hardly had the sort of strength in either House that would satisfy one of her spirit. Even if Elizabeth had otherwise been disposed to let Parliament decide the question, the chance that Mary might take offense at its verdict probably constituted sufficient reason to defer the matter.

Elizabeth had to be concerned about Mary's reaction to the Parliament of 1563. Mary was no comparatively helpless creature like her rivals for the English succession; she was a monarch in her own right, and a neighboring one at that. Nor was she irrevocably committed to seeking the succession; she had never

---

[*] In his letter of 7 February Quadra reported that a well-known Catholic M.P. had told him that "some of the nobles would like to set aside" all of the English pretenders for Mary if Philip II would consent to her marriage with Don Carlos, "in which they say all would gladly concur and receive him with open arms as king." *CSP, Span., Eliz.*, I, 297. The conclusion sounds like the sort of nonsense spies or fanatics were ever pouring into Quadra's ears, but it does seem likely that Mary had covert support in the Lords.

actually relinquished her present claim to Elizabeth's throne by fulfilling her "obligation" to sign the Treaty of Edinburgh.* If Scotland alone was not a serious threat to England, Mary might find a powerful ally in Catholic Europe, which regarded her as the rightful Queen of England. Elizabeth could not afford to allow Parliament to do anything to provoke Mary's anger.

In February 1563 Mary sent Maitland on another mission to London, ostensibly to offer her mediation in the conflict then in progress between England and France.[28] No doubt she was more concerned about what was going on in Parliament, about which she gave Maitland instructions that he was to use "at his discretion." If the succession came up in Parliament, he was to ask Elizabeth to see that nothing prejudicial to Mary's interests was done. If necessary, he was to gain access to Parliament and plead Mary's cause. If Parliament was then still unwilling to accept the validity of her title, Mary told Maitland, "you shall, in our name and upon our behalf, publicly and solemnly protest that we are thereby injured and offended, and [shall look] for such lawful remedies as the law and consuetude have provided for them that are enormously and excessively hurt."[29]

Once in London Maitland apparently found it convenient to exercise his right to be discreet about his instructions. He may have made representations and threats about the alleged plan of the Lords to limit the succession to four lines, but if so, this was as far as he went in following his instructions.[30] Perhaps he realized that Elizabeth was not going to permit Parliament to do anything about the succession. He also may have found Parliament so hostile to Mary that there was no purpose in appealing to it in her behalf. Moreover, his bargaining position was weakened by the news of the assassination of the Duke of Guise, which, wrote Quadra, made Mary's negotiations for peace between England and France "ridiculous and contemptible."[31] Anyhow, Maitland was not long in London when he evidently concluded that a different approach than that outlined in his instructions was in order.

---

* The Treaty of Edinburgh (1560) required Mary to abstain from using the title and arms of England. For her reasons for refusing to ratify it, see her letter to Elizabeth of 5 January 1562 in Labanoff, I, 123–27.

He paid a visit to Quadra and made Mary's matrimonial prospects the main topic of conversation. At the time Mary had several marriage projects under consideration, the most important of which involved Don Carlos of Spain, Charles IX of France, Archduke Charles of Austria, and Lord Darnley. Maitland dismissed the last three as unsatisfactory. Darnley would only bring with him the union of the Stuart claims, which was not enough for Mary at this stage of the game. The Archduke would mean little to her unless Philip II of Spain would guarantee him more effective aid than that King was then probably willing to offer. Charles IX would be desirable except for the difficulties that would arise from his being the brother of Mary's late husband. It was the demented Don Carlos whom Mary really wanted. Even during Elizabeth's lifetime he might bring Mary England; he offered her prospects of an eventual empire that would make her former state as wife of Francis II blush with comparison. Therefore, Maitland let Quadra know that his Queen's main interest would now be to arrange a match with the Prince of Spain.[32]

The potential menace to England of such a marriage was obvious. We do not know if Elizabeth was aware that Maitland had approached Quadra in its behalf. Possibly Maitland, who may have been insincere about the business, saw to it that she got news of the proposal.[33] Then again, she may have heard about it from a spy. Anyway, she probably knew that something was in the wind. A little earlier Quadra had reported that the English suspected a match between Mary and Archduke Charles was in the making.[34] Such a marriage might seem to Elizabeth nearly as bad as one between Mary and Don Carlos, especially since she had no way of knowing how far Philip was prepared to commit himself in the Archduke's behalf. Consequently, Elizabeth had some reason to fear that Mary was about to embark on a matrimonial venture that would be a definite threat to England. It was now Elizabeth's turn to try a new move.

On 28 March Quadra reported that she had told Maitland "that if his mistress would take her advice and wished to marry safely and happily, she would give her a husband who would ensure both, and this was Lord Robert, in whom nature has implanted so many graces that if she wished to marry she would prefer him to all the princes in the world."[35] The notion of tempting Mary to abandon the prospect of a Hapsburg match by using a man of Dudley's background as bait may sound absurd, but it is likely that Elizabeth was serious in making the proposal. She may well have seen it as a logical solution for her own difficulties and Mary's. Dudley as Mary's consort might assure Elizabeth of a friendly Scotland. He might also win Mary to Protestantism and thus make her claim more acceptable to an English Parliament. In time even Elizabeth might become willing to recognize the wife of her favorite as her successor. The proposal, as Sir John Neale has commented, "was neither unstatesmanlike nor unfriendly to Mary."[36]

Once Elizabeth advanced the proposal, it behooved her to bring the Parliament of 1563 to a close as soon as possible. The negotiations for the Dudley match could be conducted more effectively without the potentially explosive presence of the Lords and Commons at Westminster. On 10 April, the required business having been completed, Elizabeth prorogued the Parliament.[37] Immediately before doing so she made, through Lord Keeper Bacon, a sort of response—it cannot be called an answer —to the petitions of the Houses: those who believed that she was determined not to marry were mistaken; the succession was too great a cause for her to speak on until she had further advice.[38] This was all there was to it as far as her Lords and Commons were concerned; they could now return to their homes.*

This abrupt postponement could not have been received favorably by many of the Parliament men. Most of the knights and burgesses had believed that the Queen had called them to Westminster to help settle the succession; now they knew differently and perhaps felt that they had been duped. But Eliza-

---

* In her speech Elizabeth may have given a hint of her real thoughts: "I have good record in this place that other means than ye mentioned have been thought of." This was, according to Neale, "surely a covert reference to her as yet secret plan for marrying Dudley to Mary." Neale, *Parliaments*, p. 128. Be that as it may, Parliament was in no position to appreciate Elizabeth's secret thoughts.

beth had blundered in merely proroguing Parliament; the men of 1563 would be back to fight again. Many of them probably realized that they themselves were in part responsible for their present failure. The Commons had committed a major tactical error in not making at least a show of withholding supplies; next time they would know not to yield so quickly. Both Houses had been at a disadvantage in dealing with the Queen because they had been divided over the choice of a succession candidate; this too might be corrected by the next Parliament. Indeed, one M.P. had already commenced activities aimed at "clearing up" the confusion over the claimants in the interest of Lady Catherine Grey. This man was John Hales of Coventry.

5. The Tempestas Halesiana

John Hales of Coventry had a singular bent for taking dangerous positions. During Somerset's Protectorate he was the most
energetic of that party of agrarian reformers known as the
"Commonwealth's men," and took the lead in the Protector's
unsuccessful campaign against unlawful enclosures.[1] During the
Marian Exile, Hales was much in evidence in the quarrels between the English congregation at Frankfort and their pastor,
Robert Horne, future Bishop of Winchester; he joined David
Whitehead, a fellow left-wing Anglican, in leading the demo-
cratic revolution of the majority, which was based on the prin-
ciple that "the church was above the pastor and not the pastor
above the church."[2] On his return to England he presented *The
Oration of John Hales to Queen Elizabeth ... at Her First En-
trance to Her Reign*.[3] A modern commentator has said that the
Oration appears to be "a violently loyal tract; but the writer's
support is dependent on the Queen's fulfilling a definite Puritan program, taken largely from Ponet's *Politike Power*."[4] In
1563 Hales decided to meddle with the succession in behalf of
Lady Catherine Grey.

A record of insurgency was not his only qualification for his
task. Hales was reputed to be a scholar, though the extent of
his knowledge of the classics may be debatable.[5] He evidently
picked up a smattering of law while working for his uncle, Sir
Christopher Hales, who had been Solicitor General and Attorney General under Henry VIII.[6] His was probably the super-

ficial learning that makes for a good pamphleteer. Hales was also a gentleman of consequence. He had large holdings of abbey lands, and held the lucrative Chancery office of Clerk of the Hanaper.[7] His political connections, as we shall see, were considerable.

Hales sat for Lancaster Borough in the Parliament of 1563.[8] There is no record of his having taken part in its succession debates, but it is difficult to believe that he did not. The *Lewd Pasquil*, a lampoon aimed at the radicals of the Parliament, called Hales "the hottest."[9] If he did not speak, he was engaged in other activities that proved more provocative than any words uttered in either of the Houses.

We have read Lord John Grey's testimony that each of the leading claimants had some support in the Parliament. Hales's awareness of the obstacle that this division of sentiment presented to any succession settlement no doubt inspired him to try to do something about it for the benefit of his favorite candidate. Grey also testified that Hales approached him during the Parliament and asked if Lady Frances Brandon, Catherine's mother, was legitimate. Lord John gave him some affirmative evidence, and a little later he learned that Hales had written a "book" on the question.[10] The "book" was a tract entitled *A Declaration of the Succession of the Crown Imperial of England.*[11]

As the title indicates, Hales did not confine himself to showing the legitimacy of Lady Frances. The mere validation of the marriage of Charles Brandon, Duke of Suffolk, and Mary Tudor, younger daughter of Henry VII, would not be enough to establish the primacy of Catherine's claim. Hence Hales also maintained that Mary Queen of Scots and Lady Margaret Lennox, descendants of Henry VII's elder daughter, were excluded from the succession by the common-law rule against inheritance by aliens. Moreover, there was another matter that probably made the questions about the Grey descent and the Stuart Englishry of small import. If Henry VIII's will was valid, Catherine's right was almost undeniable in law. Accordingly, Hales argued as best he could from the evidence available to him that Henry's will was genuine.

This is not the time to elaborate on Hales's arguments, but it is relevant to consider briefly the way in which he made his case. His main themes had already been implied in *Gorboduc*. What the *Declaration* did was to drop the mask of suggestions: names were named, and arguments based on law and history were expounded in detail. It did not matter to Hales that Elizabeth loathed Catherine Grey, and wanted above all to keep on friendly terms with Mary Stuart. He boldly rejected the latter's claim, and specifically proclaimed the former's right. Small wonder he was called "the hottest."

Something else that may be significant about the strategy of the *Declaration* is that it reads as if it were a speech made in Parliament. Though it was composed before the session of 1563 was over, it clearly was not read in Parliament.[12] Nevertheless, its peculiar form seems deliberate. Hales probably wrote the *Declaration* mainly to convince his fellows in Parliament of the justice of Catherine's claim. He apparently was attempting to plead a case that even he would not dare present in open Parliament; his tract may be regarded as a secret motion that he intended to circulate among the Parliament men.

Such an approach had dangerous implications. Hales had probably concluded that Elizabeth was not interested in any succession settlement. Thus he addressed Parliament alone, and not the Queen. This might be an appropriate procedure for ordinary matters; it was improper in a case that touched the Queen so closely as the succession. Did Hales expect Parliament to reach its verdict, and then urge Elizabeth to accept it? Or did he regard Parliament as competent to establish the succession on its own? If he was thinking in terms of the second course, his tract may be considered a harbinger of rather revolutionary constitutional ideas.

Hales did not confine his efforts in Catherine's behalf to the *Declaration*. It was not altogether satisfactory just to maintain her right to the succession. Parliament might hesitate to accept a woman who had had sons by a man who was not legally recognized as her husband, and whose sons could not follow her on the throne if the law regarded them as bastards. It would be unwise to settle the present succession question in a way that might open the door for future ones. Therefore, Hales took steps designed to establish the validity of Catherine's marriage with Edward Seymour, Earl of Hertford.

He sent Robert Beale, an able young Puritan, on a trip to the Continent, where he was to obtain the opinions of eminent canonists.[13] Beale carried out his assignment with dispatch and success. He secured three discourses from German canonists dealing with the "former marriage" between Catherine and Lord Henry Herbert, and two discourses from doctors of the Imperial Chamber of Spires and the University of Paris concerning the "marriage" of Catherine and Hertford. To these the indefatigable emissary added a large discourse of his own on the latter subject. As Hales must have expected, the writings reached conclusions favorable to Catherine's honor.[14] Beale alone had accomplished about as much for Hales as Cranmer and sundry other agents had been able to do for Henry VIII in the case of Catherine of Aragon.

The topics of the discourses show that there were really two aspects to the problem of Catherine Grey's matrimonial status, namely, her old contract with Herbert and her clandestine marriage with Hertford. The latter, though questionable in itself, was dependent on the former. If Catherine had completed her contract with Herbert, there could be no marriage between her and Hertford. There is no evidence, however, that the Herbert business was actually brought up in 1563. Beale perhaps only secured opinions on it to play safe. We may more appropriately go into it when it comes up in a later succession tract and confine our attention now to the more immediate matter of the Hertford affair.

We have already dealt at some length with the case of Catherine and Hertford as it arose in 1561–62. The couple had then told their stories, maintaining that they had made a contract to marry and performed the same with an Anglican solemnization. The Queen's Commission of Inquiry had heard their testimonies and had ruled that there had been no marriage. This verdict, just or not, was going to stand. There was little use in continuing to argue that there had been an ecclesiastical ceremony. A different approach was required. This was found in the expedient of pleading that Catherine and Hertford had made what might be termed a canon law marriage. The new argument ran, as Hales is said to have put it, *"that their very consent made them man and wife."*[15] It was to buttress this argument that Hales sent Beale on his mission to the foreign canonists.

Hales's efforts apparently were supplemented by those of Hertford's lawyers. An anonymous and undated letter addressed to Hertford, which internal evidence seems to place about the first half of 1563, speaks of an appeal that has been devised and urges the Earl to keep it secret for a while. It further tells him that Aubrey, his counsel, wants him "by some pretty means" to acknowledge Catherine as his wife in conversations so that about three persons can say they have heard him do so at least three times since sentence was given against him. The letter suggests the Lieutenant of the Tower, his wife, and Hertford's servitors as possible witnesses. It closes by informing the Earl that Catherine will be admonished to follow a similar course.[16] The obvious purpose of the proposed acknowledgments was to help establish consent. The mention of the Lieutenant of the Tower probably means that the letter was written before August 1563, when Catherine and Hertford were transferred to other and separate custodies.[17]

The case that emerged is presented in an undated paper endorsed by Cecil: "A case of matrimony: Edward Hertford, Lady Catherine." Its substance is as follows:

First, I say that if [there was] only *sponsilia de futuro* [followed by] carnal copulation not forced . . . , it is a perfect marriage [according to canon law]. But in this case secret marriage is confessed by both parties. [This] the Church cannot refuse [because] it is the consent of the parties that chiefly ties man and woman together. And the omission of ceremonies does not make their marriage void if there be no other impediment.

Secondly, I say [neither do] they need . . . witnesses in this case [nor are they] bound to prove their marriage [so long as] they both confess it. [Nor ought they] be examined of the circumstances. [Clandestine marriages are permitted by God's Law. And Christ said:] "judge not, that ye be not judged." [Only God can judge secrets. Any mortal judge who wrongly tries to dissolve a clandestine marriage] doth sin himself.

Thirdly, I say that the omission of the ceremonies appointed by the Church [should] be corrected according to the censures of the Church

[only] if they be omitted of malice.... If they be omitted [neither] of malice nor of set purpose, there ought to be an equity admitted.

Fourthly, although the parties upon examination do differ or vary in circumstances ..., it forceth not if they agree and abide by the consent which is the substance and the principal: for the examination of them done contrary to the law is to be counted as not done and of no effect. And ... a sentence thereupon is against God's Law [because by the judgments of divines and canonists] such secret matrimony is matrimony before God. [Such a sentence is also] against the law of nature because consent is a sufficient test of marriage amongst all peoples. [It is also against man's law] because the law saith that they ought not ... be compelled to part.

Fifthly, I say that ... their agreement and confession of marriage before the judges [(i.e. the Commission of Inquiry) is as good as if it had been] published according to the common order. [The purpose of] the common order of publication is to no other end than to avoid slander [by one's neighbors. In this case there is no need for such publication since the parties have confessed their marriage] in open and solemn judgment.

Sixthly, I say that such confession both by man's law and God's Law shall perpetually bind them as man and wife. [Man's law does not allow those who have confessed marriage to marry again. According to God's Law,] knowing themselves to be man and wife they should do against their consciences if they should marry ... again and so sin. [And therefore] if they may not marry again, it must of necessity be said [that] this was a true marriage.[18]

Here we have Hales's argument written large, and the views of Beale and the canonists epitomized. The main case is simple. Clandestine marriage is acceptable to God. Neither ceremonies nor witnesses are necessary for such a marriage; only consent is essential. And God alone is capable of judging secrets; man sins when he judges them wrongly. Hence the Church should not refuse a clandestine marriage if it is confessed by both parties. And Catherine and Hertford had confessed their marriage before the Commission of Inquiry. Thus the very investigation initiated by the Queen to "judge" the "pretended marriage" is adroitly used to help in making that marriage valid.

Of course, this argument is subject to an obvious question. What if Catherine and Hertford really never had been married secretly? Then their confession was false and the commissioners had committed no sin in giving their judgment. But this could not be proved, and even if it was true, the case was not lost. Confession of marriage before the Commission of Inquiry was in itself a binding act of consent. Moreover, it was a consent made before unexceptionable witnesses, and this was followed by copulation that produced a second child. Witnessed consent followed by intercourse constituted a true marriage according to the canon law, which was still the matrimonial law of England.[19] If, according to a later Catholic writer, the original clandestine marriage was not established, Catherine's first son "might be legitimate before God and yet illegitimate before men, and consequently incapable of all succession as otherwise he might pretend by his said mother." But, as the same writer pointed out, it certainly might be argued that her second son was legitimate before men, since his parents had openly confessed their marriage before his conception.[20] And establishing a canon law marriage between Catherine and Hertford, and the legitimacy of one of their sons, would be sufficient for Hales's purposes.

Hales must have been satisfied with what he and his associates had done for the Suffolk cause. The new approach to the problem of Catherine's matrimonial status had much to be said for it from a legal viewpoint. An ecclesiastical court would have found it difficult to deny an appeal based on it. Hales's succession tract was also promising. It was then the only detailed discussion of the subject in existence, and it presented a strong case in law. It was bound to make an impression on the men who someday would be called back to Parliament, where they again could raise the succession question. However, appeals have to reach courts and tracts have to circulate, and such things could hardly be accomplished in secrecy. This meant there would have to be trouble ahead.

Early in 1564 Elizabeth got wind of Hales's doings. To say she was displeased would be an understatement. She could not fairly object if Hertford's lawyers entered an appeal against the verdict of the Commission of Inquiry, so long as they did this through the proper channels, but she could hardly be expected to tolerate Hales's sending Beale overseas to obtain the opinions of foreign canonists on the matter. True, Henry VIII had engaged in a similar venture to seek a way out of his own matrimonial difficulties, but for Hales, a mere subject, to call on alien divines in a case that was clearly within the competence of the Church of England was entirely different. Cecil wrote, "This dealing of his offendeth the Queen's Majesty very much."[21]

Elizabeth also was irritated about Hales's succession tract. The mere advocacy of Catherine's claim would have been enough to rouse her anger, but Hales, as Cecil pointed out, had been "foolish...in writing the book so precisely against the Queen of Scotland's title."[22] The *Declaration* was likely to impress Mary as indicating English Protestant hostility to her claim; it was not going to make her think better of the idea of marrying Dudley. Hales was endangering what small chance of success Elizabeth's Scottish policy had. Add to this Beale's mission, and it is not surprising that Hales's activities engendered a storm: a storm that Walter Haddon called the *Tempestas Halesiana.*[23]

The Queen was quick to suspect that Hales was not alone responsible for what had happened. Beale's journey had to be financed, and it was unlikely that Hales was supplying the cash as well as the brains. And the succession tract perhaps displayed more knowledge of law and history than Hales possessed. Indeed, both ventures were too risky for one man to be likely to undertake on his own. The ever-suspicious Elizabeth must have feared that there had been a conspiracy; she perhaps was uncertain whether it was just a conspiracy to have Catherine's claim to the succession recognized, or one aimed at a more immediate transfer of the crown. No time was lost in launching an investigation.

Incomplete records of this investigation are extant. They mainly consist of the testimonies of Hales; Lord John Grey; Francis Newdigate, Hertford's stepfather; and Anthony Penn, one of Hertford's servants. Though these testimonies do not tell all, something resembling a coherent account can be gleaned from them. We shall consider them first in terms of the succession tract, and then see what they reveal about the case of matrimony.

Nothing in the testimonies indicates that the idea of writing the *Declaration* originated with anyone but Hales, but there is evidence that others supplied him with information that he used in it. We have already referred to his conversation with Lord John Grey about the legitimacy of Lady Frances Brandon. Here he learned of litigation between Lady Frances and Lady Powes, a daughter of Charles Brandon by Anne Browne, that showed the former to be legitimate.[24] Francis Newdigate's testimony reveals that Beale sent back a "book of Charles's case" to use for the "book of succession."[25] "Charles's case" doubtless refers to the complex matrimonial business of Charles Brandon, which Hales discusses at some length in the *Declaration*.[26]

Then there is the important thirteenth interrogatory put to Hales on 25 April 1564: "Where had he the writing under the great seal concerning King Henry VIII's last will? To how many hath he shewed the same since he began to deal in the case of the Earl of Hertford? Where is that writing and how many of them doth he know to be in any other place? How many copies are thereof . . . and in whose custody?"[27] Though Hales's answers are lacking, the questions are significant in themselves. In the validity or invalidity of Henry VIII's will lay the legal heart of the succession question. The *Declaration* mentions the existence of diverse constats of a missing chancery enrollment of the will that were made under the great seal during Edward VI's reign.[28] The thirteenth interrogatory implies that Hales had help in obtaining this important evidence. He probably did.

A major aim of the investigation was to find out what sort of plot was behind Hales's tract and who was involved. The examiners evidently tried to show Lord John Grey to be Hales's chief ally in the succession business. They got little out of Grey. When they asked him if he had ever conferred with any person about the succession, he evasively replied that "many communed thereupon in the Parliament." As for the *Declaration*, Grey admitted having it "in his keeping four days," but maintained "that he neither did retain copy thereof, nor did ever commune with any person thereupon, but did restore it again to John Hales."[29] This was all Grey would say about the matter in spite of the apparent dissatisfaction of his examiners.*

Nor did the examiners get Hales to involve Grey any deeper. Hales confessed showing him the tract, but denied ever discussing the succession with Grey, who "had no skill in the law." Hales also went on to absolve himself and Grey from intending any conspiracy:

And being examined whether there was any conference with my Lord John what should be the end of this matter, either in the Queen's life or if God should take her Grace to His mercy, if the marriage [of Catherine and Hertford] should be found good or the title of succession to be in the right of my Lady Catherine; he refuseth the merits of Christ's passion if there was any change meant or thought by him thereupon. And moreover he said always, and doth say, that there is great cause of thanks to be given to God that it [the succession] lighteth upon such a poor woman ... who hath no friend ... able to do any hurt to the Queen's Majesty or the state, nor any so foolish that if they could would enterprise any such thing. And as for my Lord John, he thinketh him to be the most faithful man in England to the Queen. . . . And being examined whether he had any conference in the Parliament time touching the succession with my Lord John to make any friends in the Parliament House for my Lady Catherine's title; he saith that he doth not know anything there at all, and the only dealing in this matter came of himself touching the making of his book.

Nonetheless, Hales did bring two other names into the picture. When asked to whom besides Grey he ever showed the *Declaration,* he answered "that he remembreth no more but Fleetwood and Foster with whom he hath talked in the Parliament last."[30] These were William Fleetwood, who sat for Lancaster Borough with Hales, and John Foster, who sat for a Wiltshire borough, as did Francis Newdigate.[31] Thus Hales only admitted showing the *Declaration* to Grey, Fleetwood, and Foster. He apparently also discussed the succession with the last two. Newdigate knew of the existence of the tract, but no

---

* "I moan my Lord John who ... hath no better consideration ... but ... to choose the willful and obstinate way in defending stoutly such an untruth, so openly and plainly seen, than by an humble and dutiful declaration of a known truth submit his fault to the clemency of so gracious a prince...." Dudley to Cecil, 26 April 1564; *HM* 6990, fol. 28.

one said that he ever had seen it. This evidence provided some basis for the indictment presented by a Middlesex jury: "that John Hales...presumptuously and contemptuously did debate with diverse persons concerning the right, title, limitation, and succession of the Imperial Crown of England; and did, without license, distribute copies of a pamphlet on this subject."[32] It did not, however, indicate that anything really dangerous had taken place. This will require further consideration, but first let us turn to the case of matrimony.

Here the initiative evidently did not come from Hales. He testified that Newdigate first moved him to meddle in the question of the marriage of Catherine and Hertford.[33] Newdigate, as Hertford's stepfather, naturally wanted to see the marriage validated. It would seem that this, and not the succession, was his primary concern. Knowing of Hales's support of Catherine's claim, he probably suggested to him the importance of doing something about her marital status. Hales then must have conceived the idea of sending Beale to the Continent.

The testimonies indicate that Beale's mission was not solely a matter between Hales and his emissary. According to Newdigate, Lord John Grey was made cognizant of the project and became its "chief commender."* Newdigate had much to do with the successful carrying out of the scheme. It was from him that Hales obtained the money to finance Beale's trip. Newdigate seems to have secured these funds from Hertford. He also supplied Hales with a copy of the appeal that had been devised for Catherine and Hertford by their lawyers. It apparently furnished Beale with the details of the case to pass on to the foreign canonists.[34]

The discourses sent back by Beale presumably were intended to be used in the execution of the appeal, but difficulties seem to have been encountered with Hertford's lawyers on that score. Anthony Penn testified that Beale's own discourse was delivered to him by Thomas Dannett, a cousin of Cecil and a veteran conspirator.[35] Dannett told Penn to show it to Hertford's law-

* *Burghley Papers*, I, 416–17. Grey denied that he was at all privy to Beale's mission (*ibid.*, I, 412–13), but this seems almost inconceivable. We have already seen that Grey was not regarded as a cooperative witness.

yers in order to "quicken their wits." When he showed it to
them they "nothing liked it," but their resistance evidently was
short-lived.[36] Newdigate testified that the appeal was renewed
and brought to Hertford, "done, performed, and entered by
Dr. Aubrey."

A controversy then seems to have ensued between Hales and
Newdigate over how to proceed. According to Newdigate, Hales
wanted the appeal "committed in trust and adventure into
the Chancery." Newdigate would not agree to this, perhaps on
the ground that it would be proper to go first to the Queen and
ask her permission to prosecute the appeal in a court of her
choice.* A conference was held on the question at Hanworth.
There "Mr. Whitehead"—probably Hales's former ally at
Frankfort—and others apparently sided with Hales, but there
is no evidence that an appeal was actually made in the Chancery.[37] Newdigate probably prevailed with Hertford and his
lawyers to prevent that.

Later the course of events made Newdigate less hesitant about
carrying out the appeal. In February 1563 Hertford was fined
£15,000 in the Star Chamber.[38] This heavy sum was only intended as a warning to others; Elizabeth promptly remitted
£10,000 of the fine.[39] Nonetheless, £5,000 was still a considerable amount. In March Hertford asked Dudley to use his influence to obtain Elizabeth's forgiveness, but this produced no
result.[40] The Earl remained in the Tower and heavily in debt.
Clearly little was to be expected in the way of mercy from the
Queen. Hence Newdigate began to show "earnestness for the
appeal."

He took it upon himself to pay visits to several men of position in an effort to enlist their support. The most important
of these was Secretary Cecil. Newdigate informed him that he
had the "opinions of the greatest learned civilians" on Hertford's case—doubtless a reference to the discourses sent back
by Beale—and offered to let him see them. Cecil "made light"
of the case, and refused to examine the opinions. He obviously

---

* *Ibid.*, I, 416. Hales testified that an appeal to the Queen was the only procedure he advocated (*ibid.*, I, 415), but one suspects that this was merely an
attempt to cover his own tracks.

was trying to be as cautious as possible. It was bad enough to be approached by Newdigate in behalf of the marriage of Catherine and Hertford; it would be dangerous to give him the slightest encouragement.

Another prominent official whom Newdigate called on was Sir Nicholas Bacon, Lord Keeper and head of the Chancery. Newdigate described the meeting as follows:

I was with my Lord Keeper and prayed him, upon information what was learned by law for the fine and books I had touching the defense of my Lord's [Hertford's] case, that it would please him to use these knowledges and arguments for the better helping us to some tolerable end at the Queen's Majesty's hands: whose answer was that by way of petition he was ready to help us; but if we fought by justice, he would be against us. Now whether I left a copy of one of these books or papers . . . with his Lordship I do not perfectly remember.

Though Bacon did not give Newdigate much more satisfaction than Cecil, this testimony was somewhat incriminating. Bacon, as a great law officer and a privy councilor, was within his province in promising to help petition the Queen, but he was playing with fire when he apparently looked at the books and perhaps kept one of them. Newdigate's testimony must have helped to place the Lord Keeper in an uncomfortable position, but more on that soon.

Newdigate also solicited the aid of several other privy councilors. They too were apparently given the opportunity to see the discourses sent back by Beale. Newdigate, however, failed to reveal the identity of these men. Nor did he indicate what their reactions were. He did imply that he made all of these suits while Hertford was still in the Tower.[41] It would seem that Newdigate lost his "earnestness for the appeal" after the Earl was transferred to the custody of Newdigate's wife, the Duchess of Somerset, in August 1563.[42]

We are now ready to return to the question of whether a serious conspiracy had been discovered. The testimonies about the succession tract did not show much in the way of a plot, but those about the case of matrimony added a few coals to the fire. Beale's mission had not been promoted by Hales alone. The idea of proceeding with the appeal in Chancery without first obtaining the Queen's permission had been considered. The leaders of Elizabeth's government had been approached. And the names of Francis Newdigate, Thomas Dannett, and probably David Whitehead were added to the list of notables involved.

Those who had something to do with the succession tract and/or the case of matrimony make a rather impressive group: Lord John Grey; William Fleetwood, future Recorder of London; John Foster; Francis Newdigate, husband of the Duchess of Somerset; Thomas Dannett, diplomatist; David Whitehead, theologian; and John Hales, Clerk of the Hanaper. All of these men belonged to the religious left; all were prominent subjects of the English crown who had not always acted in ways calculated to please its wearer. Grey and Dannett had participated in the Duke of Suffolk's second rising in 1554.[43] Hales, Whitehead, Dannett, and possibly Grey had been Marian exiles.[44] In 1558–59 Grey had served with the Marquis of Northampton, the Earl of Bedford, and Cecil on the secret committee of the Privy Council for the alteration of religion.[45] Whitehead had been a member of the committee for Prayer Book revision and a disputant on the Protestant side at the Conference of Westminster in 1559, and was to be sequestered for nonconformity in 1564.[46] Fleetwood, Foster, Hales, and Newdigate had sat in the House of Commons in 1563, and were among those lampooned as troublemakers.*

These "conspirators" could not be dismissed as nonentities, and they were representative of the most vigorous segment of the Elizabethan population. Nevertheless, there was no really formidable figure among them. If any alteration of the status quo had been intended, greater men than they must have been involved. This obviously was what the Queen feared. And the names of Cecil and Bacon had been raised in the testimonies. The Principal Secretary and the Lord Keeper were the most important men in Elizabeth's government and they were brothers-in-law at that. If they had been participants in the doings

---

* They appear in the *Lewd Pasquil* as "Fleetwood the pleader," "Foster the frier," "Hales the hottest," and "Newdigate the crier."

of Hales and the others, the Queen's fears may not have been
groundless. But had they been involved and how deeply?

That Cecil and Bacon were mentioned in Newdigate's testimony proved little. They had been approached by Newdigate
in behalf of the case of matrimony. He had offered to show
them the discourses from overseas; only Bacon had looked at
them. There was nothing too serious here. Bacon had been
foolish to receive the discourses, and both he and Cecil should
have let Elizabeth know of the existence of the discourses; they
apparently had not. But these seem more like mistakes in judgment than crimes.

Nonetheless, Bacon soon found himself in trouble. In November 1564 Cecil wrote, "My Lord Keeper ... is kept from the
Court and from intermeddling with any other thing but with
the Chancery, whereof surely the affairs take great harm and
he himself is not void of peril by heaviness of mind."[47] Cecil
escaped without punishment but was, as he put it, "not free
from suspicion."[48] Bacon's troubles and Cecil's being suspected
could not have resulted entirely from Newdigate's testimony
about the case of matrimony. The two must have been suspected
of being involved more deeply with Hales and his friends than
the records of the investigation reveal.

In this connection there is an interesting passage about
Hales's *Declaration* in a later Jesuit tract:

Sir Nicholas Bacon, then Lord Keeper, was presumed also to have had
a principal part in the same, for which he was like to have lost his
office if Sir Anthony Browne ... would have accepted thereof when
her Majesty offered the same unto him and my Lord of Leicester ear-
nestly exhorted him to take it. But he refused it for that he was of
different religion from the state. And so Sir Nicholas Bacon remained
with the same at the great instance of Sir William Cecil, [who] was
thought to be privy also to the said book. Yet was the matter so wisely
laid upon Hales and Bacon as Sir William was kept free, thereby to
have the more authority and grace to procure the others pardon, as he
did.[49]

Some of this can be confirmed from other sources and some
cannot. True, Bacon was soon restored to favor, and Hales was
transferred from the Tower to confinement in his home.[50] But

there is no proof that Cecil was responsible for these things. Nor can the allegation that the Queen offered Bacon's office to Sir Anthony Browne be substantiated. If she did, however, it seems likely that Dudley, created Earl of Leicester in September 1564, was behind the move. The presumption that Bacon had a principal part in the making of the *Declaration,* and the belief that Cecil was privy to the tract, require fuller consideration.

To begin with Bacon, the notion that he had much to do with the *Declaration* cannot simply be dismissed as a product of a Jesuit imagination. Another, later tract by Sir John Harington, Elizabeth's godson, went so far as to call Bacon the author of the *Declaration.*[51] Nor was this a new idea when Harington expressed it. During the *Tempestas Halesiana* Guzman de Silva, Quadra's more capable successor, reported that the book on the succession was written by Bacon.[52] Though Silva's main source of information was probably Leicester, who then was apparently seeking Spanish support in an effort to disgrace and displace Bacon and Cecil, Bacon's exclusion from Elizabeth's inner circle perhaps signifies there was some fire behind the smoke.[53]

Indeed, certain conjectures seem to lend weight to the supposition that the Lord Keeper at least helped Hales with the *Declaration.* Bacon was Hales's chief at the Chancery; his knowledge of the law has been appraised as "remarkably full and sound."[54] He was the obvious man for Hales to approach to solicit aid in writing his tract, the official most likely able to inform him about the missing chancery enrollment of Henry VIII's will and about the existence of constats of the same, and one who probably knew much about whether the law against alien inheritance applied to the crown: a matter that Hales devoted a considerable portion of his tract to.[55] Moreover, it is likely that Bacon's sentiments on the succession were similar to those of Hales.[56] So long as Elizabeth did not marry and have issue, the Lord Keeper's religious preferences and political connections made a Suffolk succession his logical choice.

On the other hand, Bacon wrote to Cecil on 16 November 1564 protesting his innocence, that never did he support any claimant or advise any person to do so, nor would he ever enter into judgment of the succession without authorization. He stood "at this hour . . . indifferent and upright" without any commitments. He hoped that Leicester and Cecil would obtain his restoration to the Queen's favor. "My time hath been long and my grief overgreat, as appeareth by what hath happened to me since my troubles [began]: first the gout, then sickness of the spleen, and now want of sleep. . . . I pray for the best and yet [am] not altogether unprepared for the worst. God give me grace to endure all things."[57]

Bacon's defense is not very convincing. It leaves one with the impression of a man close to desperation. He seems to protest too much. One who is "not altogether unprepared for the worst" is not confident of vindication. This may indicate that the investigators discovered more about Bacon than has come down to us. Nor is the fact that he wrote to Cecil, who also was supposed to be involved with Hales in the succession, necessarily a sign of either's innocence. True, it would be absurd for a conspirator to make a private denial of guilt to a fellow conspirator, but the Lord Keeper's letter reads as if it was intended more for the Queen's attention than for the Secretary's. Having no access to Elizabeth while he was in her displeasure, Bacon probably expected Cecil to act as an intermediary who would pass on his letter or its substance at the appropriate moment.

Of course, nothing that had been said establishes Bacon's guilt or innocence. That probably cannot be determined from the evidence available. Perhaps the best clue to the solution of the problem lies in the question of Cecil's involvement. The Lord Keeper, though a man of great talent, doubtless owed his position to his brother-in-law. Bacon was far from a bold man. It is difficult to see him acting on his own in so dangerous a business as the succession. It is equally difficult to see him keeping out of it if Cecil was in it. But what about Cecil?

One thing somewhat suspect is the way in which Cecil took charge of the investigation of Hales and his friends. He certainly was far from enthusiastic about it. In a letter of 1 May 1564 he complained, "In this matter I am by commandment occupied, whereof I could be content to be delivered; but I will go upright, neither *ad dextram* nor *ad sinistram*."[58] Just how well this reluctant inquisitor managed to keep on the straight and narrow is open to question. One wonders why no answers to the interrogatory addressed to Hales about the will of Henry VIII are extant in Cecil's records.* Did Cecil have the answers suppressed to protect his brother-in-law? And hints of other peculiarities in the conduct of the investigation have come down to us.

For example, on 26 April Dudley wrote to Cecil, "I perceive you mean to have Fleetwood there, so I hope the Queen's Majesty shall not think we be negligent in observing her commandment."[59] This seems to indicate that Cecil kept for himself the task of examining William Fleetwood: a task that apparently was never carried out. Fleetwood does not seem to have suffered at all for his involvement with Hales. It is quite possible that Fleetwood owed his parliamentary seat to Cecil.† Did he also have Cecil to thank for his being cleared in the Halesian affair?

Also on 26 April Dudley, Northampton, and Mildmay wrote to Cecil: "What you think good to do touching Dannett? If he be there, we refer that to you; yet we mean and think it meet that you speak with him if he be there."[60] It appears from this that the handling of Thomas Dannett was regarded as within the special province of Cecil. There is also a hint that Cecil's associates were not sure about his zeal in the matter. We have no evidence that Dannett was ever questioned about his role in the "conspiracy." Dannett obviously was close to Cecil: he was his cousin; he had been Cecil's candidate to succeed Sir Nicholas Throckmorton as ambassador to France.[61] Did Cecil deliberately shield Dannett in 1564?

Attached to the letter concerning Dannett is a note:

After the writing hereof came Mr. Dale and Mr. Wilson with the examination of John Hales wherein he hath declared divers particularities touching the book of succession, but of the matter of the appeal ... there appeareth nothing. Neither do we find that matter at all remembered in the instructions, which we think was very requisite and most needful to be remembered of all the rest.[62]

---

* They are neither in Hales's answers of 25 April nor in those of 27 April. See *Burghley Papers*, I, 414–15.
† Like Hales, he sat for Lancaster Borough. The will of the Chancellor of

This is interesting. The instructions were deficient concerning
the appeal; Cecil was doubtless their author; and Newdigate
had approached him about the appeal. Was Cecil's forgetful-
ness in making up the instructions an attempt to cover his own
tracks? Moreover, the appeal was a matter that could most in-
criminate Hales, since it was here that he seems to have advocated bypassing the Queen. Hales too had his links with Cecil:
both men had been important figures during the Protectorate
of Somerset; it is possible that Hales, like Fleetwood, owed his
parliamentary seat to Cecil.* Was Cecil also trying to conceal
as much as he could for Hales?

It should be apparent by now that at least several of the "conspirators" were no strangers to Cecil. To this must be added the
fact that he had connections with both the Seymours and the
Greys. He owed his start in political life to Edward Seymour,
Duke of Somerset. Indeed, if we may believe Cecil's servant
turned historian, he even remained loyal to his benefactor at
some danger to himself after the Duke of Northumberland
gained the upper hand.[63] Cecil's associations with the Seymours
evidently did not end with Somerset's execution. In 1561 the
Duchess of Somerset solicited Cecil's advice and help in handling her "unruly" son, the Earl of Hertford.[64] Later in the
same year Hertford and young Thomas Cecil, the Secretary's
elder son, were traveling companions in France.[65]

Cecil's links with the Greys were of a different kind. He had
of course known Lord John Grey for years, and had been associ-
ated with him in Reformation politics, but the relationship
was more than social and political.[66] In their correspondence
with Cecil the Greys invariably called him "cousin."[67] This
derived from Lady Cecil's brother's marriage to Catherine
Grey's cousin.[68] Though this was not a close connection, to one
of Cecil's humble ancestry it was probably flattering to be con-

the Duchy usually prevailed in elections in the six parliamentary boroughs
of Lancashire. Neale, *Commons,* p. 224. Sir Ambrose Cave, a great friend of
Cecil, was Chancellor of the Duchy in 1563. Hence Cecil may have been connected with Fleetwood's election.

* On Hales and Somerset see Pollard, *Somerset,* pp. 200–237. Under Somerset
Cecil was advanced to the office of Master of Requests, his first important
position.

sidered a cousin by a noble family that contained two princesses of the blood royal, Ladies Catherine and Mary Grey, among its living members. But do Cecil's links with the Greys, the Seymours, and Hales and his friends mean that he was a party to a conspiracy?

Of course, the premise does not necessarily justify the conclusion. Of some interest here, however, is a letter of 2 September 1564 to Cecil from Sir Thomas Chaloner. Sir Thomas wrote that he was "sorry for the accident of Lady Catherine's case, and also for Mr. Hales, his friend."[69] This at least indicates that Chaloner thought it safe to express his sympathies to Cecil on the matter; it also may be interpreted as meaning that he suspected that Cecil had something to do with the Halesian business. Others must have been thinking along these lines. Two months later Cecil deemed it necessary to attempt to absolve himself in a letter to Sir Thomas Smith: "I have been . . . noted a favorer of my Lady Catherine's title, but my truth therein is tried; and so I rest quiet, for surely I am and always have been circumspect to do nothing to make offense."[70]

This was not a forthright denial by Cecil that he was a supporter of Catherine Grey's claim; he was too cautious ever to be precise about his succession preferences. About all one may safely say is that he was against Mary Stuart's claim. In 1561 he wrote to Sir Nicholas Throckmorton:

There hath been a matter secretly thought of which I dare communicate to you, *although I mean never to be an author thereof*; and that is, if an accord might be made betwixt our Mistress and the Scottish Queen, that this [Mary] should . . . surrender unto the Queen's Majesty all matter of claim, and to the heirs of her body; and in consideration thereof, the Scottish Queen's interest should be acknowledged in default of heirs of the body of the Queen's Majesty. [Italics mine.][71]

In a minute of 1566 Cecil gave as one reason why Elizabeth should marry Archduke Charles that "The Queen of Scots pretendeth title to the Crown of England, and so never did foreign prince since the Conquest."[72] This may indicate that Cecil accepted the view that the common-law rule against alien inheritance applied to the crown; moreover, the very fact that he wrote a minute advocating the Hapsburg match gives a clue

about what were probably his real thoughts on how to deal
with the succession.

There can be little doubt that Cecil saw Elizabeth's marrying and having issue as the ideal solution. This would be best
for England; it would also be likely to ensure the Secretary's
position and influence, so long as the Queen did not choose
Leicester or a Catholic fanatic as her consort. Elizabeth's marriage was probably the primary consideration to Cecil, and
settling the succession only secondary. In 1566 he also wrote
a memorandum expressing his views on the marriage and succession questions:

To urge both marriage and establishing of succession is the uttermost
that can be desired. To deny both is the uttermost that can be denied.
To require marriage is the most natural, most easy, most plausible to
the Queen's Majesty. To require certainty of succession is the most
plausible to all the people. To require succession is the hardest to be
obtained both for the difficulty to discuss the right and for the loathsomeness in the Queen's Majesty to consent thereto. The difficulty to
discuss it is by reason of the uncertainty of indifferency in the parties
that shall discuss it [and] the uncertainty of the right pretender. The
loathsomeness to grant it is by reason of natural suspicion against a
successor that hath right by law to succeed. Corollary: the mean betwixt these is to determine effectually to marry, and if it succeed not,
then proceed to discussion of the right of the successor.[73]

This was Cecil's conservative and sensible approach in 1566;
it is difficult to believe that he felt differently in 1563.

None of this takes us far in the way of discovering Cecil's
succession preferences. That he was opposed to Mary Stuart's
claim is merely negative, and that his first choice was for Elizabeth to marry and have progeny does not mean he had no ideas
about an alternative. Here there is nothing to quote, but an
inference seems safe. The logical succession candidate for Cecil
was Catherine Grey, so long as the Queen continued to follow
her virgin course. We have already noticed his connections
with Catherine and her relatives and backers. "Cousin" Catherine was the only Protestant claimant whose accession would,
in all likelihood, in no way result in the diminishing of Cecil's
power; indeed, he might emerge even stronger under her than
under the exceptionally capable and self-reliant Elizabeth.

But if Cecil was really a favorer of Catherine's title, it does not necessarily follow that he was involved in a conspiracy in her behalf. Newdigate's testimony has told us that Cecil knew something about what was being attempted in the case of matrimony. He also may well have been privy to the succession tract; it is even possible that he induced Bacon to help in its composition. It is conceivable that Cecil gave his sanction to these activities as trial balloons to test the reactions of Queen and Parliament, but he surely was too circumspect to be a party to anything more serious. Consequently, we may say that if the wary Principal Secretary and the timid Lord Keeper were involved in the doings of Hales and his fellows, it is probable that no sinister plot such as an immediate change of monarchs was intended. And conversely we may say that if Cecil and Bacon were not implicated, it is unlikely that Hales and his cohorts would have dared even to consider any such conspiracy. Therefore, whether one is justified or not in implicating Cecil and Bacon, there is little reason to believe that anything too dangerous had been contemplated.

What doubtless made the affair seem more serious than it actually was was the lasting anger of the Queen. Of course, she was greatly incensed when she first heard about Hales's activities. Moreover, she evidently deemed it politic to keep up her show of rage for a while to impress the Queen of Scots.* It is difficult, however, to believe that Elizabeth's anger would have lasted as long as it did if Leicester had not made a deliberate effort to fan the flames in order to embarrass Cecil. The nature of Leicester's mischief is apparent in a letter of 27 June 1564 from Silva to Philip II:

A great friend of Lord Robert has been to visit me on his behalf, and has informed me of the great enmity that existed between Cecil and Lord Robert, even before this book about the succession was published, but now very much more, as he believes Cecil to be the author of the book, and the Queen is extremely angry about it, although she signifies that there are so many accomplices in the offense that they

---

* "The bruit is more common that some are in the Tower for making a book against this Queen [Mary]. By their imprisonment, though he [Randolph] told her it was not in the Tower, she thinks much kindness in the Queen [Elizabeth]." Thomas Randolph to Cecil, Edinburgh, 22 May 1564; *CSP, For.*, ser. iii, VII, 137.

must overlook it and has begun to slacken in the matter. This person has asked me from Robert with great secrecy to take an opportunity in speaking to the Queen (or to make such opportunity) to urge her not to fail in adopting strong measures in this business, as if Cecil were out of way, the affairs of your Majesty would be more favorably dealt with, and religious questions as well, because this Cecil and his friends are those who persecute the Catholics and dislike your Majesty, whereas the other man [Leicester] is looked upon as faithful, and the rest of the Catholics so consider him, and have adopted him as their weapon. If the Queen would disgrace Cecil it would be a great good to them, and this man tried to persuade me to make use of Robert. I answered him that I intended to avail myself of him in all things, and I was quite sure that your Majesty would be pleased that I should do so.[74]

The manifest opportunism involved in this sometimes "friend" of the Puritans now posing as the champion of the Catholics requires no comment. Leicester's game, however, would not be played for long. It took until 6 August for Philip the Prudent to indicate that he would approve of Silva's offering Leicester covert support, and it must be remembered that in June Silva was already reporting that Elizabeth had "begun to slacken in the matter."[75] About all Leicester apparently succeeded in doing was prolonging her anger for the duration of 1564. In December Cecil wrote his last letter concerning the Queen's displeasure toward Hales, Bacon, and company.[76] It seems safe to conclude that by early 1565 the *Tempestas Halesiana* was well-nigh over.*

How much had been accomplished? Elizabeth had been angered, but eventually had calmed down. Her Scottish policy certainly had not been helped, but this was hardly the cause of its ultimate failure. A few men had been in serious trouble, and several others (Cecil, Fleetwood, Foster, Dannett, etc.) had been embarrassed, but only for Hales was the suffering long-lived.† Leicester had been given the opportunity to make

---

* "Is glad to hear that the Lord Keeper is restored to her Majesty's favor." Smith to Cecil, Bordeaux, 10 April 1565; *CSP, For.*, ser. iii, VII, 330.

† Besides Hales's imprisonment and Bacon's exclusion from Court, Lord John Grey was in custody for a time, and Francis Newdigate was confined to his house. Wright, I, 174; *CSP, Dom.*, I, 241. As late as February 1568 Hales was still under bond not to leave his house without the Queen's permission. *Ibid.*, I, 306.

an unsuccessful attempt to displace Cecil. The marriage of Catherine and Hertford had not been validated. When all is said and done, only one thing remained that was to influence the events of the next few years: John Hales had written a succession tract.

PART II

The Succession Tracts

6. *The Tracts*

No sooner did the Halesian storm subside than a battle of succession tracts began. This was to be expected. Though the Queen might still prefer to regard the succession as her private business, and though Hales's *Declaration* was addressed to Parliament, John Hales had really brought the issue out into the open. He had pronounced the succession a "great and weighty" matter "which concerneth the whole realm universally" and had challenged those who felt so moved to answer his arguments "in writing."[1] Manuscript copies of his tract continued to circulate despite his confinement.[2] Hales had opened the door to the making of tracts, of which there would be almost no end. In 1565 new tracts were written, and *Gorboduc* was published surreptitiously.[3] Parliament's meeting in the next year helped to inspire additional writings. Mary Stuart's troubles and then the prospect of the accession of her son would keep the tract business going until the turn of the century. Hales had initiated a more lasting tempest than the one named after him.

Our particular concern, of course, is with the tracts that followed Hales's in the 1560's. Although there were few of them by modern standards, those few are significant. Given Elizabeth's attitude, which had been made obvious by the fate of Hales, the succession was dangerous to deal with. Only a genuine demand for knowledge about it can account for the apparent ease with which the tract writers entered the risky business. The tracts must have been written to influence a politically conscious reading public that was deeply concerned about the succession. Clearly it was a sophisticated and educated public. Although none of the tracts rank as classics of political thought or as literary masterpieces, they are well above the popular political writings of our own day. To understand them required no little knowledge of history and law, and the ability to follow rather complicated arguments.

It is difficult to be precise about the composition of this reading public. Vague terms like "aristocracy" and "middle class" are hardly helpful. Certainly the readers of the tracts were primarily laymen, and very few of them came from the lower levels of the social ladder. They represented a new force of public opinion in England, independent of court influence and of growing political importance. We shall meet evidence that this public opinion put pressure on the Parliament of 1566. It was a force that had to be reckoned with, and that our tract writers found it worth taking risks to reach.[4]

One of the earliest tracts after Hales's was one that produced nearly as many replies as the *Declaration*. This was an anonymous tract, dated 7 December 1565, called *Allegations against the Surmised Title of the Queen of Scots and the Favorers of the Same*; we shall call it *Allegations against Mary*. What made this tract particularly dangerous to the Stuart cause was that it was printed.[5] The potential circulation of a printed tract was obvious. Mary made representations to Elizabeth over the tract, and received a promise of satisfaction.[6]

As its full title indicates, *Allegations against Mary* was mainly a rejection of the Scottish Queen's claim to the English succession. The author made much of the common-law rule against inheritance by an alien, which we shall postpone discussing until we finish introducing the tracts. He also pointed out what he thought would be the consequences of Mary's accession for England. The English would be "bound and subject unto a foreign nation." Mary would appoint Scotsmen to the great offices of the realm, an intolerable situation for Englishmen. The Scots were "a people by custom and almost nature our enemies, thirsty of our blood, poor and miserable by their country and envious of our welfare." What laws and devices might be made "that the Scots may trade and communicate the commodities of our country?"[7] The same objections would be raised against an Anglo-Scottish union on sundry future occasions.

Another ground given by the author for Mary's exclusion was her "corrupt religion."[8] Here he was anticipating—albeit from the other side of the fence—a later Jesuit argument against the accession of Mary's son.[9] This argument was dangerous in sixteenth-century England. It cut more than one way religiously; if "corrupt religion" could be used to justify excluding an heir to the crown, it could also be used to justify deposing a reigning monarch. Moreover, when our author said Mary's religion was corrupt he made no attempt to prove it. There was no need to prove a "known truth" to those at whom his tract was aimed, to wit, the majority of Englishmen (perhaps it would be safer to say, the majority of those Englishmen who counted politically). Our author, though he probably did not realize it, really was not rejecting Mary for her "corrupt religion"; he was rejecting her because her religion was not that of the "English people." He was, by implication, reversing what had been in practice the accepted and safer doctrine in Tudor England, namely, *cuius regio eius religio*.

Though *Allegations against Mary* may well have come from the Suffolk camp, it does not once mention Catherine Grey. Perhaps Hales's fate made it prudent to avoid open advocacy of her claim. The tract contains at least one statement that seems to point to Catherine. In discussing whether Scotland was a part of England, the author wrote that if one acknowledged Scotland as belonging to England, Mary's claim had to be recognized "if there were no other person that had better title by statute or else by the will of King Henry VIII."[10] By December 1565 it was widely known that Henry's will, if valid, gave Catherine the best claim. At any rate, a tract rejecting Mary's title was almost bound to help the candidacy of her leading rival most.

The first reply to *Allegations against Mary* came in an anonymous manuscript tract of uncertain title; we shall call it *Answer to Allegations against Mary*.[11] Its writer admitted that he did not consider himself sufficiently skilled in English law "to go about to confute" *Allegations against Mary*, but he felt compelled to attempt a refutation because he found the tract "full of lying, slander, and malice."[12] His lack of skill in English law shows in his somewhat unimpressive answers to *Allegations against Mary* on the important question whether the common-law rule against alien inheritance could be applied to the Scottish Queen. He is more successful in dealing with its author's views on the consequences of Mary's possible accession:

> In the first part of the book the author thereof discourseth upon the title of the Queen of Scots by conjectures what may fall if her Majesty comes to the Crown of England, viz., that then we should be bondsmen and slaves, to a foreign nation. . . . Of his conjectures he maketh no proof but uttereth that which his malice persuadeth him.[13]

This seems a deserved criticism. Mary's devotion to the Scots was hardly such that she would have ruled England in their interest. The author's rejection of his adversary's contention that Mary's claim ought to be rejected on account of her "corrupt religion" is not so fair. "If he were put to answer to defend his own religion . . . , it might be found as corrupt as the other if he be of any religion at all, for it appeareth by his words he neither liketh the old nor the new but would have religion of his own framing."[14] This attack on the other writer's religion seems a mere evasion of discussing the doctrine that he had by implication embraced, namely, that a princess of the blood royal could be deprived of her birthright because her religion differed from that of the majority—or the most influential segment—of her potential subjects. This, however, was an idea that few men were yet prepared to consider openly, though most men were undoubtedly swayed in their succession choices by their religious preferences.

Answer to Allegations against Mary clearly was not too satisfactory an answer. Moreover, it ignored Hales's *Declaration*, the fullest statement of the anti-Stuart case. These deficiencies were soon made up in a manuscript tract in two parts: the first was called *A Treatise Proving that If Our Sovereign Lady Queen Elizabeth . . . Should Die Without Issue . . . , the Queen of Scots by Her Birth in Scotland Is Not Disabled by the Law of England to Receive the Crown of England by Descent*; the second, *A Brief Declaration of the Invalidity of the Last Will of the Late King of Famous Memory, King Henry VIII.*

The origin of this tract was explained by its author in a prologue to the first part. It merits some consideration.

There came to mine hands a printed book [*Allegations against Mary*] containing among other things certain allegations and reasons supposed to be the common law made in disability of the Queen of Scots to receive the Crown of England if it should chance our Sovereign Lady the Queen ... to die without issue: by reason that the same Queen of Scots is a stranger born out of the allegiance of the Crown of England. ... There came also to mine hands, and that very lately, the book of Mr. Hales in which book amongst other things he treated of the same matter. ... When I had read I could not but marvel at the audacity of their authors who seemed to be very insufficient in learning of the laws of this realm to treat of that matter. ... And albeit to the learned their ignorance is well perceived, yet to the unlearned (to whose hands also the said books come) it is not so. ... Therefore, I thought it should be very well done of him whosoever he were that, being learned in the laws of this realm, would with learning confound that opinion. And as I was thinking upon that matter there was delivered to me a written treatise [*Answer to Allegations against Mary*] made in confutation of the printed book, upon the reading whereof I conceived that the man that made it was furnished with much learning in other sciences howbeit he seemed to me to lack sufficient knowledge in our temporal law. And therefore I thought it needful that it were taken in hand by some temporal lawyer.

Being esteemed learned in the temporal law, the author spent "a great part of Christmas 1566" searching "the reasons and grounds of the law in the point." After the dissolution of Parliament on 2 January 1567 he decided to write his tract. His purpose then was only to refute the arguments of Hales and the author of *Allegations against Mary* that Mary's birth in Scotland disqualified her from the succession. He was not yet prepared to question the will of Henry VIII: "It is not mine intent to meddle with all: for if the crown in default of heirs of the Queen's Highness' body be by testament and last will of King Henry VIII or otherwise given to any, it shall not be impugned nor will I not [*sic*] enter into discussion of it."[15]

This prologue confirms and amplifies much of our previous discussion. It indicates that both *Allegations against Mary* and Hales's *Declaration* were circulating before Parliament opened on 30 September 1566. It implies that the printed tract was the easier of the two to obtain,* yet both were reaching the hands

---

* Maitland had difficulty obtaining a copy of the *Declaration* in April 1565. *CSP, Span., Eliz.*, I, 424, 427.

of the "unlearned" as well as the "learned." The prologue reveals that even on the Stuart side *Answer to Allegations against Mary* was not regarded too highly, and enables us to place that tract in 1566.* The prologue also indicates that the first part of the tract it introduces was probably completed shortly after Parliament's dissolution. Most significant of all, the prologue shows that the author was reluctant to cast doubts on Henry VIII's will. According to the opening of the second part, it required the urging of others to make him do so.[16] Earlier we met with a similar hesitancy on the part of Maitland of Lethington.

In the case of this tract we can make a highly likely identification of the author. A note in a comparatively modern hand on one copy of the tract says he was Sir Anthony Browne.[17] This is most doubtful. Browne, as we shall see, had written another succession tract just a little earlier. A far more probable author was Edmund Plowden, an eminent Catholic lawyer whose ability was much admired by Sir Edward Coke.[18] In a list of Plowden's works is the following entry:

3. 'A Treatise of Succession written in the lifetime of the most virtuous and renowned Lady Mary, late Queen of Scots. Wherein is sufficiently proved that neither her foreign birth, nor the last will and testament of King Henry VIII could debar her from her true and lawful title to the Crown of England,' manuscript preserved at Pensax Court, Worcestershire. It is referred to by Sir Matthew Hale. . . . The dedication to James I is signed by Francis Plowden [Edmund's son].[19]

This certainly sounds like the tract in two parts, which we shall therefore consider to be Edmund Plowden's.[20]

Now let us turn to Anthony Browne's tract. Written in answer to Hales's *Declaration,* it advocated Mary Stuart's claim.[21] Browne, a Catholic judge, probably wrote his tract in the first half of 1565.† If Elizabeth knew of it, says Sir John Neale, "it is perhaps some comment on her views that she knighted its author in 1566."[22] Browne certainly made a strong case for Mary;

---

* Since the writer of the prologue saw it before Christmas 1566. *Allegations against Mary* was dated 7 December 1565.
† On 25 June 1565 Paul de Foix wrote to Catherine de Medici about a manuscript tract answering Hales and showing Mary's right to the English crown. Teulet, II, 211. At the time this could only be Browne's tract.

indeed, the second or succession book of Bishop Leslie's more
famous *A Defense of the Honor of . . . Mary, Queen of Scotland
. . . , with a Declaration as well of Her Right, Title, and Interest
to the Succession of the Crown of England, as that the Regiment
of Women Is Conformable to the Law of God and Nature* is
little more than an enlargement of Browne's tract. In the 1571
edition of Leslie "the portion dealing with the succession is described as partly [mostly might be a better word] a result of 'the
advice of Anthony Browne, knight, one of the Justices of the
Common Pleas, an. 1567.' "[23] Consequently, we shall say no
more about Browne's tract; henceforth we shall use Leslie's *Defense of Mary,* which is fuller, easier to obtain, and barely removed from our period.

There was still another writing in behalf of the Queen of
Scots that ought to be included here, though it was not, properly
speaking, a tract. This was a letter of 4 January 1567 from
Maitland of Lethington to Sir William Cecil.[24] We may think
of it as a sort of private tract written to win Mary the support
of Elizabeth's leading minister. Maitland argued that neither
her Scottish birth nor Henry VIII's will excluded Mary from the
succession. His intention obviously was to refute Hales. It is
interesting that Mary's most important minister (Maitland), the
Bishop who had the most influence over her (Leslie), and two
of England's most prominent Catholic lawyers (Plowden and
Browne) all found it necessary to write answers to Hales's tract.
This certainly constituted no small tribute to the *Declaration,*
and may be considered evidence that it had wide influence and
circulation.

Still another tract answering Hales was one dated 20 March
1566, and with the prolix and perhaps misleading title of *Alle-
gations in behalf of the High and Mighty Princess the Lady
Mary, Now Queen of Scots, against the Opinions and Books Set
Forth in the Part of the Lady Catherine, and the Rest of the
Issue of the French Queen, Touching the Succession of the
Crown*; we shall call it *Allegations in behalf of Mary.*

Manuscript copies of this tract contain a preface by the
"printer." He has seen "matter put forth in print against the
right and title that" the Queen of Scots "hath unto the Crown

of England" (doubtless *Allegations against Mary*). Since Mary
has not yet answered "by the same means in print" those who
seek to "obstruct" her title, he has seen fit to "put . . . likewise
in the meantime abroad . . . certain allegations put forth a year
ago against the heirs of the Lady Mary, the French Queen."*
This preface raises doubts.

It implies that the "printer" was publishing a tract written
a year before 20 March 1566, but it is questionable that *Allegations in behalf of Mary* actually went to press in 1566. No such
printed copy is extant.[25] The publisher of the edition of 1690
wrote: "whether ever printed or no I cannot say."[26] Maybe the
"printer" originally intended to publish the tract, but then decided that a limited and controllable manuscript circulation
would be safer.

The preface of the "printer" also indicates that the author of
the tract had presented "certain allegations . . . against the heirs
of . . . the French Queen"; it does not state that he had made
the allegations in behalf of the Scottish Queen. This is in agreement with the author's own preface, where he fails to say that
he was writing in the interest of Mary Stuart's claim. Moreover,
he then went on to devote two thirds of his tract to "the illegit-
imation of the Lady Catherine and the rest of the issues of the
French Queen," and the other third to the invalidity of the will
of Henry VIII; nowhere did he even mention the Queen of
Scots.[27]

This leaves the problem of whether *Allegations in behalf of
Mary* was a proper title for the tract or merely a purposeful in-
vention of the "printer." Though calling in question the legitimacy of the Suffolks and the validity of Henry's will was to
Mary Stuart's advantage, it was equally to the advantage of the
Earl of Huntingdon, who also was not a Suffolk and not mentioned in the succession provisions of the will. Moreover, if the
author really intended to make a case for Mary, it is strange
that he ignored entirely the alleged common-law exclusion
of aliens from the succession, a vital problem for Mary that

---

* Cotton MS. Caligula B IX, vol. II, fol. 233. Mary Tudor was usually referred to as the French Queen; she was rarely remembered as the Duchess of
Suffolk.

touched Huntingdon not at all. Perhaps, though not necessarily, another indication that he was not on Mary's side is his strongly anti-Catholic tone: "And herein it is to little purpose to cavil with canons or decretals of the pope (against the plain and manifest Word of God) from whose usurped power this realm is most happily delivered."[28] This could easily have been written by a Puritan adherent of Huntingdon. It is possible that we are dealing with a tract composed in Huntingdon's interest that fell into the hands of the "printer," who found that he could use it for Mary. Anyway, one sure thing about *Allegations in behalf of Mary* is that it was written against Lady Catherine Grey. Maybe a more appropriate title would be "Allegations against Catherine," but we won't presume to make the change.

A final writing to be introduced is one that I have discussed at length and published elsewhere.[29] Internal evidence places it in 1566. Though we shall call it *The Letter,* more than likely it was a tract in the guise of a letter. Its anonymous author accused its addressee, an unnamed "sir," of holding a private conference that resulted in a resolution favoring Mary's claim. Neither conference nor resolution can be substantiated; they may well have been invented by the writer as foils for debating certain aspects of the succession question. The author also charged the addressee with causing a tract to be "set forth in print." Over half of *The Letter* is concerned with this tract, *Allegations in behalf of Mary. The Letter* was, though not avowedly, a Suffolk tract. Its discussions of the private conference, the resolution, and *Allegations in behalf of Mary* appear to be impartial summaries of the Stuart and Suffolk viewpoints, but the Suffolk side always has the last word and is usually presented more cogently, especially in matters directly touching Catherine Grey.[30]

This concludes our introduction to the tracts. The next three chapters will be devoted to the main issues they dealt with. I deem these issues to be the applicability of the common-law rule against alien inheritance to the succession and to Mary Queen of Scots, the legitimacy of the Suffolks, and the validity of the will of Henry VIII. The law of succession as it stood in the first decade of Elizabeth's reign depended on the resolution of these issues; it is now our purpose to attempt to discover what that law was. Hence we shall not confine our discussion to what was said in the tracts, but shall call on other evidence or arguments, whether from the sixteenth century or not, whenever it seems worthwhile to do so.

7. The Rule Against Alien Inheritance

The common-law rule against aliens' inheriting ordinary property in England doubtless had its origin after the loss of Normandy, when the English found it expedient to deprive Frenchmen of their lands in England.* Hales cited opinions of Bracton and Littleton that indicate that in the middle of the thirteenth century the rule applied only to aliens in the allegiance of the King of France, and in the second half of the fifteenth to aliens generally, but it must have had the wider application long before the latter time.[1] Hales also brought up legislation of Edward III that had by implication given statutory confirmation to the rule.

This Act of 1351 did not in so many words state the common-law rule against alien inheritance. Nevertheless, it did say that children of the Kings of England could inherit in England, no matter where or when they were born. It also gave the right of inheritance in England to children who after the day of enactment might be born abroad of parents in the allegiance of the King of England.[2] From this Hales drew an obvious inference: "Those that be born of father and mother that be not in the

---

* "The King shall have escheats of the lands of Normans" and also "where any inheritance descendeth to any that is born in parts beyond the sea, whose ancestors were from the time of King John under the allegiance of the Kings of France." *Prerogativa Regis, SR,* I, 226. "It was because the king had seized the lands of these Normans, that the common law arrived at its settled rules as to the right of the king to the lands of aliens, and the incapability of an alien to hold English land." Holdsworth, IX, 83.

faith and allegiance of the King of England be not inheritable
within this realm."[3] Thus the statute was a corroboration of
the common-law rule.

The Stuart tract writers would not get very far by challenging
this rule, but they could raise two questions about its applicability against the Scottish Queen's claim to the English crown.
Did the rule apply to the succession? Did it apply to Mary
Stuart? If both questions could not be answered affirmatively,
Mary could not lawfully be excluded from the succession on the
ground of her birth in Scotland.

Perhaps the most effective way to answer the first question
would be historically. Precedents were good legal arguments in
England. If it could be shown that definite aliens had succeeded
to the crown in the past, then the rule did not apply. If it could
be shown that such aliens had been rejected in the past, then
the rule did apply. Accordingly, the tract writers used much
space debating over possible precedents, one way or the other.

This debate was largely waged over cases of succession since
the death of Henry I.* Henry was succeeded by Stephen of
Blois, a manifest alien. Stephen was, as Leslie said, a Frenchman
and not an immediate child of an English king—a perfect exception to the terms of the Act of 1351 as Hales would define
them. Leslie regarded Stephen's accession as proof that the
common-law rule did not apply to the succession.[4] However, an
obvious objection could be raised in Stephen's case: he could
be, as he was by Hales and the author of *Allegations against
Mary,* dismissed as a "usurper."[5] Hales pointed out that Henry I
had twice exacted solemn oaths from his nobility and clergy
that they would recognize the right of his daughter Maud—
modern writers usually refer to her as Matilda—to succeed him;
Stephen was crowned in violation of these oaths and of Maud's
"just" title.[6] And a usurpation, being illegal by definition, could
not be called upon as evidence of what the law of succession was.

A more complicated case was that of Henry II, Maud's son by
Geoffrey of Anjou. Henry Plantagenet was about as French as

* Aliens had been Kings of England before that time, but the precedents
were too ancient to count for much, the law of succession was then too in-
definite, and the alien usually owed his accession to force rather than law.

Stephen, but this did not settle the matter. Hales maintained that Henry was entitled to the crown, his foreign birth notwithstanding: "For albeit that Maud were not Queen of England *de facto,* yet she was *de jure* for Stephen was but an usurper. And so King Henry II was the Queen's child, which you see by the Statute of Edward III is free [to inherit in England], wheresoever they be born."[7] Leslie replied: "Although Maud . . . had a right and good title to the crown, yet was she never in possession but kept from the possession by King Stephen. And therefore King Henry II cannot justly be said to be a Queen of England's child."[8] Though it may sound peculiar coming from a man writing in behalf of a hereditary title, Leslie's argument seems to leave us with a stalemate on the issue.

Another objection to calling Henry II's accession in 1154 a proof that the common-law rule did not apply was raised by the author of *Allegations against Mary.* Henry "did not come in by order or common course of law": he came to the throne "by force and virtue of certain capitulations or agreements of peace" (the Treaty of Wallingford, 1153), the parties to which "did not regard or respect what the law was." If the succession had been determined according to law, the crown should have gone to Maud.[9] The author of *Answer to Allegations against Mary* replied:

As for the agreement . . . which Stephen made with Henry that Henry should succeed Stephen and not Stephen's son [who was dead, it] doth not make a new title to Henry but confirmeth his former right and title to be good. . . . And where it is said that Maud . . . was the next right heir before her son it is true; but who can let [prevent] her to assign over her right and interest to her son, seeing her husband [who was dead] would not pursue the claim in her right for himself but was contented that his son should have it.[10]

The assignment of roles to the dead is a good example of the answerer's scholarship, but it does not affect the substance of his argument. His "refutation," however, rather corroborates his adversary's view that Henry's accession was more a matter of practical politics than of law. And Maud's unwillingness to assert her claim in 1153–54 does not, strictly speaking, justify its being ignored. Anyhow, if we add the argument brought

up in *Allegations against Mary* to that of Hales, Henry II's case
is scarcely more convincing than Stephen's as a precedent to
establish that the rule against alien inheritance did not apply
to the succession.

The next case considered was that of Arthur of Brittany and
John Lackland. Arthur, the posthumous son of Henry II's
fourth son, had a better right by the rule of representative
primogeniture to succeed Richard I than John, Henry's fifth
son. But Arthur was born in France and John at Oxford. And it
was John whom England accepted as Richard's successor. The
author of *Allegations against Mary* claimed that this meant that
Arthur was rejected because of his alien birth.[11]

The author of *Answer to Allegations against Mary* would
have none of this. John came to the throne not because of his
English birth "but by might and usurpation." When the nobility was deceitfully persuaded to accept John, "the place of
Arthur's birth was not mentioned but only that Arthur was a
child and John a man."[12] This time the answerer's points are
worth considering.

It is almost inconceivable that the birthplace of either John
or Arthur had much to do with the decision of the largely Anglo-
Norman nobility. Surely John's manhood was more important
to the nobles, but there was another factor that probably influenced their preference for John. Though we cannot call it
nationality, it was something that approached that concept. At
the time John could not possibly be called an Englishman. A
modern authority has estimated that in 1199 John had spent
less than five of his thirty-odd years in England. But his experience and connections were Anglo-Norman. Arthur was a
stranger to the Anglo-Norman barons, but they knew John as
one of their own.[13] After the loss of Normandy this feeling
could easily develop into one that the King must be English.

As for dismissing John as a usurper, this was not as apparent
to John's contemporaries as it was to the answerer. At least some
of the men of 1199 held that they were not bound by considerations of hereditary right in "electing" a monarch.[14] Moreover, even if hereditary right were the determinant in the succession, it was not yet established in the law that Arthur, the

son of Henry II's fourth son, had a better title than John, Henry's fifth son;[15] indeed, it probably was easier in 1199 to view the claim of John, Richard I's brother, as superior to that of Arthur, Richard's nephew.* Therefore, calling John a usurper may be an *ex post facto* judgment. Now if John were a usurper, it cannot be said that Arthur was rejected because of his French birth. However, if John had a lawful title, it still does not necessarily follow that Arthur was excluded as an alien. If John was judged at the same time to have the superior hereditary right, Arthur might still be recognized as next in line. And if John's was only an elective title, it remains to be proved that Arthur's place of birth had anything to do with the decision.

Again we have failed to find a conclusive precedent for applying the common-law rule against alien inheritance to the succession. The difficulty seems to be that our tract writers were bringing up cases of succession from the twelfth century, and trying to judge them according to the standards of Elizabethan England. For one thing, they were trying to apply their matured idea of hereditary right to an England where the idea of an elective monarchy was not yet dead. It was only with the accession of Henry III in 1216 that a period of nearly two centuries of direct hereditary succession began; it was only with the accession of Richard II in 1377 that a grandson of the senior line succeeded while his uncles were still alive; it was only with the accession of Mary I in 1553 that a female actually inherited the crown. Accordingly, arguments that Maud had a right before her son, that Arthur had a better claim than John, and even that Stephen was a usurper may not be as valid as they appeared to be to the sixteenth-century pamphleteers.

Second, our tract writers were seeking to confirm or deny the applicability of a rule by using evidence from an age in which that rule probably was inconceivable. Stephen of Blois and Henry of Anjou, both born in France, had worn the English crown, but the English-born John Lackland had been advanced to the throne instead of the French-born Arthur of Brittany.

---

* "The claim of proximity of blood, which the uncle possessed, was much more obvious in early times than the subtle doctrine of representative primogeniture." Taswell-Langmead, p. 540.

That we have such contradictory cases in the twelfth century is perhaps proof in itself that place of birth was then not even considered in connection with the succession. Indeed, there was probably no rule against aliens inheriting any kind of property. In an age when the King of England, to say nothing of the Anglo-Norman nobility, held fiefs of French overlords, the danger of reciprocation alone would have precluded such a rule. It is significant here that Hales did not first find the rule in Glanville, the great English law treatise of the second half of the twelfth century, but in Bracton, written about a century later.

If the search for precedents out of the twelfth century involved reading into the past much that was never there, the situation was quite different when the next case came up. Change began in John's reign. Arthur's murder in 1203 left John's the only male line descending from Henry II. John was followed on the throne by his descendants according to the rule of primogeniture until 1399, when Henry IV's accession violated the direct hereditary order. And even in the "usurpation" of 1399 it is significant that the Lancastrians deemed it expedient to circulate the fantastic "crouchback" legend to give Henry the appearance of having the best hereditary claim.* Therefore, from the thirteenth century on, it is at least reasonable to bring up hereditary right in considering the succession.

John's reign also doubtless marks the starting point of the development of the common-law rule against inheritance by aliens. The primary factor must have been the loss of Normandy in 1204. This led to an important modification of the status quo in real estate: barons who held lands on both sides of the Channel had to decide whether to drop their English or their Norman fiefs; they could not keep both.† This really amounted to a choice of being English or French; the Anglo-Norman nobility was no more. Hence the most influential class of landholders in England became almost wholly English in interest,

---

* The legend was that Edmund "Crouchback," Earl of Lancaster, was really the firstborn son of Henry III, but, because of his deformity, his "younger" brother was made King Edward I.
† William Marshal, Earl of Pembroke, and Robert de Beaumont, Earl of Leicester, were exceptions to this rule. Painter, p. 55.

albeit still French in culture. A rule against alien inheritance could now begin to make sense to the baronage; it probably always could have to the lower classes. Moreover, Henry III, John's successor, must have provoked matters considerably by his placing of Poitevins and Savoyards in high offices in Church and State, and by his permitting the pope to provide Italians with English benefices. Here was a situation in which church-man, nobleman, and commoner alike shared resentment of the foreigner; here was the atmosphere in which judges like Brac-ton must have started making the rule against alien inheritance a definite part of the common law. The rule evidently was so well established by the time Edward III and his Parliament met in 1351 that it was superfluous to state it; the obvious reason for their statute was to specify certain necessary or justifiable exceptions to the rule.* Therefore, by 1351 there was a com-mon-law rule against alien inheritance whose applicability to the succession might be tested in future cases.

The first was that of Richard of Bordeaux, the son of Ed-ward, the Black Prince, and Joan of Kent. Richard was born in France; he was, as Maitland of Lethington put it, not a child of the King of England "if the words be taken in ... strict sig-nification."[16] Yet he became King Richard II of England in 1377. Did this, as the author of *Answer to Allegations against Mary* maintained, show that the rule against alien inheritance did not apply to the succession?[17] Hales refuted the idea quite adequately:

And other objection there is of Richard II, how he was born at Bor-deaux out of the realm and yet was King. To that I answer, he had it justly: for he was born of father and mother English, in the King's allegiance, which is sufficient and also for advantage; for Bordeaux was then in the faith and allegiance of the King of England.[18]

Hales's first point is obvious. Richard was the son of the Black Prince and the Countess of Kent, manifestly loyal subjects of Edward III; he was born in 1366. Hence his birth clearly ful-filled the requirements of the Act of 1351. Hales's second point,

---

* "The disability of an alien to hold land ... inspired the Act of 1351." Holdsworth, IX, 93.

that Bordeaux was in the allegiance of the King of England, was no doubt based on an Act of 1368, which declared infants born in Calais, Gascony, and Guienne "as able and inheritable of heritage in England as other infants born within the realm of England."[19] This statute apparently soon came to be interpreted broadly as meaning that children born in any territory belonging to the King of England were capable of inheritance in England.[20] As for Richard's case, Bordeaux, originally part of Gascony, was in Guienne under Edward III. It is interesting to note that the statute was enacted two years after Richard's birth and was retroactive. Was its principal purpose to strengthen Richard's right to the succession? More on that later.

Richard II's was the only case after the Act of 1351 that the Stuart tracts could bring up; it was a poor one. On the anti-Stuart side there was also only one case; it was no better. This was Henry VII's accession in 1485 over aliens who had superior hereditary claims. Henry's case seems to have escaped the notice of both Hales and the author of *Allegations against Mary*. It was raised in an undated fragment of a tract against the Queen of Scots. Its writer maintained: "if strangers might succeed, then after" the extinction of Henry IV's line the succession "should fall to the King of Portugal" (John II), who descended legitimately from John of Gaunt by his first wife, whereas Henry VII descended from "Gaunt's third wife, called his concubine by Froissart."[21]

This argument rested on the untenable premise that the best hereditary claim in 1485 was Lancastrian. A Lancastrian title could only be superior to a Yorkist one on the basis of a Salic law; the hereditary priority of the Yorkists came from their descent from Lionel of Clarence, John of Gaunt's elder brother, via two females. After the extinction of Henry IV's line in 1471, all male Lancastrians descended from Gaunt through females. Hence a Lancastrian claim on the ground of a Salic law, if ever valid, was no longer possible in 1485. If hereditary right had then been the only consideration, the crown should have gone to an English Yorkist—to Elizabeth of York if a woman might succeed, to the Earl of Warwick if a male was required—and not to the King of Portugal.* Consequently, the accession of Henry VII was a poor example of the applicability of the rule against alien inheritance to the succession.

We have no more found a convincing precedent after 1351 than we did before 1351. The matter has been considered for three reasons. First, our tract writers brought it up. Second, it has afforded an opportunity to explore the medieval background of our present topic and of hereditary right. Last, our very failure to find a satisfactory precedent is in itself significant. It indicates that our tract writers, whether they realized it or not, were dealing with a problem that actually had never been faced before. Answers would have to be found in law rather than history if one were to decide whether an alien might come to the throne.

One way in which the Stuart side undertook to find an answer in law was by posing the general question of whether common-law rules of inheritance applied to the crown at all. If the general question could be answered in the negative, the same obviously would go for the specific one about whether the rule against alien inheritance applied to the succession. The simplest method of ruling out the common law was by calling on the argument raised earlier by Lord James Stuart that there was a universal law, presumably decreed by God, that governed the inheritance of kingdoms. This law of all nations was the only binding law of the succession to the English crown; whatever English municipal law had to say about the matter was of no consequence. This type of plea, however, was not likely to get far in Elizabethan England. It was difficult to believe that God would not permit the English to determine their monarch by their own law of succession, whatever that law happened to be. To use a pointed illustration, if God allowed those wretched French to have a Salic law, He surely would permit the English to have a rule against alien inheritance if they so desired.

A more promising case could be made by maintaining that the crown had its own rules of inheritance, which were not the

* See Appendix, charts I and V.

same as those of the common law. It could best be presented by giving examples of common-law rules of inheritance that did not apply to the crown. There were six such examples: (1) the rule of tenant by courtesy, which gave a man the right to a life tenancy of the lands of his deceased wife; (2) the rule of dower, which gave a woman the right to enjoy for life a third of the lands of her deceased husband; (3) the rule of goods and chattels, which gave the goods and chattels of a testator to his executors; (4) the rule of coheiresses, which provided that females of equal consanguinity inherit together; (5) the rule of attainder, which forbade a man attainted of treason or felony and his heirs from inheriting land; and (6) the rule of the half blood, which prevented those related to the *propositus* only by half blood from inheriting from him. All six of these rules were brought up by Leslie.[22] It was undeniable that they applied to cases of ordinary inheritance; it was just as certain that they did not apply to cases involving the royal succession.

The problem is whether these examples were just special cases that proved nothing generally. Were there reasons for them to be exceptions? Why the first four rules could not be applied to the crown is clear. One only has to consider how they would have worked out in Tudor history: (1) Philip II of Spain would have had a life tenancy of Mary I's lands; (2) Catherine Parr would have enjoyed for life a third of Henry VIII's lands; (3) the executors of Henry VIII's will would have received his goods and chattels; and (4) Mary and Elizabeth would have reigned jointly. One can imagine the difficulties that might have arisen in the first three cases, where the crown's properties would have been in the hands of others than its wearer; the possibilities of the fourth case are too weird to contemplate. These were all common-law rules that could not sensibly be applied to the crown.

Why the fifth and sixth rules (attainder and the half blood) could not be applied to the crown is not so evident. An explanation in the case of the fifth was offered by the author of *Allegations against Mary* when he was considering Henry VII's accession despite his attainder under Richard III. He maintained that Henry's attainder disabled him as a subject of Richard, but that disability ended when the crown "was cast upon him"; when Richard's authority ceased with his death, the judgment against Henry also ceased, for his offense was then committed against himself.[23] Though it may not seem reasonable that a traitor against the crown should have a right to wear it, Henry's contemporaries perhaps saw the matter differently, considering the ease with which claimants to the crown found themselves attainted.

However, the rule of the half blood is a case in which the inconsistent is added to the unreasonable. The exclusion of children of the half blood from the inheritance of ordinary property makes little sense; a half brother is a more logical heir than a distant cousin.[24] Nonetheless, to include the rule of the half blood in the laws for the inheritance of the crown would be at odds with the general rule. Maybe expediency made the law more sensible at the comparatively late date (1553) when the question of the half blood was first raised in connection with the royal succession.*

At any rate, all six of our examples are of rules that for one reason or another probably could not very well be applied to the inheritance of the crown. It seems likely that they were merely special cases, and if so, they could not be called on to prove that common-law rules of inheritance were generally inapplicable to the crown. Moreover, against our six "exceptions" stands the fact that all the other rules for the inheritance of the crown conformed with the common-law pattern. It is significant here that when representative primogeniture was yet a somewhat strange doctrine in England, John came to the throne rather than the son of his elder brother; when that doctrine was better known to English law, Richard II received the crown instead of one of his father's younger brothers. This does not mean that the order of the succession to the crown was determined by the development of the common law.† Rather, there was a parallel growth of royal and ordinary rules of inheritance that tended

---

* One of the reasons given by Northumberland to justify the exclusion of Mary and Elizabeth in favor of Lady Jane Grey was that they were Edward VI's half sisters. Nichols, *Queen Jane*, p. 93.

† Maitland, *History*, p. 97, says that it was usually the other way around.

to approximate each other unless such a course proved impractical.* The hypothesis that the crown generally followed rules of inheritance similar to those of the common law seems at least as acceptable as the contrary hypothesis. Apparently we have again reached a stalemate.

There was, however, still another way to maintain that common-law rules of inheritance did not apply to the crown. This was by invoking the notion that the crown was a corporation. The substance of this argument, as Leslie presented it, is as follows:

The crown is a "thing incorporate." Consequently, it "doth not descend according to the common course of private inheritance but goeth by succession as other corporations do." An indication that the crown follows corporate rules is that the king cannot "avoid by law his grants and letters patents by reason of his nonage as other infants . . . may do." The king may "always be said to be of full age in respect of his crown" just as "a parson, vicar, or dean, or any other person incorporate" is in respect of his office. Another indication is that the king cannot avoid the letters patents made by a usurper of the crown ("unless it be by act of Parliament"), just as other persons incorporate cannot "avoid the grants made by one that was before wrongfully in their places; whereas in the descents of inheritance the law is otherwise."[25]

This was a particularly pertinent argument. It was undeniable that an alien could become a parson, a vicar, or a dean. If the kingship was subject to corporate rules of succession rather than common-law rules of inheritance, it might follow that an alien could become king. But Leslie offered no convincing evidence that the kingship followed corporate rules of succession. He merely brought up two instances where the crown was subject to rules similar to those to which corporations were subject. In both cases it was reasonable that the crown's authority be limited. If the grants and letters patents made in the king's name during his nonage might be rescinded when he came of

* "The inheritance of the crown has at all times been closely analogous to the contemporary idea of inheritance generally, and each has influenced the other." Taswell-Langmead, p. 531.

age, normal and legitimate transactions involving the crown could only be conducted precariously in the time of a minority. Much the same would go for the king's voiding the letters patents of a usurper, especially when one remembers that "usurpations" like the Lancastrian might last over sixty years. These instances cannot be said to establish anything generally; again we may be confronted with mere exceptions.

Moreover, Leslie's simple statement that the crown descends "by succession as other corporations do" was vague and dangerous. He named the parson, the vicar, and the dean as examples of persons incorporate. The succession of parsons and vicars commonly went by presentation; that of deans was theoretically determined by election. Leslie, who was writing in behalf of a hereditary title, certainly did not desire the monarchy to be appointive or elective, but his statement was open to interpretations whereby Queen or Parliament might be considered capable of deciding the succession without regard for claims of blood. He should have been more specific lest he put his own cause in peril.

A better case along similar lines was presented by Plowden; the following is the purport of it:

The king has two bodies, namely, a mortal body natural and an immortal body politic. His body politic is the superior body; in fact, it includes his body natural. In his body politic "his subjects, who be of divers degrees and sorts, be his members . . . they be incorporate to him and he to them, and they both make a perfect corporation."* All other bodies corporate in England "go by succession, which succession cometh by election, presentation, donation, and other like means, and not by descent." The crown also goes by succession, but its succession is determined by descent. This is so because the king's body politic "was founded without letters patents by common law only." It "was first devised for necessity of the people, and for their good direction placed in someone; [it] is by the law of the realm descendible in his blood." Though this succession by blood works

---

* The words and ideas up to here are almost identical with those in Plowden's *Commentaries*, p. 234. This lends additional support to our assumption that Plowden was the author of the tract under consideration.

out in the same way as the common-law rule of representative primogeniture, the crown is not subject to common-law rules of inheritance generally. This is shown by cases of attainder. If a man has two sons and the elder is attainted, the elder cannot inherit his father's land, but neither can the younger because he is unworthy in blood. The land escheats to the lord of whom it was held. If a similar case arises involving the crown, such common law cannot possibly apply. The younger son is also unworthy in blood, and there is no lord to escheat. The elder son becomes king because his attainder only touches his inferior body natural. This is just as an attainted man may become a bishop or a mayor of a city. A member of a corporation has capacity to take use of the corporation; so the attainted prince has capacity to receive the body politic.[26]

This is not the work of a mere pamphleteer. Plowden, unlike Leslie, attempted to explain the origin and nature of the crown as a corporation. He did not do as well with the former as the latter. His hypothesis that the body politic of the king originated out of the "necessity of the people" and was founded "by common law only" is mainly interesting in terms of political philosophy. Not only is it a departure from the earlier Stuart approach, but it anticipates the views of the political theorists of the turn of the century, particularly Sir John Hayward and Sir Thomas Craig, on the origin of government.[27] In fact, Plowden may be more modern than Craig and Hayward, since he does not mention God at all in this connection. God apparently had absolutely nothing to do with the matter; an immortal body politic was created entirely by man. This would rule out completely the idea of any divinely ordained order of succession; hereditary kingship was merely a law of the realm, which, we might add, evidently came into being with the accession of Henry III. Indeed, Plowden's hypothesis seems to break down altogether on this business of sequence. We learn from Sir Frederick Pollock that the crown could not have been a corporation "in the earlier Middle Ages when the king's peace died with him and 'every man that could forthwith robbed another.' "[28] Presumably Plowden did not mean that the body politic of the

King of England was created when the Kingdom of England was already centuries old.

Plowden's concept of the nature of the crown as a corporation is more satisfactory. There are two elements here. The first was the notion that the king and his subjects made a "perfect corporation." This was not new; it was a restatement of the medieval idea of the king as the head of a "corporation aggregate of many."[29] This doctrine had found statutory expression in an Act of Henry VIII: "This realm of England is an empire ... governed by one Supreme Head and King having the dignity and royal estate of the Imperial Crown of the same, unto whom a body politic, compact of all sorts and degrees of people divided in terms and by names of Spirituality and Temporality be bounden."[30] What it amounted to was a picture of the Kingdom as an incorporated borough written large. If nothing else this was a convenient way of thinking about the state.

The second element of Plowden's concept of the nature of the crown as a corporation was his notion of the king himself. The king had two bodies; one was mortal and natural, the other immortal and politic. His body politic was the superior body; it apparently absorbed his natural body. Moreover, the king's two bodies gave him two capacities. Suppose he had been attainted during his predecessor's reign. As an attainted man he would not have had capacity to inherit an acre of land in England; yet as a member of the corporation he would have had capacity to succeed to the Crown of England despite his attainder. How well did this king with two bodies and two capacities fit the monarchs who actually reigned in Tudor England?

One may certainly take exception to some of what Plowden wrote in light of the realities of sixteenth-century England. Consider, for example, the implications of his case of the attainted prince. If the attainted prince could not inherit land and yet could succeed to the kingship, it might follow that the lands of the crown were only held by the king in his corporate or politic capacity. This could give rise to the radical doctrine that those lands really belonged to the entire corporation of England; the king just held them in trust for the nation. The bulk of the

royal lands, however, must have been regarded as belonging to
the king in his natural capacity. The medieval expectation that
the king should "live of his own" was still strong in Tudor England, and this implied the view that the lands of the crown
were held by the mortal king.[31]

Plowden's ascribing superiority to the king's politic or non-
natural body is also open to question. Probably few of Plowden's contemporaries gave any thought to the bodies politic
of their sovereigns. The body politic was an abstruse notion,
and rulers like Henry VII, Henry VIII, Elizabeth I, and even
Mary I had very definite bodies natural whose activities were
often quite manifest to all and sundry. The personal side of
monarchy was still an important consideration in the sixteenth
century; Tudor Englishmen probably thought of a Henry VIII
or an Elizabeth I in much the same terms as their ancestors had
thought of an Edward I or a Henry V.*

Nevertheless, Plowden's concept of the king seems generally
acceptable, though somewhat overstated. All of the crown's
property was not regarded as belonging to the king in his
natural capacity. For example, gifts to the king were assumed
to be to his corporate capacity.[32] Far more significant was the
growing distinction between the king in his natural capacity
and the king in his politic capacity in the constitutional sphere.
First we must mention the Statute of Treasons of 1495, which
made it no offense to serve a king *de facto*.[33] If a king *de jure*,
when he came to the throne, was permitted no lawful vengeance
on those who had served a king *de facto*, then a recognition of
an allegiance to an immortal body politic was implied because
a king *de facto* had no lawful capacity to wear the crown.
Furthermore, there was the distinction between what the king
did on his own prerogative and what he did in Parliament.[34]
The king could certainly be regarded as acting in his corporate
capacity when he was in Parliament. In 1552 Chief Justice
Fineux declared that "the Parliament of the King and the
Lords and the Commons are a corporation."[35] Henry VIII im-

* At the beginning of the next century the judges in *Calvin's Case* declared
that allegiance to the king was personal. McIlwain, p. 95; Holdsworth, IX, 81.

plied the same in 1543, when he told his Commons that in Parliament "we as head and you as members are conjoined and knit together in one body politic."[36] Indeed, Henry, that great practitioner of "Tudor despotism," could not have created the new treasons needed to enforce the royal supremacy and his alteration of the succession without acting in his corporate capacity, i.e., in Parliament.[37]

Therefore, Plowden's concept of the crown as a corporation had some foundation. It remains to be considered whether he managed to apply it to the question at issue. He did better than Leslie in this respect. From the premise that the crown was a corporation, both writers concluded that the kingship went by succession like other corporate offices, but Plowden avoided Leslie's rather dangerous conclusions by suggesting that the royal succession might be determined by claims of blood, and yet not follow common-law rules of inheritance generally. Moreover, Plowden's "proof" of his argument was more relevant than Leslie's. His example of cases of attainder at least had something to do with inheritance and succession.

Nonetheless, Plowden did not make a conclusive case. We have already seen that although the rule of attainder did not apply to the succession, this did not necessarily prove that common-law rules of inheritance in general could not be applied to the same. Moreover, Plowden's statement that the crown went by descent was an admission that England was an unusual corporation. Hereditary succession was not its only peculiarity. For example, its council and Parliament, if in session, ceased to exist with the demise of its head; the new king had to appoint his own council, and issue writs for a new Parliament if he desired one. The death of a mayor did not ordinarily have such consequences for the equivalent institutions of an incorporated borough. The corporation of England evidently had its own rules, and they were not always the same as those of other incorporated bodies. Therefore, it was at least possible that the succession to its kingship followed common-law rules of inheritance generally, the rule against alien inheritance included.

This ends our discussion of whether common-law rules of inheritance applied to the succession to the crown. It has failed

to produce anything definitive one way or the other. When all
is said and done, we are left with a rule against alien inheritance
whose applicability to the crown had never been put to test.
If the question had to be decided under such circumstances,
practical considerations undoubtedly would have prevailed.
And the sixteenth-century Englishman's dislike of the foreigner
surely would have been a most important factor in the making
of such a decision. Consequently, the Stuart tract writers found
it insufficient merely to argue that the rule against alien inheritance did not apply to the succession. They also had to maintain that even if the rule applied, it did not reach Mary Stuart.

One way to do this was by calling on the very statute that
Hales had brought up in support of the rule against alien
inheritance. One provision of the Act of 1351 read: "the children of the Kings of England (*les enfantz des Rois d'Engleterre*)
in whatsoever part they be born, in England or elsewhere, be
able and ought to bear the inheritance after the death of their
ancestors."[38] Did "children of the Kings of England" only refer
to sons and daughters of English monarchs? Or was it also meant
to extend to their remoter descendants? If the second question
could be answered affirmatively, everyone knew that the Queen
of Scots was a great-granddaughter of Henry VII. Therefore, the
Stuart tract writers maintained that the makers of the statute
intended "children of the Kings of England" to be interpreted
broadly.

Their case consisted of four points. First, the words *enfantz*
and ancestors in the statute were "in *predicamento ad aliquod*
[somewhat close status] and so correlatives in such sort as the
meaning of the law was not to restrain the understanding . . . of
enfantz so strict as only to the children of the king's body, but
to others inheritable in remainder."[39] Second, *enfantz* is the
French equivalent of the Latin *liberi,* which in the civil law
"doth comprehend . . . not only the children of the first degree,
but other descendants also."[40] Third, it is absurd to believe that
Edward III would accept a law that might disinherit his foreign-
born great-grandchildren. Fourth, if the statute excluded such
descendants, John of Gaunt and Thomas of Woodstock, Edward's fourth and youngest sons, would not have married their
daughters to foreign princes.[41]

These points are not unexceptionable. The words *enfantz* and ancestors, as used in the statute, did not have to be correlatives. The Stuart argument is that the men of 1351 intended to give a foreign-born great-grandson of Edward III, for example, the right to bear the inheritance of his ancestor, namely, Edward III. They could as easily have been thinking only in terms of allowing only the immediate children of the Kings of England to bear the inheritance of their ancestors as well as of their fathers. For instance, when Edward III ascended the throne, he could be considered as bearing the inheritance of Henry III and Edward I, as well as of Edward II. If this was the meaning of the Act of 1351, *enfantz* and ancestors were not correlatives, at least not in the sense of the Stuart argument.

Nor was the fact that the French word *enfantz* could be extended to include children beyond the first degree proof that such was the intention of the statute. *Enfantz* also could mean sons and daughters only. As the author of *Allegations against Mary* put it, "if such had been the intention of the Parliament that not only the children of the first degree should inherit, but likewise that all offspring generally of the king should be inheritable . . . , they might as easily have named the descendants generally as the king's children particularly."[42] Of course, the logic of this argument was capable of a contrary application, to wit: Parliament should have shown its intention by specifically naming Edward III's immediate children. Unfortunately the men of 1351, knowing their own meaning and not anticipating the debates of Elizabethan pamphleteers, did not see any need to be more precise than they were in wording their statute.

Nor do we have to accept the view that Edward III and his sons must have understood the word *enfantz* in the Act of 1351 to include children of further degrees than the first. It was not unreasonable for Edward III to allow his foreign-born descendants to be disinherited under the conditions provided in the statute. They could not, according to another of its provisions, be disinherited if they were born of parents in the allegiance of the King of England. If they were born of parents in the allegiance of a foreign king, Edward might be glad to see them set aside in favor of other descendants, of whom there was no likely scarcity. He may have had some inkling of the succession troubles that could arise from his having too many direct descendants—the reverse of the Tudor problem—and concluded that it would not hurt if a few were excluded. We cannot prove that he thought in these terms, but neither can the assumptions of the Stuart tract writers be substantiated.

As for Edward's sons, the evidence offered to show that they must have known the word *enfantz* was subject to a broad intrepretation is unconvincing. That John of Gaunt and Thomas of Woodstock married their daughters to foreign royalty was hardly significant. Those princesses were not very close to the throne. Woodstock himself was but a youngest son in a family of several. When Gaunt's eldest daughter Philippa married the King of Portugal in 1387, the children of her father's elder brothers, her father himself, and her own brother were all living. Moreover, we must remember that the capacity of females or their heirs to succeed to the crown was still questionable. Hence Gaunt and Woodstock probably would have made the appropriate matches for their daughters that they did, no matter what their understanding of the word *enfantz* in the Act of 1351.

Furthermore, we have previously alluded to another statute that perhaps indicates that Parliament itself regarded that word as only covering immediate children of the Kings of England. This was the Act of 1368 permitting infants born in English territories in France to inherit in England. Its date seems significant. Edward of Angouleme and Richard of Bordeaux, the sons of the Black Prince, had been born in such territories in 1365 and 1366, respectively. By 1367 the Black Prince, Edward III's heir apparent, had contracted a mortal disease.[43] When Parliament met in 1368, it must have been obvious that the Black Prince might predecease his father. Though the Englishry of young Edward and young Richard was established by the Act of 1351, since they were born of parents in the allegiance of the King of England, Parliament perhaps feared this would not be sufficient to assure their places in the succession under any contingency, what with the powerful John of Gaunt, Edward III's favorite son, around to claim the crown.[44] Therefore, the Act of 1368 might be considered a sort of insurance measure for the sons of the Black Prince. If this was its chief purpose, Parliament must have understood the word *enfantz* in the Act of 1351 to refer only to the King of England's own children.*

The main trouble with the arguments of the Stuart tract writers—and with our objections to them, for that matter—is that they are simply speculations. In 1351 Edward III and his Parliament knew exactly what they meant by the word *enfantz* when they used it in their statute. They did not realize that their language would not be so clear to later ages. What our tract writers really did was to try to read the minds of the men of 1351. They would have done better if they had paid more attention to statute reading.

Toward the end of the Act of 1351 they would have found that the Parliament men had been

of one mind accorded that Henry son of John de Beaumond, Elizabeth daughter of Guy de Bryan, and Giles son of Ralph Dawbeny, and others which the King will name, and which were born beyond the sea out of the allegiance of England, shall be from henceforth able to have and enjoy their inheritance after the death of their ancestors, in all parts within the allegiance of England, as well as those that should be born within the same allegiance.[45]

The important name in this list of those born abroad who evidently were to be exempted specially from the common-law rule against alien inheritance is "Henry son of John de Beaumond." He was a great-grandson of Edmund "Crouchback," Earl of Lancaster, the second surviving son of Henry III.† If Henry Beaumond or Beaumont had been regarded as included among "the children of the Kings of England," there would have been no reason for his name to appear in this special clause.

---

* No doubt there were other reasons for giving the right of inheritance in England to infants born in English territories in France, but it is difficult to imagine any more compelling reason at the time than the fact that the birth of the Black Prince's sons was followed by his mortal illness.

† The younger son of "Crouchback," Henry, Earl of Lancaster, was married first to Maud Chaworth. Their daughter Eleanor married Lord John Beaumont. Henry Beaumont was their son. *Complete Peerage,* II, 61; VII, 378, 387, 396, 400.

This is substantial evidence that the men of 1351 did not intend the word *enfantz* to apply to any but the sons and daughters of the Kings of England. The significance of Henry Beaumont's inclusion in the list of exemptions seems to have escaped the notice of all of our tract writers, Stuart and anti-Stuart.* It would have been difficult for the Stuart side to argue that Beaumont's name did not settle the matter against them. One might maintain that the Henry Beaumont of the statute was not the descendant of Henry III, but this would be most unlikely. Possibly there was another man of that name, but only *the* Henry Beaumont, the cousin of the Blanche Plantagenet who was soon to wed John of Gaunt, would be important enough to rate such special mention.† One might also argue that the naming of Beaumont was superfluous and accidental, but this too would be improbable. Those who actually drafted the statute no doubt knew just who Beaumont was, and would hardly have named him if he were already covered by the words *"les enfantz des Rois d'Engleterre."*‡

If the argument that Mary Stuart was a "child" of Henry VII according to the terms of the Act of 1351 was untenable, there was yet another way to maintain that the common-law rule against alien inheritance did not apply to her. We have said that the Act of 1368 came to be interpreted to mean that an infant born in any foreign territory of the King of England, in France or elsewhere, was capable of inheritance in England. Mary was born in Scotland. And she was Queen of Scotland. The full import of this last fact will be more apparent shortly. If Scotland was indeed a fief of the English Crown, the Queen

---

* I have only found two instances where writers have recognized that the appearance of the name of Henry Beaumont in the statute is important. The first was in a later tract, which seems to have been an answer to Leslie, *HM* 780, fol. 6. The second was in 1690 in Atwood, pp. 96–97.

† Henry and Blanche had a common grandfather in Henry, second son of Edmund "Crouchback."

‡ It is true that statutes in the reign of Edward III were often not so well drafted as those of Edward I's reign. But this was usually because they were composed of parts of various unrelated and unskillfully worded Commons' petitions. Sayles, pp. 461–62. This apparently was not the case with the Act of 1351. It only dealt with one subject, the divisions of which were presented in logical order. It probably was drafted by men skilled in such matters.

of Scots was not an alien in England. The status of Scotland and its Queen, however, was not easily determined. The question produced much debate among our tract writers.

The anti-Stuart side was best presented by Hales. He claimed that Scotland of right belonged to the Crown of England, but so did Normandy. This no more proved the Scots to be in the allegiance of the Crown of England than it did the Normans. The Normans owed allegiance to the King of England, but gave the same to the King of France. This lost them their Englishry as shown by the fact that their lands were escheated.

So in like manner, albeit Scotland belongeth of right to the Crown of England . . . and the Kings of Scotland have ofttimes* done their homage therefore to the Kings of England; yet we say they have long forsaken their faith and allegiance of England and have become rebels, but rather have been taken for enemies to England; for they have usually ransomed upon their taking, as enemies, and not been executed, like rebels. And by that means King James, father to their Queen that now is, was at the time of her birth, and of his death, out of the faith and allegiance of England. Wherefore, to say that she was born within the King's allegiance because she was born in Scotland is a mere cavillation.[46]

The case for the Stuart side was a delicate one for some of the Scottish Queen's supporters to make. Maitland, in his letter to Cecil, said that he, as a Scot, could not admit that Scotland was a fief of England. He told Cecil that "the argument" is "fitter for your assertion than mine."[47] Maitland was doomed to disappointment if he really expected Cecil to assert that the Queen of Scots could not be regarded as an alien in England, but there were others who would assert the argument without requiring any special invitation from Maitland. This was being done by the Englishman Plowden about the same time that Maitland was writing his letter.[48] Some two years later Leslie—a less scrupulous Scot—was also maintaining the Englishry of Mary Stuart.[49] No matter what the source of this argument, however, there was a certain amount of hypocrisy in its making.

---

* "Ofttimes" is misleading. Many Kings of Scotland did homage to the Kings of England for their fiefs in England; few did so for Scotland itself. See Wycoff; Bain; and Rait.

It was asserting a claim for the Queen of Scots that she herself would almost have to deny because of her birth and rank.

Though Maitland would not admit his Queen and people to be in the allegiance of England, he indicated how a case for it might be made. He pointed out that the English had long considered Scotland to be subject to England. He said that sundry old English proclamations, treatises, and histories could be called upon as evidence of this.[50] But perhaps the most striking illustration—albeit Maitland was loath to refer to it—was the fact that the Kings of England had many times demanded, and sometimes received, the homage of the Kings of Scotland. Still another indication that Scotland was not regarded as being outside the allegiance of England was brought up by Leslie:

> England, Scotland, and Wales be all within one territory and not divided by any sea. And all old records of law concerning service to be done in those two countries [Scotland and Wales] have these words *Infra quator maria,* within the four seas, which must needs be understood in Scotland and Wales as well as in England because they be all within one continent compassed by four seas.

And very pertinent, the Act of 1351 was entitled "A Statute for those who are born in parts beyond sea . . . , whereby," Leslie added, "it seemeth that no part of the Statute toucheth those that are born in Wales or Scotland."[51]

One notices that the evidence presented to support this case came from the England of the past rather than from the England of Elizabeth. And the relationships of those two Englands with Scotland were not the same. This leaves room for doubts about the applicability of the evidence. For instance, consider the Act of 1351. By 1351 David II of Scotland had acknowledged Edward III as his suzerain, and was himself a captive in England. David was something of an Anglophile, and was not averse to the idea of having a member of the English royal family follow him on the throne of Scotland. Edward's Scottish policy must have seemed on the verge of complete success in 1351. The English no doubt thought of Scotland in much the same way as they thought of Wales, where things were well under control.[52] This might well explain why the title of the

Act of 1351 only mentioned "those who are born in parts beyond sea."

The situation was quite different during the first decade of Elizabeth's reign. The Queen of Scots had done no homage to the Queen of England. Nor did Elizabeth make any serious effort to receive it. She evidently did not inherit her father's ambition to subjugate Scotland. An independent and unhostile Scotland was doubtless enough for Elizabeth, and safer and less costly for England. Moreover, Scotland's sovereignty was, for all practical purposes, undeniable. Though most Englishmen must have still believed with Hales that Scotland rightfully belonged to the Crown of England, this did not mean that they would consider a Scot to be in the allegiance of the Kings of England; indeed, their views on the matter undoubtedly were quite the contrary. After all, the Kings of England claimed the very Crown of France, but no one would say that a Frenchman was anything but an alien. Therefore, most of those who knew about the Act of 1351 would probably regard it as applying to those born in Scotland as well as those "born in parts beyond sea."

But would English law agree with English opinion on the status of a Scot in Elizabethan England? Court decisions do not answer this question. As for the Act of 1351, no court ever seems to have made a direct ruling on its applicability to a Scot. Otherwise there are two later cases. In 1571 in the Queen's Bench, a Scot was denied a foreigner's privilege to be tried *per medietatem linguae*, i.e., that half of the jurors be his own countrymen. One of the three reasons given by the judges for their ruling was that "a Scot was never here accounted an alien, but rather a subject."[53] Against this stood the more famous *Calvin's Case* of 1608. There the question, argued before all of the judges in the Exchequer Chamber, was whether a Scot could bring suit in an English court concerning English lands. If he could he certainly was not an alien. The effect of the decision of the judges, as far as it concerns us here, was that a Scot born before James VI of Scotland became James I of England was an alien in England.[54] These two *ex post facto* decisions, which con-

tradicted each other and may well have been politically inspired, hardly establish anything for us.[55]

Court decisions aside, there is evidence that the law was
clearly against the Englishry of a Scot. To go back to Henry
VII's reign, Parliament in 1491 evidently regarded Scots as
aliens when it required all Scots not made denizens to leave
England.[56] That they were still considered aliens may be indicated by the numerous denizations of Scots during our period.[57]
And long afterward, some four years before the decision in
Calvin's Case, James I had to have his Parliament naturalize
those Scots whose services he required in England.[58]

Plowden apparently was afraid that Mary Stuart's birth in
Scotland would not be an acceptable proof of her allegiance to
England. Consequently, he also called on the fact that she was
Queen of Scotland. Even if Scottish subjects were out of the
allegiance of England, he argued, their Queen could not be
so. This was because she was in homage to the Crown of England, and it would be "too too strange" to say that one in
homage to a crown was out of its allegiance.[59] Thus the Queen
of Scotland was a kind of special subject of the Queen of
England. And therefore Mary could be Elizabeth's heir, no
matter where she was born.

There were practical difficulties—to say nothing of theoreti-
cal difficulties—with this doctrine. If the Queen of Scotland
owed homage to the Queen of England, Elizabeth had never
received any from Mary. This might make Mary technically a
rebel. Then her position might be similar to that of an attainted
prince, who could inherit the Crown of England. But James V,
Mary's father, had, as Hales pointed out, been considered an
enemy rather than a rebel when he went to war with Henry
VIII. This might imply that James was regarded as an alien
monarch, Henry's previous assertions of suzerainty over Scotland notwithstanding.[60] Moreover, this would be a particularly
distasteful way for the Queen of Scots to claim Englishry. Indeed, at her trial in 1586 Mary declared that she "would not
offend against her progenitors the Kings of Scots by acknowl-
edging herself a subject of the Crown of England, for this were
nothing else but to profess them openly to have been rebels and

traitors."[61] Obviously Plowden's alternative idea on how to show Mary to be in the allegiance of England was not too useful.

This ends our study of the applicability of the common-law rule against alien inheritance to the succession and to Mary Queen of Scots. It has not produced definitive answers, and such answers probably cannot be found. The main obstacle here undoubtedly is the lack of any genuine precedent, legal or historical. There may be another matter that, though it is perhaps somewhat vague and no doubt debatable, is at least worth advancing. During the revolutionary decade of the 1530's, England had become, in the words of G. R. Elton, "an independent state, sovereign within its territorial limits."[62] If this national sovereignty was lost temporarily under Mary I, it certainly was restored in 1559. A corollary to the development of national sovereignty would be the replacement of older, "feudal" concepts of allegiance by national concepts. The problem is that thought and language had not yet caught up to the new situation. Our tract writers necessarily argued in terms of homage, of allegiance, direct or indirect, to an overlord whose title happened to be king. But allegiance which doubtless had been changing in nature long before the 1530's, was now to Elizabeth as Queen of England, to the Queen as symbolizing and synonymous with the nation of England. If this were so, the terms used, and even the laws referred to, by the tract writers had lost much of their original relevance. They had to be seen in a light that was not yet bright enough to perceive.

At any rate lacking definitive answers our conclusions must be qualified. My inclination is to accept the view of F. W. Maitland: "Mary Stuart was born in Scotland; she could not inherit an acre of English land, and it was highly doubtful whether English law would give the crown to an alien who was the child of two aliens."[63] The very existence of the rule against alien inheritance would seem to place the burden of proof on the Stuart side. And the Stuart tract writers hardly offered convincing proofs. Nonetheless, they did raise sufficiently impressive arguments to allow the favorers of the Queen of Scots to accept with a clear conscience her eligibility to ascend the English throne.

8. *The Legitimacy of the Suffolks*

Now we turn from the question of whether the Queen of Scots was eligible to be included in the succession to the Crown of England to ask the same about her chief rivals. Here we are mainly concerned with the legitimacy of the descent of Lady Catherine Grey and her sons from Henry VII. Catherine's blood royal could only be pure if two marriages were valid: the first was that of Charles Brandon, Duke of Suffolk, to Mary Tudor, younger daughter of Henry VII and widow of Louis XII of France; the second that of Henry Grey, Marquis of Dorset and later Duke of Suffolk, to Lady Frances Brandon, elder daughter of Mary Tudor and mother of Catherine Grey. The legitimacy of the royal descent of Catherine's sons also depended on the validity of the same marriages, but in their cases there was a third questionable marriage to be considered. We have already discussed at length Catherine's marriage with Edward Seymour, Earl of Hertford, and have reached conclusions mostly in its favor; we shall not investigate it further. That marriage, however, could not stand if Catherine and Lord Henry Herbert had completed the contract of matrimony that their parents had made for them late in the reign of Edward VI. Therefore, it is now our task to deal with three cases of matrimony: Mary Tudor and Charles Brandon, Frances Brandon and Henry Grey, and Catherine Grey and Henry Herbert.

The issue in the first case was whether Lady Margaret Mor-

timer was Charles Brandon's lawful wife when he married Mary
Tudor. If she was, his cohabitation with Mary was adultery.
This matter was debated in three of our tracts: Hales's *Declaration, Allegations in behalf of Mary,* and *The Letter.* We begin
with the first part of Hales's argument:

Is it like ... that if Duke Charles had had another wife living when he
married the French Queen ..., King Henry [VIII] would have consented that his sister should have received so great injury that she
should have been kept like a concubine? Would his Council have suffered so great an infamy to have come to his Majesty's stock? Or would
the nobility ... have honored so unlawful an act? Or would the common people ... have holden their tongues in so manifest adultery?
Is it like that in so long time that the French Queen and the Duke
lived together as man and wife ... she should not have heard of it? ...
Is it to be believed that she ... would have been contented that another should have been partaker of that flesh which she ... took only
to be her own? Or can any man think that any woman can be contented to live in mean degree when she may be a duchess, as ... Lady
Mortimer might have been justly, if she had been the Duke's wife? ...
Suppose that the Duke had had another wife living at the time he married the French Queen; yet for as much as he and she were married
together openly, continued all their lives as man and wife together,
and nothing said against them ..., and that the Lady Frances and the
Lady Eleanor [their daughters] were not taken to be bastards during
their lives; now, after their death, neither they nor their children may,
by the laws of this realm, be accounted so.[1]

The author of *Allegations in behalf of Mary* dismissed Hales's
points as "conjectures," but saw fit to make a lengthy reply.
Though it is likely that Henry VIII, "if he had known that the
Duke had another wife living ..., would not have consented
that his sister should have married him ..., there be ... perfect
clerks ... that are of opinion certain that the French Queen and
the Duke were matched before the King was privy thereof."
About Mary Tudor's supposed ignorance of Brandon's marriage with Lady Mortimer, he said:

[Though] some ignorance in some sort might ... shadow the illegiti-
mation of the children ..., [not] every kind of ignorance might be
accepted to bolster forth such causes ... for the law tendeth to the favor of the vigilant and diligent in their own causes, and not to the
willful, slothful, or negligent.... [Since] the French Queen, if she had
liked ... to have hearkened, searched, or demanded, might easily have

had intelligence whether the Duke had any wife living . . . , it is as much as if she had known it: so doth it manifestly appear that the children born in such matrimony cannot by any means be reputed or taken for legitimate. . . . [As for the long continuance of the marriage without anything said against it, this] might have had some color or show of reason . . . if the persons against whom any such controversy should have risen had been of such degree or condition as any might freely have proceeded against them. . . . [But Brandon and Mary were] in great favor with the Prince in such sort that the great and imminent danger and peril that did depend thereof was, and is, the apparent and manifest cause why no man did or durst begin with them, or attempt any such matter, and specially in a thing that touched any whit the displeasure or dishonor of the King himself. And therefore that long continuance in matrimony . . . without controversy is not to be counted for quiet and peaceable, but rather injurious and violent. . . . [As such it] cannot help anything to the legitimation of the children.[2]

There were rights and wrongs on both sides of this debate. No doubt the author of *Allegations in behalf of Mary* was generally correct that the peculiar positions of the French Queen and the Duke of Suffolk made it almost impossible to voice objections to their marriage. Nonetheless, when the marriage was openly solemnized in England in May 1515 there were manifestations of displeasure, Hales's implications to the contrary notwithstanding. A report was sent to Venice that "there were no public demonstrations because the kingdom did not approve of the marriage," and a large faction in the Council was strongly opposed to the match.[3] Such sentiments, however, probably were motivated mainly by a natural jealousy over the rapid rise of Charles Brandon, the son of a simple esquire; it is unlikely that there was real concern for Lady Mortimer at the time.

As for Henry VIII's attitude, the author of *Allegations in behalf of Mary* probably was right in indicating that "the French Queen and the Duke were matched before the King was privy thereof." They had been married secretly in France in February 1515, prior to their return to England.[4] This could not have come as much of a surprise to Henry, however. He had promised to let Mary choose her next husband when she first consented to marry the aged and sickly Louis XII, and Henry, according to Mary, well knew that she had "always been of good mind" to Suffolk.[5] Nor was the King obliged to accept the match as a *fait accompli*. It would have been a simple matter to have the Duke removed from the picture by the headsman's ax. And if Henry liked Suffolk too much for that, the match could have been undone in the ecclesiastical courts if the King believed that the Duke had another wife.

Nor was Henry beyond going to the trouble of securing an annulment, especially in a case where the ecclesiastical authorities, English and Italian, would have no difficulty in complying. Henry was very moral about such matters—at least when his own marriages were not involved. In 1528, at the very time he was seeking the divorce from Catherine of Aragon, Henry severely lectured his elder sister, Margaret, for divorcing the Earl of Angus in violation of "the divine ordinance of inseparable matrimony first instituted in Paradise."[6] Moreover, in 1515 he had his younger sister and her Duke completely at his mercy. Though Mary and Suffolk were two of his favorite people, it seems improbable that this would have stood in his way if he had doubts about the validity of their marriage. After all, its dissolution would leave him with an unmarried sister who might be useful in future diplomacy. Therefore, there is still much to be said for Hales's view that Henry's acceptance of Suffolk as a brother-in-law meant that he did not think that the Duke had another wife living.

Perhaps Hales's most impressive point was his assertion that Mary would not have continued to live with Brandon if he really belonged to Lady Mortimer. It is easy to doubt Henry VIII's motives, but it is difficult to see Mary Tudor as one who would feign ignorance. "Her moral character," writes an eminent historian, "stands out with singular freshness, in contrast to the cold selfishness and heartless ambition of the grasping politicians by whom she was surrounded." Later this woman of integrity espoused the cause of Catherine of Aragon against her mighty brother and in behalf of "the divine ordinance of inseparable matrimony."[7] Though it would be naive to assume that Mary never knew anything about Charles Brandon and Lady Mortimer, a woman of her character probably satisfied herself that Brandon had no other wife during their cohabitation.

This was the real issue that Hales and his adversary were hesitant about tackling. It was undeniable that Lady Mortimer had once been regarded as Brandon's wife.[8] The problem was whether she was still his wife in 1515. The author of *Allegations in behalf of Mary* accused Hales of making conjectures, but conjectures were what he offered in reply. Both writers devoted the larger part of their case to speculation. This was the typical technique of polemicists faced with a question about whose facts they were uncertain. But the real issue remained, and they could not ignore it entirely.

Again we begin with Hales's side of the story:

Charles Brandon . . . made a contract of matrimony with one Mrs. Anne Browne; but before any solemnization of marriage, not only had a daughter by her (which after was married to the Lord Powes) but also broke promise with her, and openly and solemnly married with the Lady Mortimer; which marriage . . . Mrs. Anne Browne judicially accused to be unlawful for that . . . Sir Charles Brandon had not only made a precontract with her, but also had carnally known her; which things being duly proved, and sentence of divorce between . . . Sir Charles and the Lady Mortimer given and denounced [proclaimed]; he married solemnly . . . Mrs. Anne Browne, at the which marriage all the nobility were present and did honor it. And afterwards . . . Sir Charles had by . . . Mrs. Anne Browne another daughter, which was married to the Lord Monteagle. After this . . . Mrs. Anne Browne continued with him all her life as his wife . . . without any impeachment of the marriage: after whose death King Henry . . . intended he should for his better preferment have married the Lady Lisle, being a young maid and an inheritor; whereupon . . . Sir Charles was created Viscount Lisle. But that marriage by reason of her youth took no place. After this he was created Duke of Suffolk, about which time Louis the French King died: and leaving the . . . Lady Mary . . . widow; the . . . Duke of Suffolk was sent to France for her; and with the consent of King Henry married her twice, first secretly in France, and after openly here in England. . . . After this they had issue between them, that is, the Lady Frances and the Lady Eleanor. Against whom the Lady Powes, their base sister, in the time of King Edward VI, alleged bastardy. But . . . they were both by the laws of the realm and by the canon laws declared to be legitimate, and approved to be born in lawful matrimony; so as no man can say they be bastards.[9]

This certainly makes obvious what a complicated subject the matrimonial history of Charles Brandon is. And Hales even left out one of Brandon's most ambitious projects, his vain suit for the hand of Margaret of Savoy, daughter of the Emperor Maximilian I.[10] Brandon apparently saw matrimony as a road to wealth and power, and cared little about how many hearts he broke along the way. Moralizing aside, such a career was almost bound to leave in its wake questionable arrangements that would be difficult for posterity to fathom. The truth was hardly as simple—I use the word comparatively—as Hales's story would have it.

Two of Hales's points were probably unassailable. The proposed match between Brandon and Lady Lisle must have been no more than just that. It appears that no objections were ever raised about it. But it would only have been an added complication. More important is the likelihood that Hales was correct about the failure of Lady Powes in her suit to obtain the bastardization of Brandon's daughters by Mary Tudor. We have previously found out that the source of Hales's information was Lord John Grey, a man who might well know about such a matter. That no attempt was made by the author of *Allegations in behalf of Mary* to refute Hales on this point would seem to indicate his accuracy.

That author's neglect to consider Lady Powes's case was, according to *The Letter,* fatal to his whole argument. He held that since Mary Tudor's children had been born while Lady Mortimer was living, they could not be regarded as legitimate according to the common law unless their legitimacy had been proved before an ordinary while they were still alive.[11] The Ladies Frances and Eleanor were, to quote Lord John Grey, "proved legitimate, both in the Arches [and] the Star Chamber"; the Arches, the Archbishop of Canterbury's court, certainly had ordinary jurisdiction.[12] "And this being done in their lifetime," said the writer of *The Letter,* "by his [the author of *Allegations in behalf of Mary*] own judgment they stand clear of all bastardy at the common law."[13] Lady Powes's case cannot be regarded as conclusive, however. Lord John Grey's testimony only tells of the courts that heard it and their finding. Powerful men were interested in the Suffolks during Edward VI's reign, and it is possible that undue pressure was exerted in securing the verdict. We would have to know something of the details of the proceedings and the grounds of the decision before we could accept Lady Powes's case as proving anything.*

The really crucial question involves Charles Brandon's relationship with Anne Browne and the subsequent Mortimer divorce. Here Hales's story was challenged by the author of *Allegations in behalf of Mary*. He maintained that since the supporters of the Suffolk claim could "prove no lawful divorce within the realm," they supposed a suit between Anne Browne and Charles Brandon,

whereof should arise the displeasure between . . . Lady Mortimer and the said Charles, her husband, seven years and more after their marriage: during the which time . . . Anne Browne . . . never . . . once complained to the law, or ever thought of the matter, nor as it seemeth would ever have done, if in this time . . . Charles had not consumed . . . Lady Mortimer's wealth and . . . found her years not answerable to his youth and wanton disposition; for the satisfying whereof, this acquaintance, that belly rising, and these practices with . . . Anne. Whereof riseth now these feeble grounded histories . . . that she forsooth should be precontracted to him before and had a child; which child, eight years after, is known well enough, but was but two or three years old at the most. A strange case; and yet she had it at seventeen or nineteen, and was but twenty at the time of this supposed divorce, when . . . Charles and she came together.[14]

Though this account, the full accuracy of which cannot be checked, seems to fit the character of Charles Brandon, it suggests good reasons for the divorce whose existence its writer denied. The exhaustion of Lady Mortimer's wealth and the attraction of Anne Browne would explain Brandon's desiring a new wife, and the birth of a child would be cause for Anne Browne to fall in with the scheme. Even if we allow that there never was a precontract, such circumstances would make it politic to pretend there had been and bring suit for an annulment. Nev-

---

* It is difficult to guess what was argued before the tribunals. If the Ladies Brandon were illegitimate, so was Lady Powes. In both cases legitimacy depended—though not entirely for Lady Powes, who apparently was born before the solemnization of Brandon's marriage with her mother—on the invalidity of the Mortimer marriage. Since Anne Browne was not living when Brandon married Mary Tudor, there could be no question of bastardy on that account.

ertheless, Hales failed to document any such divorce, and the burden of proof would seem to be his. Hence one has to conclude that the author of *Allegations in behalf of Mary* had the better of this particular argument with Hales.

There was, however, a pertinent matter that Hales did not bring up. His adversary stated that the friends of the Suffolk claim could "prove no lawful divorce within the realm." This suggests the possibility of a divorce outside the realm. And we are dealing with a period when England was still under Roman jurisdiction. Bulls from the Holy See then had meaning in English cases of matrimony.

By March 1527 Henry VIII had commenced proceedings to annul his marriage with Catherine of Aragon, an annulment that would bastardize Princess Mary.[15] The elder Mary Tudor must have been duly shocked. It was not simply that her sympathies were with her sister-in law and namesake; she doubtless realized that her own marriage and the legitimacy of her own daughters were also open to question. And her husband was probably as much of a rogue as her brother. Accordingly, a bull was obtained from Clement VII in 1528 to ensure the status quo in the Suffolk household. The author of *Allegations in behalf of Mary* never definitely admitted the existence of any such bull; he merely hinted that one was alleged.* The copy of the bull at the Public Record Office, however, proves that it was promulgated.[16]

Clement VII issued the bull at Orvieto on 12 May 1528; it was exhibited and attested before the Bishop of Norwich and other witnesses on 20 August 1529. The bull stated that Charles Brandon married Lady Mortimer on the strength of an invalid dispensation, though he had previously contracted matrimony *"per verba licentiae de presenti"* with Anne Browne. Later Brandon brought Lady Mortimer before the Archdeacon of London, the judge of matrimonial affairs in the Diocese of London, and secured a divorce. This was granted on three grounds: (1) that Brandon and Lady Mortimer were in the second and third de-

---

* "And if they seek their relief by any dispensation from Rome, as is said, it serveth not, although there were a divorce to be proved by any such instrument." Atwood, Appendix, p. 10.

grees of affinity; (2) that Lady Mortimer and Anne Browne were within the prohibited degrees of consanguinity; and (3) that Brandon was first cousin once removed of Lady Mortimer's former husband.* Brandon then solemnized his marriage with Anne Browne, and after her death wedded Mary Tudor. This history recited, the bull went on to declare the legitimacy of Brandon's children by both Anne and Mary. It concluded by visiting with ecclesiastical censure any who might challenge its contents.[17]

Two relevant points of this bull deserve mention before we proceed to consider its validity. First, it indicates that the Archdeacon of London annulled Brandon's marriage with Lady Mortimer because of their consanguinity and affinity, not because of a precontract with Anne Browne. Hales's version of the divorce is thus contradicted. Second, that those who questioned the bull were made liable to ecclesiastical censure perhaps explains why none of our Catholic tract writers attacked either the marriage of Charles Brandon and Mary Tudor or the legitimacy of their children. The author of *Allegations in behalf of Mary* had a near monopoly of those mischievous pursuits.[18]

That author was quick to attack the validity of the bull, whose existence he refused to acknowledge. For one thing, he pointed out that the realm had been "most happily delivered" from the pope's "usurped power." Hence his laws had "lost their force and vigor" in England.[19] Second, the author maintained that such a bull had never "been of valor" in England, not even "when the pope was here in greatest authority." Issues of matrimony and legitimacy raised "at the common law ... should then have been tried by the certificate of the ordinary. ... The pope's dispensation carrieth not in our law the jurisdiction of the ordinary." Therefore, no "such sleightful certificate, the unlawful doing of the pope," would have been of any validity.[20]

The first of these arguments seems unimpressive. That the England of Elizabeth was not under the obedience of the pope

---

* Anne Browne and Lady Mortimer were first cousins. Strickland, p. 52n. The father of Lady Mortimer's late husband was the brother of Brandon's grandmother. M. A. E. Green, V, 19.

did not necessarily void his doings when he was in authority. As the writer of *The Letter* suggested, though bulls from Rome were no longer allowed in England, they were accepted there in 1528 and 1529.[21] Thus it could be argued that Clement VII's bull had not lost its "force and vigor" for the matter under consideration. The second argument, however, seems more cogent. English law had long assigned jurisdiction in cases of matrimony and legitimacy to the ordinary. We find in Glanville that once an accusation of bastardy is made, "the plea shall cease in the king's court, and the archbishop or bishop of the place shall be commanded to inquire concerning such marriage."[22] Elsewhere the pope might be recognized as the universal ordinary, but in England "the archbishop or bishop of the place" or either's delegate were regarded as the only lawful ordinaries. Hence Clement's bull was not "the certificate of the ordinary" and did not in itself meet the common-law requirement.

But this does not settle the matter. If Clement lacked authority to decide the case, his bull said that the marriage of Charles Brandon and Lady Mortimer had been annulled by the Archdeacon of London. And the Archdeacon of London, the representative of the Bishop of London, evidently was the ordinary having jurisdiction over matrimonial affairs in the Diocese of London. Though the divorce he awarded could not be produced, it could be maintained that the document was lost or destroyed. Then the bull could be regarded as, to quote *The Letter,* "a good testimony, record, and writing that the divorce . . . was lawful and good, seeing that it was a ratification of the ordinaries."[23]

Of course, this is open to an obvious objection. It is easy to allege that the bull did not confirm the ordinary, but instead invented it. It is our only source specifically indicating that the Archdeacon of London annulled Charles Brandon's marriage with Lady Mortimer. The story of the divorce could have been made up by the Suffolks, and could have been accepted by the pope without any serious investigation. Clement VII was not beyond doing such a favor for the King's sister and the powerful Duke. No Italian real estate was at stake in this case, which

it was in that of Henry VIII and Catherine of Aragon, where
the Emperor Charles V was an interested party. Consequently,
we cannot rule out the possibility of fabrication. Nevertheless,
this is merely conjecture, and the burden of proof would seem
to belong to the conjecturers. Unless concrete evidence of fraud
can be found, one feels that the word of the Holy See ought to
be taken, and the reality of the divorce admitted.

Moreover, the fact that Henry VIII's successors always regarded the daughters of Charles Brandon and Mary Tudor as
legitimate is not without significance. We may dismiss Edward
VI as a child controlled by men closely connected with the
House of Suffolk, but the same cannot be said for Mary I and
Elizabeth I. In spite of Suffolk attempts to deprive her of her
throne, Mary never treated Lady Frances Brandon, her personal
friend and godmother, with anything but the respect due to a
princess of the blood royal.[24] And Elizabeth, despite her dislike of the Suffolk claim, surely affirmed the marriage of Charles
Brandon and Mary Tudor when she issued this warrant to her
Kings of Arms in December 1559 on learning of the death of
Frances Brandon:

Letting you to understand that for the good zeal and affection which
we of long time have borne to our dearly beloved cousin the Lady
Frances, late Duchess of Suffolk, and specially for that she is descended
lineally from our grandfather King Henry VII . . . , we have thought
it requisite and expedient to grant and give unto her and to her posterity an augmentation of our arms to be borne with the difference to
the same by us assigned . . . which shall be an apparent declaration of
her consanguinity unto us.[25]

What perhaps should be the final point on this subject was
made by Hales. "Albeit it were true that the Lady Frances and
the Lady Eleanor were not lawfully born . . . , it hurteth not the
title of their heirs given by King Henry his will; for it is appointed to the heirs of them, and not to themselves, as the will
plainly declareth."[26] In other words, if the will of Henry VIII
was valid, whether Charles Brandon and Mary Tudor were
lawfully married was not really important to the succession
question. This does not mean that the above discussion is irrelevant. If the will was invalid, the marriage would be vital

to an hereditary Suffolk claim, which would be good if the Stuarts were excluded as aliens. But assuming the validity of Henry's will, the main question of legitimacy did not concern Lady Frances Brandon, but her elder surviving daughter, Lady Catherine Grey. And Catherine's legitimacy depended on the resolution of our second case of matrimony, that of Frances Brandon and Henry Grey.

The issue here also was a previous "marriage" of the husband. Thomas Grey, Marquis of Dorset, had contracted his very young son Henry to Lady Catherine Fitzalan, daughter of William, Earl of Arundel. Possibly a child marriage was celebrated. After his father's death Henry Grey, then Marquis of Dorset, became the ward of Charles Brandon, Duke of Suffolk. Brandon wanted to match the young Marquis with his elder daughter Frances. Grey apparently was released from his marriage with Catherine Fitzalan on his promise to pay her an annuity for life. In March 1533 he married Frances Brandon with the full approval of Henry VIII.[27]

This account does not give enough information about the marriage of Henry Grey and Catherine Fitzalan to permit a definitive judgment of its effect on Grey's subsequent match with Frances Brandon, but it seems safe to assume that he obtained a proper divorce before marrying that royal lady. As has been pointed out, however desirable the union with Frances might have been to Grey, it was hardly so essential to the interests of her parents that they would have let her marry a man who already had a lawful wife. Nor would Henry VIII have been likely to approve a questionable match for a niece whose descendants might someday inherit the crown.[28]

None of our tract writers made a single allusion to the invalidity of the marriage of Henry Grey and Frances Brandon.[29] They probably knew of, or could have found out about, the Lady Fitzalan business.* That none of our anti-Suffolk writers saw fit to challenge the marriage upon which Catherine Grey's legitimacy depended seems to indicate that the charge against

---

* Simon Renard, Charles V's ambassador, had written about it in 1553. *CSP, Span.*, XI, 334–35, 393. The author of *Leycester's Commonwealth* knew of it in 1584. It was the type of story that would readily become common gossip.

it was not regarded as worth pressing. Moreover, Elizabeth I, in spite of her aversion to Catherine Grey, evidently was satisfied that her second cousin was a legitimate child of her first cousin. Though it was only "our cousin the Lady Catherine," as compared to "our entirely beloved cousin the Lady Frances," the Queen did not allow her personal feelings to prevent her from recognizing the purity of her blood ties with Catherine.[30] In fact, Elizabeth was sufficiently convinced of Catherine's legitimacy to grant her and her sister Mary the rents and profits of certain lands that doubtless had belonged to Henry Grey.*

This is all we have to say about our second case of matrimony. It is difficult to take it seriously. Lacking substantial evidence to the contrary, the issue ought to stand resolved in favor of the marriage of Frances Brandon to Henry Grey, and the legitimacy of Lady Catherine. This leaves the question of the legitimacy of Catherine's sons by Edward Seymour, Earl of Hertford. The aspect of that question that we have not as yet discussed is our last case of matrimony, namely, between Lady Catherine Grey and Lord Henry Herbert, son and heir apparent of William, Earl of Pembroke.

A match between Catherine Grey and Henry Herbert was part of the Duke of Northumberland's attempt to bring about a Suffolk succession on the death of Edward VI. It is our task to find out how far the marriage proceeded at the time, and what happened to it in the years that followed. We shall introduce this subject by presenting for consideration the account in *Allegations in behalf of Mary*, the only one of our tracts that dealt with the marriage of Catherine and Herbert.[31]

The marriage was perfected by all necessary circumstances. There was consent of the parents, open solemnizing, continuance after till lawful years of consent, and in the meantime carnal copulation, all of which, save the last, are commonly known by diverse that saw them, and the

---

* In June 1567 the Queen issued a warrant "to permit Lady Catherine and Lady Mary Grey, daughters and coheiresses of Henry, Duke of Suffolk, and Frances, his wife, to receive the rents and profits of certain lands, late parcel of the College of Astley, co. Warwick." *CSP, Dom.*, I, 294. The manor of Astley was held by Henry Grey. Salzman, VI, 17–18.

last, which to all others might be most doubtful, is known by the confession of them both, and so made the more likely to be true, because
she herself, though in such things that sex be most covert and shame-
faced, hath yet acknowledged the same: after which consummation
every man knoweth that albeit the matrimony had been before for
lack of years not available . . ., yet thereby it cometh and is made perfect and of full force and valor. In sort that the divorce and sentence
that was so driven, procured, and practiced by the means of the Earl
of Pembroke in Queen Mary's reign (for respects then well enough
known) against both the parties' wills—as most manifestly appeared,
not only by their great unwillingness unto it then, but also by their
affectionate and willing manner of living continent many years after,
continuing in mutual love testified by sundry means, many tokens,
messengers, and other signs of the same—cannot be of any force to
break the said matrimony, *nisi de facto*. But during this delay, she by
dalliance fell to carnal company with the Earl of Hertford, which was
not descried till the bigness of her belly betrayed her ill hap. . . . But
this done the Lord Herbert, seeing himself deceived by his wife, did
(as he might lawfully) join himself in marriage with another woman;
and that life and usage between the Lady Catherine and the Earl being confirmed by double issue . . . was . . . found unlawful before such
bishops and other commissioners as had the hearing of the same, and
their issue bastardized.[32]

This account, a combination of facts and allegations, requires careful consideration if we are to get anywhere near
the truth about the marriage of Catherine Grey and Henry Herbert. To begin with the perfection of the marriage, some kind
of ceremony involving Catherine and Herbert did take place
on 21 May 1553.[33] The author of *Allegations in behalf of Mary*
evidently regarded it as a solemnization of marriage, but this
cannot be verified. At the time Catherine was at the most thirteen years old, apparently below "lawful years of consent."*
Her youth suggests that a betrothal was more likely. Moreover,
an immediate solemnization was not required for the success of

---

* An inquisition made in 1560 showed that Catherine was born in 1540. *CSP,
Dom.*, VI, 404. Herbert was perhaps nineteen. *DNB*, IX, 640. The age of
consent, according to Littleton, was fourteen; an Elizabethan lawyer said it
was twelve for a female. Hurstfield, *Wards*, pp. 134–35. From the account in
Allegations in behalf of Mary, and from a letter of Herbert (see p. 143), we
may assume that Catherine was regarded as under age in May 1553.

Northumberland's design. Nor would it have suited the Earl of Pembroke, who could not have wanted to commit his son so fully that there would be no way out if disaster overtook Northumberland's plan. Consequently, one is inclined to agree with W. L. Rutton that the celebration of 21 May was probably "a contract of marriage, not fully completed nuptials."[34] This receives contemporary support from the Venetian ambassador's report that Catherine had only "been promised" to Herbert; it is also corroborated by a later statement of Herbert himself.*

Of course, a contract of marriage followed by carnal copulation would have constituted perfected matrimony. And the author of *Allegations in behalf of Mary* claimed that Herbert and Catherine had both confessed that there had been such intercourse between them. We are unable to substantiate any such admissions, however. The closest thing to a confirmation of the author's charge is Camden's statement that when Catherine was "lawfully divorced" from Herbert she was "so far gone with child, as to be very near her time."[35] But Catherine's pregnancy was not alleged by any other writer, not even by our alleger. Catherine's tender age inclines one to dismiss the idea of sexual intercourse—to say nothing of pregnancy—as unlikely. Catherine was at the most thirteen when she was contracted to Herbert. She probably was no more than fourteen at the time that the contract was annulled; the spring of 1554 is the most likely date for the divorce.† Moreover, nearly contemporary writers indicate that Pembroke did not permit the marriage to be consummated, which would be in character for that cautious Earl.[36]

Now let us turn to the question of the effectiveness of the di-

---

* After his return to Venice, Giacomo Soranzo reported that Catherine had "been promised" to Herbert; but as Pembroke "knows that this alliance could but cause him great embarrassment, by reason of the marriage of Philip and Mary, he was on the point of breaking it off when he (Soranzo) left England." 18 August 1554, *CSP, Ven.*, V, 539. Soranzo's letters of recall were drawn up on 27 March. Mullinger, p. 529. For Herbert's letter, see p. 143.

† Philip and Mary were married on 25 July. Pembroke was one of the four noblemen who gave Mary away in the name of the realm. He also advanced the sword before Philip at the ceremony. Nichols, *Queen Jane*, p. 169. One doubts that Pembroke would have been so honored if his son had not already been divorced from Lady Jane Grey's sister.

vorce of Catherine and Herbert. The reason for that divorce is clear. Pembroke had originally consented to the match because there were obvious advantages to be derived from a union with a princess of the blood royal who would be heir presumptive to the crown once Lady Jane Grey became its wearer. The failure of Northumberland's conspiracy no doubt caused Pembroke to reconsider the now dangerous match that he had made for his son. Thomas Fuller put it charmingly: "The politic old Earl perceiving the case altered, and what was the high way to honor turned into the ready road to ruin, got pardon from Queen Mary, and broke the marriage quite off."[37] The cause of the divorce was manifestly political, and this alone makes it suspect.

Moreover, specific evidence about the grounds on which the divorce was granted is lacking. There do not seem to have been any of the usual impediments to bar a marriage between Catherine Grey and Henry Herbert. Neither of them had been previously contracted to another, nor were there past ties between their families that would have put them within prohibited degrees of relationship. About the only conceivable reason for an annulment would seem to be that the marriage had been contracted but not solemnized. A contract made *per verba de futuro* could be repudiated by either party "for any just and reasonable cause."[38] An ecclesiastical court in Mary's reign probably would have been willing to deem the prospect of a completed union with the attainted blood of Grey to be such a cause. Anyway, a divorce was obtained, and the presumption ought to be that it was granted for a valid reason. Camden expressly stated that Catherine was "lawfully divorced" from Herbert; moreover, the author of *Allegations in behalf of Mary*, though he condemned Pembroke's motives and methods, did not attack the actual divorce as groundless. Rather he maintained that the divorce could not be of any effect *de jure* because neither party wanted it, "as most manifestly appeared, not only by their great unwillingness unto it then, but also by their affectionate and willing manner of living continent many years after, continuing in mutual love testified by sundry means, many tokens, messengers, and other signs of the same." There is something to be said for this. It is possible that neither Catherine nor Herbert really wished to terminate their match at the time of the divorce. Though Herbert must have been the one who actually sued for an annulment, this was perhaps the act of an obedient son rather than of a reluctant spouse. It is certainly conceivable that young love refused to die right away because of political expediency. It is easy enough to concede this point.

The difficulty is over the apparently more important question of the longevity of the love. Here we are faced with the problem of gleaning an obscure history from sometimes sparse and sometimes confusing evidence. This requires more speculation than one would like, but it seems incumbent on us to have a go at it. We know nothing about the years immediately following the divorce. Our first piece of evidence is the testimonies of Catherine and the Earl of Hertford that their own affair began in Mary's reign when she was living with his mother. We cannot be sure just when this was, but it seems a good guess that it was late in the reign. Nor does it necessarily mean that Catherine had altogether given up the idea of marrying Herbert. It is only in March 1559 that we find Feria reporting that Catherine "has ceased to talk about it as she used to."[39] The young lady evidently was slow in making up her mind. We cannot say how Herbert felt about Catherine at this time, but in the same dispatch Feria seems to hint that the Earl of Pembroke had come around to favoring a renewal of the matrimony.* Maybe the fact that many people now regarded Catherine as Elizabeth's heir presumptive caused the "politic old Earl" to change his mind once more about her suitability as a wife for his son.

At any rate, Catherine and Hertford testified that they were married late in 1560, and one would expect the affair with Herbert then to be closed completely. The marriage was kept secret, however, and as late as June 1561—the first son by Hertford was then on the way—we find Sir Henry Neville writing about Pembroke's purpose to make Catherine his daughter-in-law.[40] And finally we are confronted with two ungentlemanly letters from

---

* "The Bishop will have told your Majesty what passed between the Earl of Pembroke and me on this matter." *CSP, Span., Eliz.,* I, 45.

Herbert to Catherine, which were probably written on 14 and 22 July respectively.*

I perceive your mind to keep my tokens back; but if I cannot have them at your hands, I will seek them at that companion's hand ... by whose practice to cover your whoredom and his own knavery and adultery you went about to abuse me. . . . Having hitherto led a virtuous life, I will not now begin with loss of honor to lead the rest of my life with a whore that almost every man talks of. You claim promise madam of me when I was young, and since confirmed as you say at lawful years, but you know I was lawfully divorced from you a good while ago. And if through the enticement of your whoredom and the practice and device of those which you hold so dear, you sought to entrap me with some poisoned bait under the color of sugared friendship; yet (I thank God) I am so clear as I am not further to be touched than with a few tokens that were by cunning sleight got out of my hands both to cover your own abomination and his likewise. You would be brought, I privy, to your trial, but let him meddle therewith that findeth himself aggrieved.

Like as a good while ago I was your friend madam, so your deserts now being so openly known to all the world makes me right sorry for that which is past of my part. For having now the mist of frail youth and abused friendship rubbed from my eyes, I can both well discern your whoredom . . . and prove it if you will further enforce me. Wherefore, without delay I require you madam to send me by this bearer those letters and tokens with my tablature and picture that I sent you when I was so blinded. For I here protest that I will never hereafter have to do with you to nor fro, being provoked hereto neither by malice . . . nor fear, but only by your own abominable and detestable deserts. Wherefore, I eftsoons require you to send me all my sendings or else, to be plain with you, I will make you as well known to all the world as your whoredom is now, I thank God, known to me and spied by many scores more.[41]

These letters suggest a pathetic story. In the spring of 1561 Catherine found herself in a precarious predicament. She knew that she was with child, and she knew who was responsible for

---

* In our MS. the first letter is simply dated "the 14th of July"; the second is dated "the 22 of July 1559." These letters do not look like originals. Both handwriting and punctuation seem too good for a sixteenth-century nobleman. The content of the letters makes July 1561 a more likely time for their composition. The references in them to Catherine's "whoredom" probably indicate that Herbert knew about her pregnancy. Though she was not officially discovered to be "big with child" until 10 August 1561, her condition was talked about at the Court before that. See *HM* 6286, p. 37.

it, but Hertford was in France, and Catherine had reason to doubt his sincerity.[42] Her later testimonies indicate that he had given her cause to have misgivings about his departure, and that she had received no letters from him when he was overseas.* Poor Catherine could not help fearing that Hertford might fail to acknowledge his marriage and paternity when the time would come for him to do so. Her situation seemed desperate.

In these circumstances she probably conceived a most dishonorable scheme. Before her pregnancy became obvious, she would renew her friendship with Herbert, and claim that their former marriage had been completed and was still valid. If Herbert would acknowledge Catherine as his wife, she could allege that the child was his. English law then probably would accept the child as his, no matter what protests he might make.† Herbert, perhaps at the urging of his father, evidently grabbed at the bait to the extent of sending Catherine letters and tokens that might later be used against him, but before he admitted matrimony he must have found out about her pregnancy. Once he appreciated the trap that Catherine had set for him, Herbert, with understandable indignation, sought to extricate himself: hence the ungentlemanly letters.

If our interpretation of their setting is correct, Herbert's letters hardly verify the arguments of the author of *Allegations in behalf of Mary* as much as they may appear to at first glance. They confirm his statement that there were tokens and messages, but considering the peculiar circumstances under which Herbert sent them to Catherine, they cannot be deemed testimonies of continued and reciprocal love. And we have no evidence of earlier tokens and messages. In the letter of 14 July, Herbert did once use the word adultery in connection with Catherine's "companion," but the word apparently was not intended to have its precise meaning. Later Herbert reminded Catherine

---

* Lady Jane Seymour told her that Hertford had applied for a license to leave the realm, but the Earl denied this when she asked him about it. When she saw a passport signed for his departure "it caused her much grief." *HM* 6286, pp. 82, 92.

† The presumption of English law was always in favor of the legitimacy of the child of a married woman. Pollock and Maitland, II, 396; *EB*, XVI, 387.

that they had been "lawfully divorced," and this seems a clearer expression of his attitude. Moreover, the same letter reveals that it was Catherine who alleged the completion of the original contract. And this, coming from her, should be taken with a grain of salt, it being made after "she by dalliance fell to carnal company with the Earl of Hertford" and shortly before "the bigness of her belly betrayed her."

If we consider our evidence as a whole, it seems to yield the conclusion that the divorce secured early in Mary's reign settled the matter between Catherine and Herbert. What happened in 1561 should be dismissed as foul play. And we certainly cannot prove that a wish to renew the match was continually shared by both parties during the period after the divorce and before Catherine's clandestine marriage with Hertford. Moreover, even if there was such a wish, it probably would not have been enough, unless there had been a perfected marriage between Catherine and Herbert before their divorce. It is difficult to accept the notion that love—and apparently silent love at that —would have been sufficient to turn an abrogated contract into completed matrimony.

There is yet a final consideration that gives strong support to the conclusion that Catherine was in no way still lawfully attached to Herbert when she began her cohabitation with Hertford. Nowhere in the records of the trial of Catherine and Hertford is there a single reference to her old connection with Herbert.[43] The men who held that trial could not have been ignorant of Catherine's first match; they surely would have used it to justify their required decision against her second union if they thought it had yet the slightest validity. The author of *Allegations in behalf of Mary,* if I read him correctly, implied that because Catherine was lawfully the wife of Herbert, her "life and usage" with Hertford was "found unlawful before such bishops and other commissioners as had the hearing of the same." Archbishop Parker, however, later told Hertford that the reason for their verdict was only "that we could see nothing for solemnization or for any marriage."[44] Therefore, one feels compelled to agree with Henry Hallam that the fact that no advantage was taken of Catherine's old contract with Herbert in the proceedings of the Commission of Inquiry "seems to show that there was no legal bond remaining between the parties."[45]

This ends our discussion of the cases of matrimony that were the determinants of the purity of the Suffolk descent from Henry VII. In each of the three cases treated in this chapter and in the one dealt with earlier—i.e. Mary Tudor and Charles Brandon, Frances Brandon and Henry Grey, Catherine Grey and Henry Herbert, and Catherine Grey and Edward Seymour —the weight of the evidence would seem to be in favor of the legitimacy of the Suffolks. At any rate, sufficient "proofs" could be produced to allow contemporary supporters of the Suffolk claim to presume the eligibility of its representatives to succeed to the Crown of England. This would put them in about the same position where we left the advocates of Mary Stuart's title. Of course, the presumptions of neither side would settle the issue in law. Indeed, the most important legal question was not that of eligibility, but that of prior right. And who possessed the prior right to the succession was dependent upon whether or not the will of Henry VIII was valid.

9. *The Will of Henry VIII*

The document known as the will of Henry VIII set aside the superior hereditary claim of the Stuarts, and appointed the Suffolks to the succession after Henry's own children and their issue; it vaguely assigned the crown after the Suffolks to the "next rightful heirs," which could mean complete exclusion of the Stuarts.[1] This may be deemed one of the strongest expressions of despotic will that ever came from an English monarch. It would have had the accepted hereditary order of succession nullified because of the wishes of a dying old man. It would be wrong, however, to let this consideration carry us too far. If Henry VIII was really the author of the will, its succession provisions cannot be considered wholly the arbitrary act of one man. Though it was not mentioned in the will, the King had Parliamentary authorization to make a limitation of the crown.* The Acts of 1536 and 1543 had given Henry "full and plenar power" to designate the succession "by his gracious letters patents under his great seal, or else by his Highness' last will made in writing and signed with his most gracious hand."[2] Moreover, even here the King's authority was not absolute. He never had power to exclude his son Edward, "the only heir whose legitimacy was undisputed."[3] Nor could he, according to

---

* Some importance has been attached to the will's failure to appeal to statute for authorization. Pickthorn, *Henry VIII*, p. 537. This, it seems to me, is mainly interesting as an example of Henry's inflated notion of his authority. His will, if genuine, was nevertheless backed by legislation.

the Act of 1543, entirely will the crown away from his daughters Mary and Elizabeth; he could only prescribe conditions they would have to comply with to maintain their eligibility.[4] Consequently, Henry's power to designate the succession was limited to Parliament's prescription, and any future monarch whose title derived from such a designation would have what was ultimately a Parliamentary title.

Why would Henry VIII, whose own hereditary title was beyond dispute and whose notion of his royal authority was high, accept such an arrangement? Clearly because the situation required it. The succession, like religion, was a matter that had customarily been regarded as ordained by God. If the King was going to tamper with it in any way, it would be desirable to have the highest sanction possible. By making Parliament his accomplice, Henry gave his acts the appearance, if not the fact, of having the consent of the nation. Moreover, that consent was bound to be far from unanimous. Any change in the succession would have to be buttressed by the dread penalties of high treason, and only Parliament could create new treasons.

Furthermore, there is no reason to believe that Henry could in any way have anticipated the modern implications of basing a royal title on Parliamentary authority. Henry VIII was "in Parliament" in a very real sense; indeed, he was largely the determining factor there. He could "pack" Parliament if he wished, but that was hardly necessary. He could usually count on his councilors in both Lords and Commons to move Parliament in the direction of his will. If Parliament dared to follow a different course, his veto provided a decisive stop. Henry most likely only thought of Parliament as providing him with an indirect, if limited, means to exercise the ultimate in kingly authority, the power to designate his successors, a means those successors might use for the same purpose if they so desired. He had no way of knowing that a changing relationship between Crown and Parliament would make Parliament's new authority in determining the succession a real problem to his daughter Elizabeth I.

A more important question than why Henry chose to deal with the succession by means of Parliament is whether either the King in Parliament or, in the case of the will, the King with Parliamentary authorization, had the right to alter the hereditary order in any way. Father Pollen has referred to the will as "that unconstitutional document known as the will of Henry VIII, which a servile Parliament had given him leave to draw up."[5] The charge of Parliament's servility, which cannot be proved, is really extraneous.[6] Even if the Parliaments of 1536 and 1543 were Henry's puppets, that would not affect the authority of their lawful legislation. The pertinent issue raised by Pollen is whether the statutes that gave Henry the power to settle the succession by will *were* constitutional.

The English constitution has never been entirely static, especially concerning the powers of Parliament. Hence the logical way to determine the constitutionality of Henry VIII's Succession Acts at particular times would be to find out how contemporaries felt about them. And the time that concerns us extends from their enactment through the first decade of the reign of Elizabeth I; the opinions of late Elizabethan writers, whose ideas emerged in—and probably as a result of—a much altered situation, ought to be dismissed as irrelevant.*

During the reign of Henry VIII, two of the King's most learned and saintly subjects evidently did not regard the succession as outside the constitutional jurisdiction of Parliament. Sir Thomas More told Solicitor General Rich that he would accept even Rich as King if an Act of Parliament so willed it: "The Parliament may well, Mr. Rich, meddle with the state of temporal princes."[7] The man who said this in 1535 would have had little trouble recognizing the constitutionality of a limitation of the crown made by Henry VIII with the authorization of two Acts of Parliament. The same may be said for John Fisher, Bishop of Rochester, who is reported to have told Thomas Cromwell, "I doubted not but that the prince of any realm, with the assent of his nobles and commons, might appoint for his succession royal such an order as was seen unto his wis-

---

* For late Elizabethan denials of Parliament's right to legislate on the succession, see Allen, pp. 256–60. Such denials probably rose out of the emergence of Mary Stuart's Protestant son as the only logical successor to Elizabeth.

dom most according."⁸ Surely the opinions of More and Fisher, martyrs for the old faith, cannot be dismissed as those of time-servers.

There is little to say about the reigns of Edward VI and Mary I. The succession provisions of the Acts of 1536 and 1543 remained on the books, and apparently were regarded as constitutional. The one serious attempt to ignore them came with the manifestly unconstitutional plan of the Duke of Northumberland to set aside Mary and Elizabeth, and turn the succession over to the Suffolk line after Edward VI. The Duke tried to give his scheme the trappings of legality by having the young King lend his royal name to a "devise for the succession." When Edward ordered his judges and law officers to draw up a will along the lines of the "devise," they protested that "it was directly against the Act of Succession [1543], which was an Act of Parliament which would not be taken away by no such device."⁹

Where one encounters the most important evidence of the constitutionality of Henry VIII's Succession Acts and of his will, if genuine, is in the first decade of the reign of Elizabeth I. The statute of Elizabeth's first Parliament that recognized her title said, "The limitation and declaration of the succession of the Imperial Crown of this realm mentioned and contained in the ... Act made in the ... five and thirty year of the reign of your ... most noble father [1543] shall stand, be, and remain the law of this realm forever."¹⁰ Pollen sees this to be a confirmation of the will of Henry VIII.¹¹ If that testament was authentic, there can be no quarrel with his view.

There is more convincing evidence in the writings of the 1560's. During that decade Sir Thomas Smith, perhaps the highest Tudor authority on English government, wrote that "the Parliament ... giveth forms of succession to the crown."¹² His precedents for this were doubtless Henry VIII's Succession Acts, which he presumably accepted as constitutional. Most significant of all, however, is that none of the writers of the 1560's who denied the validity of Henry VIII's will questioned Parliament's right to give the King the power to make a testamentary limitation of the crown. Indeed, their chief objection to the document was that it did not strictly fulfill the requirements set forth in the Acts of 1536 and 1543, the statutes from which Henry's authority was solely derived.[13] As the author of *Allegations in behalf of Mary* put it, "it is . . . certain that King Henry should have had no authority or power to dispose of the crown by will if by Parliament it had not been given him."[14] That such men, who would not have left a promising stone unturned, did not dispute Parliament's right to authorize Henry to settle the succession by will is clearly indicative that contemporaries saw nothing unconstitutional about such an authorization.[15]

Now if we may reject the charge of unconstitutionality as *ex post facto,* we must still determine whether the document known as the will of Henry VIII can be accepted as genuine and authoritative. The Acts of 1536 and 1543 had empowered Henry to designate the succession by his last will "signed with his most gracious hand." The anti-Suffolk tract writers maintained that Parliament had specifically required the royal signature to avoid the possibility of a counterfeit will, that if the will were not signed with the King's own hand, its succession provisions were invalid, and that the will had not been signed with Henry's "most gracious hand," but merely stamped by one William Clerc, moreover, stamped after the King was dead.[16] In Mary I's reign, according to Leslie, the truth of this charge was testified to by Lord Paget and Sir Edward Montague, two of the wills executors. The same was then supposed to have been confirmed by Clerc, who confessed that he "himself put the stamp to the said will." As a result of these depositions Mary "caused the record of the said forged will remaining in the Chancery to be cancelled, defaced, and abolished."[17] Plowden alleged that those who had seen the original will stated that it was "signed with the stamp and not signed with the hand of the . . . King."[18] In apparent confirmation of this is an entry in a list of documents that Henry VIII "caused me, William Clerc, to stamp" in the presence of Sir Anthony Denny and John Gate "at diverse times and places" in January 1547:

Your Majesty's last will and testament bearing date at Westminster the thirty day of December last part, written in a book of paper, signed above in the beginning and beneath in the end, and sealed with the signet in the presence of the Earl of Hertford, Mr. Secretary Paget, Mr. Denny, and Mr. Harbert, and also in the presence of certain other persons, whose names are subscribed with their own hands, as witnesses to the same; which testament your Majesty delivered then . . . to the . . . Earl of Hertford.[19]

This seems to indicate that Clerc did stamp a will of the King dated 30 December 1546; it refutes the charge that that will was stamped after Henry's death.

Hales was able to anticipate much of this case and reply in advance. He lamented that the original document, which would certainly contain the King's signatures, could not "be found." However, "after the will was once proved and allowed, which I take to be sufficiently done when it was enrolled in the Chancery under the great seal . . . by King Edward VI," the original was no longer needed, "for the record was of more strength." If that record was missing, there were constats of the same. If it was destroyed in Mary I's reign, "as the common report goeth," that was done by those who "knew the will to be lawful, and saw no other way to deprive" the Suffolk line of its right to the crown. And finally, against any testimony that the will was stamped, Hales cited the signatures of eleven "very honest and substantial" witnesses which appear on the will below Henry's statement, "we have signed it with our own hand."[20]

That the will had been enrolled in the Chancery and published under the great seal early in Edward's reign does not necessarily mean, as Hales thought, that it was then accepted as valid because it was found to be signed with Henry's hand.[21] It is possible that those who passed on the document in Edward's name were under the impression that a stamped will was sufficient, a notion that would become most doubtful later on.* Moreover, the men who approved the will in Edward's reign were those who might be accused of counterfeiting it in Henry's. Anyway, Hales could not produce the enrollment of the will; he

---

* In 1553 Parliament voided Henry VIII's assent to the attainder of the Duke of Norfolk on the ground that it was only stamped by a clerk. Bailey, pp. 150–53. If the assent to Norfolk's attainder required the royal signature, so must the King's will designating the succession have needed it, since two statutes specified the need for it.

could only call on constats of it. Exemplifications, as Maitland of Lethington pointed out, lacked the legal force of an original record.[22] And constats were too easily forged in an age when the photostat was centuries away.

The trouble was that the enrollment of the will seems to have been destroyed on the order of Mary I in 1553 or thereabouts.* Hales alleged that this was done because those in control knew the will was valid, and wished to prevent a Suffolk succession; his adversaries claimed it was done because of testimony that the original will was stamped and not signed. Both arguments seem improbable. It is difficult to believe that much thought was given to the possibility of a Suffolk succession at the time. And, as we shall see, there is impressive evidence that Mary knew her father's will was genuine. More likely, she had the record of the will destroyed for a personal reason, namely, her desire to marry Philip of Spain. The will specified that she obtain the consent of the majority of the surviving councilors and executors named therein before she married.[23] She had no intention of doing so, but if she did not, it was possible to allege that she had thereby forfeited her crown to Elizabeth. This must have been what Simon Renard, the Imperial ambassador, had in mind when he expressed the belief that Mary would have the will "annulled for the sake of avoiding all the difficulties that Elizabeth would make if she were able."[24] Indeed, Sir Henry Dudley's conspirators later tried to make trouble for Mary along these lines in spite of any destruction of the enrollment: "The men exhibit a copy of King Henry VIII's will, and pretend that her Majesty, having done contrary thereto, has forfeited the crown and right to it, and therefore they may rebel against her."[25]

Hales was on sounder ground when he pointed out that eleven witnesses signed the will immediately under Henry's declaration that "we have signed it with our own hand." Against

---

* The most likely date seems to be 1553, since that was when the assent to Norfolk's attainder was voided. It was Lord Paget who testified that the commission giving Henry's assent was only stamped. Pollard, *Somerset*, pp. 4–5. It is likely that Paget's testimony about the stamping of the will came at the same time, as Maitland seems to imply. Collier, p. 47.

this Leslie claimed that such prominent figures as Paget and Montague testified that the will was stamped. The eleven witnesses were "too slender and weak for the importance of the matter . . . the law doth as well weigh the credit as number the persons of the witnesses."[26] The list of witnesses is in fact unimpressive; more consequential men could have been selected for the purpose.* Nevertheless, Maitland acknowledged the witnesses as "honest gentlemen."[27] Nor must the word of Paget and Montague be considered trustworthy. Paget had proved himself capable of duplicity in the past, and Montague had been intimidated before.† They were not beyond testifying falsely if that was expected of them. The credibility of Hales's eleven good men may be regarded at least as highly as that of Paget and Montague.

Of course, Hales's adversaries alleged that one of his witnesses later said that he had stamped the will. But Clerc's confession was perhaps made under pressure. What else could poor Clerc have done but admit stamping the will if men like Paget and Montague testified that he had? All in all, the cases presented by Hales and his opponents seem to balance each other. What appears to tip the scale against Hales is the fact that Clerc listed the will of 30 December among the documents that he had signed with the stamp in January 1547. If we had no other evidence to the contrary, his entry would almost compel us to conclude that the will was stamped and therefore probably invalid.

There was another matter, however, that our polemicists could not write about with certainity. This was the original testament, which none of them had seen. Most of them seem to have been under the impression that it had been destroyed with the chancery enrollment. Hales, as we have seen, said that the

---

* The signers were John Gate, George Owen, Thomas Wendye, Robert Huick, E. Harman, William Saintbarb, Henry Neville, Richard Coke, David Vincent, Patzec, and W. Clerc. Rymer, XV, 117.

† When Somerset fell from power, Paget saved himself and won his peerage by an ignoble betrayal of his colleagues. Pollard, "Reformation," pp. 495–96. Montague participated against his conscience in the illegal attempt of Northumberland to alter the succession. Fuller, IV, 137–46.

original could not be found, and this was one place where Leslie was in full agreement with Hales.[28] Maitland, in requesting that Cecil examine the original, expressed his hope that God had preserved the same despite the talk that it had "been embezzled in Queen Mary's time."[29] Only two of our tract writers apparently knew that the original will was extant. Plowden wrote that it was in the custody of Lord Treasurer Paulet, and asserted that those who had seen it said it was stamped.[30] The author of *The Letter* reported that some noblemen who saw the will "said they knew not the signing thereof from King Henry VIII's own hand."[31] These conflicting testimonies of those who were supposed to have seen the document may have been invented by their reporters. Be that as it may, we need not depend on them. The original will still exists.[32]

An inspection of the document, however, does not yield a positive answer whether its two royal signatures were made in writing or with a stamp. Until lately the case presented by A. F. Pollard, and Francis Hargrave before him, was generally accepted. They maintain that an examination of the will proves the signatures to have been made in writing. The signatures are "not sufficiently uniform to have been made with a stamp," and "both differ materially from signatures known to have been so made." There is no trace of the indentation one would expect to find in a paper stamped with the dry seal used for stamping documents. "Some of the strokes of the letters are plainly uneven as drawn by a weak and trembling hand," presumably the dying King's.[33]

Recently the Pollard-Hargrave case has been rejected by Lacey Baldwin Smith. He maintains that the two signatures, which are some fourteen pages apart, deceive the casual observer. A close inspection and comparison of the spacing and individual letters reveals "that they are far more similar to examples of the dry seal than they are to known specimens of the King's actual signature." As for the lack of indentation, no such impression can be found in documents acknowledged to have been stamped: "it must be concluded that the mark was so faint that it has not lasted for some four hundred years." The "slight tremble" in the signatures is "similar to trembles in other dry stamp signatures";

it could have been produced by the pen of a clerk who filled in the impression. Nonetheless, Smith admits that the evidence is "not clear one way or the other."[34]

One must grant that the failure of the signatures to retain an impression left by a dry stamp proves nothing, and that the calligraphic evidence is not conclusive one way or the other. My own opinion, based on an inexpert examination of the document, is that there are slight differences in the two signatures. Of course, this lack of uniformity could have come from the pen of a clerk filling in indentations. Pollard, Hargrave, and Smith may all be mistaken about a tremble in the signatures. Other examiners of the will have not found it.[35] My impression is that the signatures were made by a rather steady hand, and even a dying man might have such a hand for the brief task of signing his name twice. The signatures do resemble earlier signatures of Henry VIII, notwithstanding the fact that he often changed his way of making particular letters. Indeed, a comparison of the King's signatures over a period of years suggests that those on the will are a natural product of a long development.[36]

The principal objection to accepting the signatures as written remains Clerc's inclusion of the will in his list of stamped documents. Alternative hypotheses to account for Clerc's entry have been presented by Pollard:

> Either the illegality of a stamped will was suggested some time shortly before Henry's death, and another was hastily drawn up and signed in writing by the King ..., or Clerc made a mistake in including in his schedule of stamped documents one which, though drawn up possibly at the same time as the others, was signed in writing and not like the others with a stamp.[37]

Smith rejects both of these hypotheses. "There was hardly time for a new will to be drawn up" if one was stamped on 27 January, the day before Henry's death, "as Clerc's list would suggest." That Clerc and Denny and Gate, who were present when Clerc stamped documents, "each witnessed the will ... would seem conclusively to preclude the possibility of a mistake."[38]

The possibility of a mistake is indeed remote; not so that of a new will being hastily drawn up. There is no proof that a will was stamped on the 27th, let alone, as Smith implied in another connection, "a few hours before Henry died."[39] Clerc's list is of documents stamped at "diverse times" in January. The will is the eighty-fifth item on the list; the eighty-sixth is the King's assent to the attainder of the Duke of Norfolk.[40] That Norfolk's attainder was stamped on the 27th does not necessarily mean that the will was also.[41] And even if the will was stamped on the 27th, there still could have been time to draw up a new one for signing in writing. The will appears to have been written in haste. The penmanship seems unworthy of so important a document. There are even some interlineations, "notably one after the limitation of the crown to the Lady Mary of the important words 'and the heirs of her body.' "[42] Yet the wording of the will indicates that it was the result of careful preparation. Thus the will itself can be called upon in support of the view that it was hastily copied from another document that had been found deficient because it was signed with a stamp.

If the will was signed in writing, it need not follow that the signatures were made with Henry's "most gracious hand." There is still the possibility that someone made up a will and forged the King's signatures. That someone would almost have to be Edward Seymour, Earl of Hertford, whom we had better call by his subsequent title of Duke of Somerset to avoid confusing him with his son. Clerc's entry tells us that Henry delivered the stamped will to Somerset. On 29 January, the day after the King's death, Somerset informed Paget that he had Henry's will in his private keeping; he evidently kept it until 2 February, when it was turned over to Lord Chancellor Wriothesley.[43] Hence Somerset, perhaps with Paget's connivance, had ample opportunity to replace the real will with one of his own making. In that event, however, forging Henry's signatures would not have been enough. It also would have been necessary to counterfeit the signatures of eleven witnesses or induce the eleven to sign a revised will. It is difficult to believe that this would not have come out on some occasion after Somerset was dead and gone. There is no evidence of any such leak.

Moreover, the will, as Pollard has pointed out, stood in the way of Somerset's ambitions. As a successful general and young Edward VI's uncle, Somerset was the logical man to be designated protector of the realm, but the will merely made him the equal of the other councilors and executors named therein. It required a coup d'état, which overturned the conciliar government set up by the will, for Somerset to gain "unfettered the royal power of the Tudors." He had more reason to wish that the will was nonexistent or clearly invalid than to counterfeit it.[44]

Nevertheless, there are two considerations that may be said to point to a forgery by Somerset. First, it may be maintained that the omission of Stephen Gardiner, Bishop of Winchester, from the executors and councilors named in the will was not the work of Henry VIII. Gardiner was the one forceful personality who might have blocked Somerset's plans if he had been in a position of power. Second, it may be claimed that Henry would not have set aside Mary Stuart in the succession. Somerset, who hoped to match his eldest son with Lady Jane Grey, had a personal motive for placing the Suffolks before the Stuarts in the same.

However, Gardiner's exclusion from the lists of executors and councilors may well have been Henry VIII's doing. According to John Foxe, Paget testified in the fourth year of Edward VI's reign that Henry had ordered him to remove the Bishop from his will, and told Paget that Gardiner was "a willful man, and not meet to be about his son."[45] Though Foxe's veracity here may be questionable, Gardiner himself stated that at the time "he had no access to the King."[46] Moreover, Gardiner never questioned the authenticity of the will; rather he appealed to the very part of it from which his name was omitted when he later protested against Somerset's despotism.[47] There is no real evidence to support a case for forgery based on Gardiner's exclusion.

The question of whether Henry could have set the Queen of Scots aside in the succession was discussed by our tract writers. Hales, taking the affirmative, argued that Henry had no reason to love his Stuart relations, who had caused him much trouble and even made war against him.[48] Leslie replied that it would have been dishonorable for the King to penalize a "lawful" heir for the past acts of her relatives; it was inconceivable that Henry would sacrifice honor where there was no present commodity to be gained by doing so.[49] But perhaps present commodity can be found in the idea that the peculiar succession provisions of the will were intended to convince the Scots to accept Henry's favorite project, a match between their Queen and his son. If England was not to come to the Stuarts in their own right, the Scots might be more willing to have them share it with the Tudors by uniting the families and the realms. Though this type of persuasion was not likely to succeed, Henry's entire Scottish policy showed his inability to realize that coercion was not the way to win over the Scots.[50] Henry also could have been influenced here by his love for the Suffolks, the national contempt for Scots, and the common-law rule against alien inheritance.

At any rate, we must not overrate the importance of these considerations. The succession provisions of the will were of great moment in Elizabeth's reign, when Mary Stuart's advocates found it imperative to challenge their validity, but they could not have been taken so seriously when they were conceived. Henry had three children, and the prospect that none of them would have issue must have been regarded as remote. Somerset doubtless knew that Henry's death would confront him with more pressing problems than the chances of a Stuart or a Suffolk succession. Such distant possibilities gave him little reason to take the risks involved in having a will forged.

Another approach is to consider whether Henry's mature Tudor successors accepted his will as genuine. Neither Mary nor Elizabeth needed the will to confirm their titles; their hereditary and statutory claims were sufficient without it. And both had access to the original document during their reigns, if not before. If their views on its authenticity can be determined, that would be significant evidence.

The evidence that Mary believed the will to be genuine seems convincing. During Edward's reign she twice invoked the will to defend her Catholic position.* On 9 July 1553, in a letter to the Council claiming the crown, she cited the "testament and last will of our dearest father" as one of the "circumstances ad-

* In 1549 and 1551 against the Council. Dixon, III, 145; *CSP, Span.*, X, 259.

vancing our right."[51] Though Mary, after ascending the throne, apparently ordered the chancery enrollment destroyed, she left the original will intact. This may indicate that the pious Queen scrupled to destroy a solemn testament that she knew to be signed with her father's own hand. Moreover, in August 1553 she called on the will to justify her proposal to give her brother a Catholic funeral.[52] And as late as Easter 1557 Mary's judges found it safe to show due respect for Henry's will in a case involving the Queen's property, any destruction of the chancery enrollment notwithstanding.[53]

Elizabeth's view is less easily discerned. Elizabeth, doubtless because she did not want the succession question settled, never expressed an opinion about the validity of Henry's will. We have previously heard her tell Maitland of her lack of curiosity, but it is difficult to believe that she did not investigate the signatures on the will. Indeed, there is unexpected evidence indicating that she did. The document contains a clause willing that the Dean and Chapter of Windsor shall forever have an annual revenue of £600. In return for this, masses were to be said for Henry's soul, and thirteen poor men, "which shall be called poor knights," were to be maintained at Windsor.[54] In July 1559 the Queen wrote to the Dean and Chapter commanding that her father's wishes be carried out, and approved an account of the yearly limitation and distribution of the £600 per annum "appointed for the maintenance of thirteen poor knights at Windsor for the further performance of the testament of the most noble King Henry VIII."[55] That a Protestant Queen, sometimes accused of being penurious, should allot £600 per year for the execution of such a Catholic provision would seem inexplicable, except on the ground that she knew that the signatures on the will were her father's. Perhaps another indication of this is Elizabeth's failure to permit an examination of the document, even after assuring the Queen of Scots in 1566 that she would have one.[56] If an official investigation revealed the signatures as Henry's, Elizabeth probably would have faced a Parliamentary demand for a succession settlement in favor of the Suffolks that even she might not have been able to frustrate.

All in all, the weight of our evidence points to the conclusion that the will of Henry VIII is genuine. It is significant that the first serious challenge of that testament was made by the adversaries of the Suffolk claim, and approximately twenty years after Henry's death. And their case was based on the doubtful notion that the original will was only signed with a stamp. If the will was signed in writing, the possibility of forgery is most unlikely. The genuineness of the will seems to receive important confirmation from the opinions of Henry's two mature Tudor successors, whose titles were good enough without it. Unless substantial proof to the contrary can be produced, the presumption of history should, I think, be in favor of the authenticity of the will of Henry VIII.*

Of course, contemporaries hardly found it necessary to reach the same conclusion. The concealment of the original document made it impossible for them to resolve their debate over whether it was signed in writing or with a stamp. Both supporters and opponents of the Suffolk claim were free to act on their prejudices in accepting or rejecting the succession provisions of Henry VIII's will. They were in about the same position in this matter as we have already found them in concerning Mary Stuart's birth in Scotland and the legitimacy of the Suffolks. In September 1566, however, there was a session of Parliament coming in which they might, with the Queen's leave, obtain some information and reach a succession settlement.

Before proceeding to the Parliament of 1566, however, being at the end of our study of the succession tracts and the law of succession, and being in possession of evidence that eluded contemporaries, we ought to venture to answer the important question of whether Mary Stuart or Catherine Grey had the best claim to succeed Elizabeth. The sum of the evidence from each of the three main issues considered points clearly, if not definitively, to one answer. Mary's Scottish birth probably made her ineligible according to English law to succeed to the English crown. More than likely, there was nothing in Catherine's Tu-

---

* To doubt the genuineness of the signatures on the will without convincing evidence would allow the acts of a Mary or an Elizabeth to be challenged whenever convenient, to say nothing of those of earlier monarchs who could not even sign their own names.

dor descent to bar her from the succession, though the Commission of Inquiry's verdict stood as a legal, but not irremovable, obstacle in the case of her sons. Most significant of all, the will of Henry VIII should be regarded as valid, and therefore its succession provisions should be deemed the law of the land. The answer to the question is that Lady Catherine Grey, not Mary Queen of Scots, had the best legal right to succeed Elizabeth.

PART III

*The Climax and
Transformation of the Question*

10. *The Parliament of 1566*

We left the Parliamentary story with the abrupt prorogation of
10 April 1563. The Queen had promised to marry and to consider the weighty matter of the succession, and had then sent
the Parliament men on their separate ways. Probably the main
reason for the prorogation was to remove the Lords and Commons from the scene while negotiations for a marriage between
the Queen of Scots and Lord Robert Dudley were in progress.
Elizabeth's creation of Dudley as Earl of Leicester in 1564 was
doubtless intended to make him more agreeable to Mary as a
consort. And Mary might well have accepted Leicester under
the right conditions. The question of conditions proved the big
obstacle: Mary would only marry the Earl in exchange for a
guarantee about the succession; Elizabeth was not ready to go
that far.[1] Hence the negotiations dragged on until Mary took
matters into her own hands, and found herself a seemingly more
appropriate mate.

On 29 July 1565 she became the wife of Henry Stuart, Lord
Darnley. This match, as is well known, ultimately led to Mary's
ruin, but for the present she had scored an apparent triumph.
The union of the Stuart lines ended the division among English Catholics over the succession; that Mary did not marry a
Hapsburg or a Valois made it possible for all of Catholic Europe
to back her claim. Elizabeth had some reason to see herself
threatened with rebellion from within and encirclement from

without.* On 13 August 1565 Mary and Darnley sent their
terms to Elizabeth. They offered to do nothing, directly or indirectly, against her title or that of her lawful issue, and to enter
a league with England. In return Elizabeth by Act of Parliament was to establish the succession, failing herself and her
issue, in Mary and her lawful issue, and then in Lady Margaret
Lennox and her lawful issue, "as the persons by the law of God
and nature next inheritable to the Crown of England."² Though
claiming hereditary right, Mary and Darnley evidently accepted
—a significant recognition—Parliament's authority to settle the
succession.

These terms, reasonable as they may have seemed to Mary
and Darnley, were neither acceptable nor practicable to Elizabeth. Promises made by Mary and Darnley might later be
evaded, but an establishment of the succession by Act of
Parliament would be a nearly irrevocable commitment, and
moreover, one that Elizabeth probably could not secure the
making of. It is difficult to see how the Queen could have convinced the Parliament that she had prorogued in 1563 to accept
a Stuart succession. Its members had then displayed, if nothing
else, a marked antipathy to Mary's claim. It was to be expected
that the Darnley marriage would not reverse the attitude of that
largely Protestant group, but rather confirm it, and that any
new Parliament likely to be elected would feel the same.

What the Darnley marriage really did was increase the seriousness of Elizabeth's existing predicament. She obviously had no
wish to see any succession settlement. The Parliament of 1563
had shown her that there was strong sentiment in England for
a settlement. She had prorogued it with the hope that her own
marriage, or Mary's marriage with Dudley, might provide some
way out of her difficulty. Neither project had materialized, however. Moreover, these failures were accompanied by the appearance of a succession literature that only added coals to the fire:

---

* The dangers to England had been anticipated and discussed at length by
the Privy Council even before the completion of the Darnley marriage. *CSP,
For.*, ser. iii, VII, 384–87. Though the threat of a Hapsburg-Valois alliance
against England was more apparent than real, Elizabeth did not know this.
A. M. F. Robinson, p. 48.

the dissemination of facts and fancies by the several tract writers facilitated men's taking sides and intensified public concern. The Darnley marriage topped all this off: it doubtless brought almost all Catholics into Mary's camp, augmented the determination of the Protestants to reject Mary's claim, and made all parties even more impatient for a succession settlement.

In this atmosphere Elizabeth must have preferred not to recall Parliament, which would inevitably demand to deal with the succession. If leave to do so had to be granted, a grave clash of interests between the majority of the Parliament men and the Queen of Scots might ensue. Elizabeth could attempt to evade this danger by employing the same delaying tactics that had won her a "victory" in 1563, but this time the fight was bound to be more difficult, and might get out of hand. On the one side, Elizabeth would have to face the same Parliament that she had left nursing its wounds since 1563. On the other, she would have to placate Mary Stuart, who apparently was in a stronger position than she had been in in 1563.* Elizabeth could hardly anticipate the prospect of another session of Parliament without misgivings.

By the summer of 1566, however, Elizabeth found herself unable any longer to avoid reassembling Parliament. She needed money, and consequently was forced to call on her Lords and Commons to vote supplies. This time the circumstances in which funds were required were somewhat unusual. England was not at war; the Queen was going to ask for extraordinary revenue in time of peace.[3] Whatever the justification for such a request, Elizabeth would be inviting trouble by seeking financial aid from Parliament men who expected her to live of her own in peacetime. They would certainly demand something in return, and their succession petitions of the last session had not yet really been answered. When the Queen permitted the Parliament to open on 30 September, she was committing herself to a sure ordeal.

---

* Though Mary's position had been endangered by the murder of David Riccio in March 1566, she soon recovered control of affairs. Moreover, on 19 June Mary enhanced her position considerably by giving birth to Prince James.

No sooner did the session get under way than certain outside activities commenced in London that were obviously designed to back the Parliament men and to goad them on. These activities certainly represent the new force of public opinion that was independent of court influence and at which the succession tracts were aimed; they doubtless reflect much more than London opinion alone. If the activities were largely the work of Puritans, that only made them more ominous for the Queen.

Particularly interesting is a pamphlet that has come down to us among the papers of Thomas Sampson. Sampson, an eminent Puritan divine and a veteran insurgent, may well have been its author.[4] The pamphlet is entitled *The Common Cry of Englishmen Made to the Most Noble Lady, Queen Elizabeth, and the High Court of Parliament Assembled at Westminster in the Month of October, the Eighth Year of Her Most Happy Reign.* The following is its purport:

If you O Queen do die . . . void of issue and wanting a known successor and ordered succession, as the case now standeth, what good can continue? what evil shall not come? . . . This lack is that rack whereon England rubbeth, the sand where it sticketh and sinketh daily to destruction. [Two solutions have been suggested: (1) for the Queen to marry and have children; (2) for the succession to be settled.] Of the first all are desirous, but of the second the more desirous because the first is an unlikely and uncertain help. . . . It is not your marriage . . . which can help this mischief, for a certain ruin cannot be stayed by an uncertain means. It is uncertain whether ever you shall marry; it is uncertain whether you shall have issue in marriage; it is uncertain whether your issue shall live to succeed you. [But it is] most certain that unless the succession after you be—and that in time—appointed and ordered, England runneth to most certain ruin. [Therefore, we most humbly beg] that you with your . . . Parliament do both appoint your next successor and also set the succession and inheritance of the crown in safe and sure order. [If this is not done, we are in danger of civil war. And what might happen when] civil war is ended by a stranger gaining the crown? . . . And if the Queen, either of timorousness to attempt a matter of so great weight or of any other singular respect, should seem not to be willing to hear and help, as we desire presently; then we turn our cry to you our Lords and Commons assembled now in Parliament. Though the delay made upon your last most godly request in this behalf [in 1563] did daunt and grieve the hearts of you and of thousands which loved you for your good attempt, yet assay again. . . . You know whether your last answer received was . . . a promise. [If it was a promise,] it is time to claim the performance. [If it was a refusal,] look not for it to happen again. If it should happen [despite] the peril that hangeth thereon, as you do know what your authority is, so bestow your wisdom and power to put your country out of such peril. [Princes sometimes act unwisely and go astray.] Then do not only wise councilors stand instead, but chiefly such great assemblies of such persons so authorized and therewith privileged as Parliament men are. [Parliament is the place of free speech.] Speak there![5]

Today such a pamphlet would be classified as lobbying. It presented a Puritan program for the session; the radicals in the Parliament would, to a certain extent, attempt to carry it out. One is immediately struck by the new attitude toward the Queen's marriage. In 1563 that was at least a sincere hope; it was now dismissed as "an unlikely and uncertain help," and that with little show of courtesy. Actually this skepticism was unwarranted at the time, and may well have been feigned. In 1566 Elizabeth, no doubt influenced by the political and diplomatic consequences of Mary's union with Darnley, was evidently giving serious consideration to the idea of marrying Archduke Charles. In the spring of that year, she sent Thomas Dannett to Vienna to negotiate the matter.[6] A match with the Catholic Archduke, however, was viewed as worse than no solution at all by the Protestant zealots, who, in Sir John Neale's words, "had been the most clamorous for marriage in the abstract."[7] Hence the dismissal of the Queen's marriage as a way out; Elizabeth alone should not be blamed for her failure to keep her promise to marry and have issue.

The real Puritan program comes out when our pamphlet turns to the succession. Here the plea to the Queen is little more than a replaying of the old theme of *Gorboduc*. Even so, it was rather presumptuous. A petition embodying that theme had been presented to Elizabeth by the House of Commons in 1563; it was neither necessary nor exactly proper for a private party to bring that up again. Indeed, the Queen would even become indignant when the Parliament men themselves sought to remind her of their petitions. At any rate, one doubts that our pamphleteer had much faith in his appeal to Elizabeth. If he really expected to get any results from her, the daring exhortation to the Lords and Commons would not have been worth risking.

There, to say the least, he went completely out of bounds. If a promise was received in 1563, "it is time to claim the performance." This was bad enough, but what followed was revolutionary. If the Queen should refuse to have the succession settled now, "as you do know what your authority is, so bestow your wisdom and power to put your country out of such peril." Except for reminding the Lords and Commons of their privilege to speak up, our pamphlet does not specify what powers its writer thought they had. But it does say that they should "stand instead" if Elizabeth went astray. If I read this correctly, there is a definite implication that Parliament was competent to decide the succession without the Queen if necessary, that for this purpose Parliament was complete without the Queen. Such a notion would have been unthinkable to the Parliaments that enacted Henry VIII's Succession Acts. Concern over the succession was producing a dangerous drift in the constitutional thinking of some Puritans.

Also in October 1566 a significant extracurricular activity took place at Lincoln's Inn. There the law students held a disputation on the succession in the presence of, and probably at the instigation of, William Thornton, a Reader and a Bencher at the Inn.[8] Their finding was that "by all the laws and customs of England . . . , as a foreigner, born outside the realm, Mary Queen of Scots could not succeed to the crown, even if she were the nearest in birth and the ablest."[9] Of course, this produced a protest from Mary that resulted in Thornton's imprisonment.[10] It is particularly interesting that this disputation took place at Lincoln's Inn. At least three of the men who were going to make their marks as insurgents in the Parliament of 1566—James Dalton, William Lambarde, and Robert Monson—were alumni of that Inn.[11] We recall that Thomas Norton came from the Inner Temple. The Inns of Court were already beginning to produce the type of Puritan lawyer who would become so important in the struggle between King and Parliament in the next century. Moreover, it has been calculated that 108 members of the Parlia-

ment under consideration went to the Inns of Court.[12] Though
there is no way of knowing how many of them shared Norton's
political and religious views, the doings of the Parliament suggest that the number was considerable.

There also is evidence of further outside succession activities in London. For 6 October, Cecil's diary contains the entry:
"Certain lewd bills thrown abroad against the Queen's Majesty
for not assenting to have the matter of the succession proceed
in Parliament."[13] And on 11 November, according to Silva, "a
paper was thrown down in the presence chamber, declaring that
Parliament discussed the succession, as it was necessary for the
good of the country, and that if the Queen did not consent to
the discussion, she would see some things she would not like."[14]

All indications are that London was strongly behind Parliament in wanting the succession settled without delay. And we
may be sure that Protestant London was anti-Stuart; indeed,
we remember that Quadra reported it to be pro-Suffolk in 1563.
Such surroundings must have had an effect on the deliberations
being held at Westminster that could only make Elizabeth's
task all the more difficult.

We may be sure that most of the rest of the country shared
London's desire for a quick succession settlement. Did it share
London's probably pro-Suffolk sentiments? Our only information is what we can find out about the succession preferences of
those who represented the nation—or that part of it that
counted politically—in the Parliament of 1566. We can learn
nothing positive about this from the records of their meetings.
The correspondence of Guzman de Silva is our only source.
Though Spanish ambassadors were often influenced by their
own prejudices and by unreliable informants in their reports
on English opinion, Silva was at least a more discerning observer than Quadra. Elizabeth showed some respect for Silva,
and she was no mean judge of men. At any rate, Silva's apprais-
als of Parliamentary sentiments concerning the succession do,
for the most part, coincide with what one would expect to find
in light of the situation in general.

On 14 September, a fortnight before the opening of Parliament, Silva wrote:

The heretics are furiously in favor of Catherine, although somewhat divided, some wishing for the Earl of Huntingdon, who is the man to suit them best. They are powerful in Parliament, as there was a great ado here a year and a half ago in order that all those who were elected for shires and boroughs to vote in the Commons should be heretics. And what with them and the new bishops they should thus have a majority, especially as the nobles are divided, and they can settle the succession on a heretic, if the Queen wishes it.

A fortnight after the opening the Ambassador reported on the two most influential nobles: "I am told that the Duke of Norfolk will espouse the cause of Catherine . . . in the matter of the succession, whilst Leicester will advocate the claims of the Queen of Scotland. No doubt Cecil has persuaded the Duke . . . with the idea that the daughter of the Duke may marry Catherine's son." Late in October Silva wrote:

The discussion about the succession still goes on in Parliament, and the Queen is extremely annoyed, as she fears that if the matter is carried further they will adopt Catherine, both she and her husband, the Earl of Hertford, being strong Protestants, and most of the members of Parliament are heretics, and are going on that course to maintain their own party.

Then on 13 November the Ambassador reported: "It appears that they claim the right to proceed in the appointment of a successor to the crown, and in this case, although the Scotch Queen has a large party in the House of Lords, it is thought that Catherine would have nearly all of the members of the Lower Chamber on her side." On 16 December, as the session neared its end, Silva wrote:

It is not known yet if Parliament will be ended or prorogued. It would be much better for the Queen of Scotland that it should be dissolved, as the members of the Commons are . . . nearly all heretics and adherents of Catherine, and if Parliament is prorogued, the same members will continue, whilst if it be dissolved new ones will be chosen, who in any case must be better than the present ones, as these are the worst that can be found. Melville* quite understands this, and that if the appointment of a successor were left in their hands his mistress would come out badly.[15]

---

* Robert Melville, Mary's representative in London.

The only mention of Huntingdon was in the dispatch written before the session began, and was probably a mere guess on Silva's part. Once things got started, it evidently became clear to him that all the "heretics" were going to back Catherine's candidacy if the succession was to be declared. This would be a logical consequence of the arguments about the legal questions involved in the succession that had taken place since 1563: none of our known tracts actually made a case for Huntingdon. It would also be an expected result of Leicester's apparent shift to the Queen of Scots: without the support of the powerful Leicester, Huntingdon was just another nobleman who happened to have distant claims to the crown. Therefore, it is safe to conclude that in 1566 the old Protestant division over where the succession should rest was no longer an obstacle to a final settlement.

Catherine Grey evidently had more supporters than Mary Stuart in Parliament. Silva conceded the House of Commons with its great Protestant majority to Catherine. He did think Mary had "a large party in the House of Lords," but even there her chances were probably not too good. If, as Silva predicted and as seems reasonable, the Duke of Norfolk would back Catherine, many moderate peers might be expected to join him.* Add to this the "new bishops," whose succession activities would antagonize Elizabeth particularly, and the Protestant zealots among the nobles, and it becomes likely that the larger party in the Lords would be against Mary. Consequently, if the Commons were permitted to declare for Catherine, the Lords would probably have gone along with them. This obviously would not be the session for Mary to press her demand to have the succession established by Act of Parliament; it would be a session that Elizabeth could not afford to let get out of control, no matter what the cost.

* Though Norfolk apparently had Catholic leanings, he was not committed to Rome. Norfolk's later involvement with Mary Stuart was largely due to his opposition to Cecil rather than to a desire to restore Catholicism. Pollard, *Political History*, pp. 282–91; Neale, *Queen Elizabeth*, pp. 183–87. Proposal of a match between his daughter and Catherine's son would probably have been sufficient bait to bring Norfolk into the Suffolk camp in 1566.

We may now consider what actually happened at Westminster. For over two weeks after it opened on 30 September, Parliament remained silent about the succession. During the interval, according to La Forest, the French ambassador, the Duke of Norfolk addressed the Queen in Council on behalf of the nobility. He reminded her of the petitions presented in 1563, and told her that Parliament awaited her answer. He then begged her to allow Parliament to discuss her marriage and the succession. Elizabeth's reply to Norfolk was short and angry. She would marry soon. The succession was her own affair, and she was not interested in receiving counsel from Parliament about it.[16] This reply was bound to be provocative. A deeply concerned Parliament, no doubt feeling the pressure of a deeply concerned public opinion, and remembering the precedent of Henry VIII's Succession Acts, could not really accept the idea that the succession was merely Elizabeth's affair, to be disposed of whenever and however it suited her. The Queen's hostility would soon be equaled by that of her Commons.

The quiet in the Lower House ended on 17 October, when Sir Edward Rogers, Comptroller of the Household, moved the House for a subsidy to be given the Queen. This produced a debate over whether such a grant was really needed in time of peace.[17] The next day, in the words of the *Journals,* "a motion, made by Mr. Molyneux, for the reviving of the suit for succession, and to proceed with the subsidy, was very well allowed of the House."* This was, Neale writes, "the opening, the crucial, and surely the prearranged move in the succession campaign, linking it immediately with supply."[18] The lesson of 1563 had been learned. Molyneux's move was followed by others until finally Sir Ralph Sadler, no longer an ordinary member, made an unsuccessful attempt to defer the Commons from adopting this radical course: "After diverse propositions for that purpose, Mr. Sadler, one of the Privy Council, declared, that he had heard the Queen say, in the presence of her nobility, for the wealth of the realm, that her Highness minded to marry;

---

* *JHC,* I, 74. John Molyneux sat for Nottingham County. *Return of Members,* p. 405. He is listed among the radicals named in the *Lewd Pasquil* as "Molyneux the mover."

but their mind was to recontinue their suit, and to know her Highness' answer."[19]

On the next day, 19 October, several Privy Councilors declared Elizabeth's intention to marry, and advised the House "to see the sequel of that, before further suit touching the succession." But, as the Clerk of the House added, this only resulted in "long arguments by diverse lawyers to recontinue the suit to get the Queen's answer."[20] According to the French ambassador, there was a general outcry for the succession. When one of the Council begged the Commons to have patience and to proceed with the subsidy, they replied that they were expressly charged by their respective counties and boroughs to grant nothing until the Queen satisfied them about the succession. It was a day of exceptional insurgency. La Forest concluded: "We shall see what will come of this."[21]

What did come of it was that the Commons decided to ask the Lords to join them in a suit for the succession.[22] And Elizabeth was left to find her only confidant in the Spanish ambassador. She told him that she did not think that the Lords would join with the Commons. Silva found in the Queen's anger with the Commons an opportunity to point out to her "the turbulence of the Protestants."

She answered me that she did not know what these devils wanted. I said what they wanted was simply liberty, and if kings did not look out for themselves, and combine together to check them, it was easy to see how the license that these people had taken would end. She could not avoid agreeing with me, although she wished somewhat to excuse her friends, saying that they had some show of reason in their wishes with regard to the succession.[23]

Here was the main difficulty with Elizabeth's position. The knights and burgesses indeed had "some show of reason in their wishes with regard to the succession." We know that the unexpected length of her reign permitted things to work themselves out eventually, but the men of 1566 were not prescient, and they did have counties and boroughs to answer to.

The Queen was to be disappointed in her hopes about the Lords, but they apparently did hesitate about joining the Commons. On the evening of 22 October, a delegation of the principal lay peers and several bishops sought out the Queen in private. Their spokesman was no less faithful a servant of the Tudor Dynasty than the Lord Treasurer Winchester. His speech, as reported by La Forest, clearly presented the situation to Elizabeth. The Commons had approached them to make a joint suit for the succession. Necessity "compelled them to urge this point, that they might provide against the dangers which might happen to the kingdom if they continued without the security they asked." It had been the custom of Elizabeth's "royal predecessors to provide long beforehand for the succession to preserve the peace of the kingdom." The Commons were united in their opinion,

and so resolved to settle the succession before they would speak about a subsidy, or any other matter whatever; that, hitherto, nothing but the most trivial discussion had passed in Parliament, and so great an assembly was only wasting their time, and saw themselves entirely useless. They, however, supplicated her Majesty, that she would be pleased to declare her will on this point, or at once put an end to the Parliament, so that every one might retire to his home.

After Winchester finished speaking, his views were affirmed in turn by the Duke of Norfolk and each of the prelates and nobles present.

La Forest also reported Elizabeth's sharp response on this occasion. The Commons were "very rebellious"; they would not have dared to attempt "such things during the life of her father." They had no right to "impede her affairs"; it did not become subjects to compel their ruler.

What they asked was nothing less than wishing her to dig her grave before she was dead. . . . [Then,] addressing herself to the Lords, she said: "My Lords, do what you will; as for myself, I shall do nothing but according to my pleasure. All the resolutions which you may make have no force without my consent and authority; besides, what you desire is an affair of much too great importance to be declared to a knot of harebrains. I will take counsel with men who understand justice and the laws, as I am deliberating to do; I will choose half a dozen of the most able I can find in my kingdom for consultation, and after having their advice, I will then discover to you my will." On this she dismissed them in great anger.[24]

This exchange between the Lords and the Queen covers the situation. The views presented by the Lords certainly can be appreciated. The Commons wanted the succession settled during the session. Their desire was reasonable: England had a right to see more protection than Elizabeth's single life against a prospective anarchy. Moreover, the Commons were determined to withhold supplies and do nothing whatsoever until the succession was dealt with. Therefore, Elizabeth should either act on the succession or dismiss the Parliament. These were the facts of the matter as the Lords saw them.

But the Queen also had her views, and they too can, for the most part, be appreciated. The Commons were indeed coming close to being rebellious in their threat to refuse supplies without succession. They would not have dared to try such a maneuver against Henry VIII. That they did so against Elizabeth cannot be explained merely by her sex; rather it is indicative of Parliament's growing consciousness of its strength. The Queen, however, was not going to be intimidated; she understood Silva's warning about what the tactics of the Commons were leading to. The Lords could join the Commons if they wished; whatever resolutions they might make would be of no force without her consent and authority. This last was a hard fact that Parliament had to face, the implications of certain Puritan writings notwithstanding.

As for Elizabeth herself, she would do as she pleased about the succession. She apparently was still afraid that to establish the succession would be "to dig her grave before she was dead." This doubtless was not an apprehension of assassination, but an anticipation that dissatisfied elements would tend to conspire around a known successor. Such a fear is understandable in light of her experiences during her sister's reign. Nevertheless, the Queen did tell the Lords that she was going to do something about the succession. She would not consult Parliament about it: it was "an affair of much too great importance to be declared to a knot of harebrains." She would seek out six of the best legal minds in England, obtain their advice on the matter, and then make known her will.

This, however, seems like a strategem on the Queen's part. Silva's correspondence has indicated that Elizabeth at the time was afraid that Parliament wanted to nominate Catherine Grey. The lawyers whom the Queen would consult would likely be Catholics and supporters of the Stuart claim. The Inns of Court were indeed producing their share of Puritan lawyers, but the high law offices were then mostly occupied by men like Sir Anthony Browne. In March 1566 John Hales, not yet a free man, wrote Cecil a letter illustrating this. Hales heard that Mr. Carell, Attorney of the Duchy of Lancaster, was dying. He suggested to Cecil that the replacement be George Bromley, a man who "for his religion and knowledge of the law ought above many to be preferred. . . . You shall thereby, I know, win the hearts of a great many Protestants who, now discouraged, will take some hope if they may hear a Protestant lawyer beareth some authority in Westminster Hall."[25] The Queen probably had no real intention of seeking the advice of her leading lawyers; the threat to do so was perhaps made in the futile hope of deterring the Protestant Commons.

Be this as it may, Elizabeth could not very well have accepted either of the alternatives suggested by the Lords. To allow Parliament to proceed with the succession would likely be to go against the interests of the Queen of Scots. Mary's current strong position, and the misconceptions in Protestant countries about the arrangements made between Catherine de Medici and the Duke of Alva at Bayonne in the summer of 1565, combined to make this diplomatically unwise for Elizabeth.[26] Even if she had felt differently about settling the succession than she actually did, it might still have been better to let England gamble a little longer on her staying alive. Nor could the Queen afford to send Parliament home until it granted her some money. After all, it was her financial need that caused her to call on it in the first place. Therefore, she was going to fight it out with the Commons, and with the Lords too if necessary.

In fact, Elizabeth's stand left the Lords little choice. Though most of them must have disliked the means adopted by the Commons, practically all of them were undoubtedly sympathetic to having the succession established. On 25 October the

Commons received word that the Lords would join with them "in the suit to the Queen's Majesty, viz., for marriage and succession."[27] The Lords made this decision, according to Silva, "without any dissentient vote, except that of the Lord Treasurer, who was heard unwillingly by the others." Elizabeth reacted to this news by displaying her rage against certain peers: the Duke of Norfolk was called to his face "traitor or conspirator, or other words of similar flavor"; the Earl of Pembroke, the Earl of Leicester, and the Marquis of Northampton were awarded biting personal affronts for protesting the rebuke of the Duke.[28] Cecil recorded in his diary that "Pembroke and Leicester were excluded the Presence Chamber for furthering the proposition of the succession to be declared by Parliament without the Queen's allowance."[29] Afterwards Elizabeth told Silva that all of the Lords were against her but the Lord Treasurer. She was, probably rightly so, "greatly incensed with her bishops," whose attitude seems to have been much the same as that of the Commons.[30]

The Queen's show of anger apparently frightened most of the Lords; the making of arrangements with the Commons for a joint suit dragged on.[31] The interval seems to have been seized by the Privy Council to discover some way to avoid a decisive clash between Queen and Parliament. The idea that evidently developed is revealed in a memorandum of Cecil; it is summarized by Neale as follows: "proceed with marriage; declare the necessity to establish the succession; then prorogue Parliament for a short time, see how the marriage negotiations prosper, and when Parliament reassembles deal with the succession as circumstances require."[32] Perhaps in conjunction with the Council, Cecil's friend Thomas Ratcliffe, Earl of Sussex, approached Silva, and urged him to advise Elizabeth to effect her marriage with Archduke Charles and to prorogue Parliament for six months. Silva spoke to the Queen and got the impression that she approved of the plan, "although she seemed to think it an affront to her dignity to adopt any compromise."[33] Elizabeth actually did nothing about the proposal. That was perhaps for the best. If a prorogation of six months failed to produce a satisfactory solution, matters could only be made the worse for it.

This effort to find a way out should not deceive us about the Council. There can be no doubt that its sentiments were almost entirely with Parliament's quest for a succession settlement. Possibly at the time when the idea of an "Addled Parliament" was broached, Sir Ralph Sadler made a speech to the Queen in Council, the substance of which follows.

The security of the realm requires "that it would please your Highness to establish your succession, which is the thing that all of your people of all degrees have long expected and looked for." This would not put your royal person in peril; rather, it would make you the more secure by winning "the hearts of all your people. . . . If your Majesty should now end your Parliament, and leave your people void of hope and desperate in this matter of succession," what will happen when your Lords and Commons go home? "Their countrymen shall inquire of them what is done, for your Highness may be sure that all men hearken to this matter. And some of them perchance will advisedly answer, and some others perchance . . . will say, 'We have done nothing but given away your money; the Queen hath that she looked for, but she hath no care of us.' " Then you will lose the love of your people, and really be in danger. If the succession is settled now, good laws can be made to protect you. I have heard you say that the succession is uncertain and doubtful in law. "Surely the more uncertain and the more doubtful it is, the more needful it is to make it certain." It is to be considered whether it is better to have it decided now in an orderly way, or to have it determined eventually on the field of battle, where justice may not triumph. If you act now, you may first consult those nobles and councilors whom you wish to call on. With them "the matter may be debated and in manner adjudged . . . before it be brought in question in the Parliament House."[34]

Nearly everything in this speech doubtless was acceptable to all but the most radical of the Commons. No doubt the majority in the Lords and the Council would also agree with Sadler. The Queen alone saw things differently; she was all but isolated.

This, however, was exactly the situation in which Elizabeth Tudor might be expected to show herself the most resourceful. On 4 November the insistent Commons and the reluctant Lords finally finished their negotiations, and resolved "to petition the Queen by common consent to deal with the matter of the succession."[35] On the next day Elizabeth struck back quickly by requiring that thirty of each House appear before her in the afternoon to hear her pleasure.[36] The strategy behind this move is clear. The Queen would have her say before the Lords and Commons had time to make up a petition. Moreover, she apparently had things so arranged that the delegation from the Commons could not cause her trouble. It was chosen by the Speaker instead of the House; he seems to have seen to it that most of its members were moderates. And the Speaker himself was excluded; the delegation was to be without a voice. The Queen obviously was going to state her position without hearing Parliament's case. Neale comments, "Ethics apart, the tactics were sound, for the weakness of Elizabeth's position lay in the plausibility of her opponents' arguments."[37]

What is probably a faithful report of the Queen's words to the delegations has come down to us. Elizabeth opened by localizing her anger:

If that order had been observed in the beginning of the matter, and such consideration had in the prosecuting of the same, as the gravity of the cause had required, the success thereof might have been otherwise than now it is. But those unbridled persons whose mouth was never snaffled by the rider, did rashly ride into it in the Common House, a public place; where Mr. Bell* with his complices alleged that they were natural Englishmen and were bound to their country, which they saw must needs perish and come to confusion unless some order were taken for limitation of the succession of the crown. And further to help the matter, must needs prefer their speeches to the Upper House, to have you, my Lords, consent with them; whereby you were seduced, and of simplicity did assent unto it, which you would not have done if you had foreseen before considerately the importance of the matter. So that there was no malice in you, and so I do ascribe it. ... But there, two bishops, with their long orations, sought to persuade you also with solemn matters, as though you, my Lords, had not known that when my breath did fail me I had been dead unto you, and that then, dying without issue, what a danger it were to the whole State: which you had not known, before they told you it!

---

* Robert Bell sat for King's Lynn in Norfolk. *Return of Members,* p. 405. He is listed in the *Lewd Pasquil* as "Bell the orator."

The singling out of the Commons and bishops for blame, and the excusing of the lay peers, were evidently purposeful. The Queen must have known that the nobles were frightened accomplices, and wanted to encourage them to separate themselves from the dangerous business.

After finishing her prologue, Elizabeth got down to her main task of answering a petition before it was made:

Well, the matter whereof they would have made their petition (as I am informed) consisteth in two points—in my marriage and in the limitation of the succession of the crown, wherein my marriage was placed first, as for manner's sake. I did send them answer by my Council I would marry (although of mine own inclination I was not inclined thereunto). But that was not accepted nor credited, although spoken by their Prince. . . . A strange order of petitioners, that will make a request and cannot otherwise be ascertained but by their Prince's word, and yet will not believe it when it is spoken! But they (I think) that moveth the same will be as ready to mislike him with whom I shall marry, as they are now to move it. And then it will appear they nothing meant it.

There undoubtedly was a good deal of truth in this. Parliament invariably mentioned marriage before succession, and that probably was done "for manner's sake." Marriage was not a sure way to provide a certain successor; only a definite limitation of the crown promised that. Both Houses apparently were convinced that England required the immediate security of a settled succession before anything else. The Queen also had ground to express surprise that a new petition for marriage was in the making, when she had already sent word of her intention to wed. She was only correct to a degree, however, in attacking the sincerity behind such a request. There probably was no less desire for her to marry and produce an heir of her body, but the majority of the Parliament men must have been unenthusiastic over the idea of a match with the Catholic Archduke Charles. And he, unless the Queen would rob the cradle and take the young King of France, was the only prospective husband to whom she could give serious consideration. Elizabeth was not going to marry for love; she was going to marry for reasons of state. The Hapsburg match could reverse the upset in the diplomatic balance caused by Mary Stuart's marriage. To Elizabeth, this would be as important to England's security as anything else. We can appreciate the positions of both Queen and Parliament; we can also appreciate the sarcastic tone of her address to the latter.

The Queen next spoke at length on the succession question:

The second point was the limitation of the succession of the crown: wherein was nothing said for my safety but only for themselves . . . I am sure there was not one of them that ever was a second person, as I have been, and have tasted of the practices against my sister. . . . I had great occasion to hearken to their motions, of whom some of them are of the Common House. . . . I stood in danger of my life, my sister was so incensed against me: I did differ from her in religion, and I was sought for divers ways. And so shall never be my successor.

Though the fears expressed here are understandable, given Elizabeth's background, she must have known that the possibility of intrigue around the next in line had to be faced by every monarch and every successor, whether father and son, or distant cousins. Her Lords and Commons were not likely to find this a compelling argument.

The same would apply to what came next:

I have conferred before this time with those that are well learned, and have asked their opinions touching the limitation of succession; who have been silent—not that by their silence, after lawlike manner, they have seemed to assent to it, but that indeed they could not tell what to say, considering the great peril to the realm, and most danger to myself. But now the matter must needs go trimly and pleasantly when the bowl runneth all on the one side. And, alas, not one amongst them all would answer for us, but all their speeches were for the surety of their country. They would have twelve or fourteen limited in succession, and the more the better. And those shall be of such uprightness and so divine as in them shall be divinity itself. . . . [I] am not ignorant of stories wherein what hath fallen out for ambition of kingdoms. . . . You would have a limitation of succession. Truly, if reason did not subdue will in me, I would cause you to deal in it, so pleasant a thing it should be unto me. But I stay it for your benefit. For if you should have liberty to treat of it, there be so many competitors—some kinfolks, some servants, and some tenants; some would speak for their master, and some for their mistress, and every man for his friend— that it would be an occasion of a greater change than a subsidy.

This picture was exaggerated. Parliament undoubtedly wanted more than one person named to ensure the survival of one successor, but twelve or fourteen surely were not demanded. And Elizabeth certainly was not fooling anyone when she claimed she would be pleased to have Parliament deal with the succession "if reason did not subdue will in me." The protest about too many candidates was out-of-date in 1566, when nearly all of the Commons, and a good many of the Lords, probably would have easily accepted Catherine Grey, the claimant whom the Queen was most opposed to.

After this Elizabeth turned her special wrath on the bishops, whom she called *Domini Doctores*:

Well, there hath been error: I say not errors, for there were too many in the proceeding in this matter. But we will not judge that these attempts were done of any hatred to our person, but even for lack of good foresight. I do not marvel though *Domini Doctores* with you, my Lords, did so use themselves therein, since after my brother's death they openly preached and set forth that my sister and I were bastards. Well, I wish not the death of any man, but only this I desire: that they which have been practisers herein may before their death repent the same, whereby the scabbed sheep may be known from the whole.

This is mainly interesting in that it seems to corroborate the reasonable presumption that the bishops were the chief instigators of succession activities in the Upper House. Elizabeth's prelates were naturally committed to prevent any chance of a Catholic coming to the throne; indeed, they probably were solidly for Catherine Grey.

The Queen next declared that she would "never be by violence constrained to do anything" and then gave her final answer to the unmade petition:

Your petition is to deal in the limitation of the succession. At this present it is not convenient; nor never shall be without some peril unto you and certain danger unto me. But were it not for your peril, at this time I would give place, notwithstanding my danger. Your perils are sundry ways; for some may be touched, who resteth now in such terms with us as is not meet to be disclosed, either in the Common House or in the Upper House. But as soon as there may be a convenient time, and that it may be done with least peril unto you—

although never without danger unto me—I will deal therein for your safety, and offer it unto you as your Prince and head, without request; for it is monstrous that the feet should direct the head.

We may be sure what Elizabeth meant when she said: "for some may be touched, who resteth now in such terms with us as is not meet to be disclosed, either in the Common House or in the Upper House." She obviously was referring to the Queen of Scots. Mary now appeared to be in a more powerful position than ever, and was about to have Prince James baptized in the Roman Church. She had already let Elizabeth know that if the succession was to be gone into during the Parliament, she would "send persons to present her claims."[38] Consequently, there probably was much to justify the stand that this was not an appropriate time to attempt to settle the succession. Nonetheless, one cannot help being skeptical about Elizabeth's promise to do so "as soon as there may be a convenient time." A Parliament that had been disappointed before by its Queen could only take this as another insincere delay. In fact, many of its members must have concluded that "the head" would only act when "the feet" would manage to force it to, no matter how "monstrous" such a procedure might seem.

And finally, the end of the speech: "And therefore this is my mind and answer, which I would have to be showed in the two Houses. . . . And therewith, speaking of the Speaker, that the Lower House would have had their Speaker there, wherein they did not consider that he was not there to speak: she said she was a speaker, indeed; and there ended."[39] The Queen thus made known her "mind and answer." If these were normal circumstances, the matter would have ended here. In fact, it apparently did in the now rather thoroughly intimidated House of Lords, where many peers seemed hastily to beg Elizabeth's pardon for their "offense."[40] But the Queen was mistaken if she really expected the Lower House to be satisfied without even being heard.

On the next day, 6 November, her speech was reported to the House of Commons. Its reception was succinctly described by the Clerk: "whereupon all the House was silent." The silence evidently was more ominous than words; it did not last for long.

On 8 November, according to the Clerk, "Mr. Lambert began a learned oration for iteration of the suit to the Queen's Majesty for limitation of succession; and thereupon [it was] strongly reasoned, for both parts."* This attempt to renew the suit in face of Elizabeth's "answer" was something no monarch worthy of the name could be expected to tolerate; it was open defiance. On the following day, the *Journals* tell us, "Mr. Vicechamberlain [Sir Francis Knollys] declared the Queen's Majesty's express commandment to this House, that they should no further proceed in their suit, but to satisfy themselves with her Highness' promise of marriage."[41] This order apparently produced another period of temporary silence in the Lower House. Indeed, Elizabeth, according to the Spanish ambassador, was convinced that it had put the entire business to rest. Silva commented: "I do not know if it will be sufficient to bridle the insolence of these heretics."[42] It would not be sufficient.

On 11 November Paul Wentworth† put three questions to the House, the most important of which was the first: "Whether her Highness' commandment, forbidding the Lower House to speak or treat any more of the succession and of any their excuses in that behalf, be a breach of the liberty of the free speech of the House, or not?"[43] This opened a new field for hostilities, and the Commons seemed eager to do battle. Wentworth's questions were followed by "diverse arguments, continuing from nine of the clock till two [in the] afternoon." On the next morning the Queen sent for Speaker Onslow, and sent him back to the House with a "special commandment" in which she repeated her former order for silence on the succession.[44]

The House soon responded to this second order by appointing a committee of thirty to consider what course should be taken.[45] The committee decided to draft a petition. The submissive tone of the resulting petition suggests that moderates

---

* "William Lambert, gent.," sat for Aldborough in York. *Return of Members,* p. 406. Neale, *Parliaments,* pp. 151–52, identifies "Mr. Lambert" as the antiquary William Lambarde.

† This brother of the more famous Peter sat for Buckingham Borough. *Return of Members,* p. 403. He appears in the *Lewd Pasquil* as "Wentworth the wrangler."

predominated on the committee, but there certainly was no ab-
ject surrender. The petition opened by indicating that the Commons were much grieved that Elizabeth seemed to have received
the wrong impression about "certain conferences lately held in
our Common House." Their only intention was the "renewing
of the former suit made in the last session," the obtaining of
which would be to the glory of God and the benefit of both
Queen and country. Having made this pointed reminder, they
proceeded to declare their good faith and to beg the Queen to
accept their testimony of the same, rather "than any other conjectures which . . . , by misreporting or mistaking of speeches,"
might cause her to doubt their meaning.

Excuses made, the Commons got down to business. First a
polite expression of gratitude for Elizabeth's promise to marry.
Then a reluctant acceptance of her decision to postpone the
settlement of the succession: "We your Majesty's most humble
subjects do receive this your Majesty's answer according as we
are bound by our obedience, being most sorry that any manner
of impediment hath appeared to your Majesty so great as to stay
you from proceeding in the same." There would be no allowing
her to forget her recent promise to proceed "as soon as there may
be a convenient time." Next the Commons turned to the commandments received from the Queen for silence on the succession. They reminded her of their "ancient" liberty "to treat and
devise of matters honorable for your Majesty and profitable for
your realm." They had been informed that she did not mean
by her orders to diminish their "accustomed lawful liberties."
The Commons closed by beseeching Elizabeth that they might
be permitted to continue to serve her faithfully "without the
burden of any unnecessary, unaccustomed, or undeserved yoke
of commandment."[46]

The final draft of this petition was dated 16 November by
Cecil. For some reason or other it was never presented, but perhaps Cecil gave the Queen some idea of its nature. At any rate,
by now she must have known very well that what had originally
been an issue of succession alone had also become one of Parliamentary liberty. And she doubtless realized that the question
of liberty had far more dangerous implications for monarchy

than any other. Elizabeth was confronted with the type of problem that was to plague her Stuart successors. Her first commandment for silence on the succession was the obvious step that any sixteenth-century monarch would have taken in a like situation. The novel tactics of Wentworth and his colleagues, however, put the Queen in a serious predicament. There were three courses open to her: she might continue a fight from which no good could come; she might send the Parliament home and not get her much-needed subsidy; she might surrender.

Elizabeth sensibly chose to yield with good grace. This she did by a royal message delivered to the Commons by their Speaker on 25 November. Here it was explained that the Queen's orders for silence were based on information that made it appear that the suit for the succession had been revived after her answer of 5 November. Now she understood "that albeit the speeches of some particular men seemed to incline to reiterate that suit, yet there followed no general consent nor resolution of the whole House." Therefore, it was the Queen's pleasure to revoke her commandments as unnecessary, "assuring herself that all her good and loving subjects will stay themselves upon her said answer, without pressing her Majesty any further therein at this time."[47]

This was a masterly surrender: it contained no direct recognition of the House's "accustomed lawful liberties"; it did contain a polite request to drop the succession question for the time being. Its reception by the Commons was described by the Clerk's entry: "Which revocation was taken of all the House most joyfully, with most hearty prayer and thanks for the same."[48]

Meanwhile, another storm was brewing that threatened to provoke things anew. In June 1566 at Paris, Patrick Adamson, a refugee Scot, had published a poem of thanksgiving for the birth of Mary Stuart's son. The baby James was described in its title as *"serenissimus princeps"* of Scotland, England, France, and Ireland.[49] This poem had already angered Elizabeth, who commanded the Earl of Bedford to protest it when he arrived in Scotland to represent her at the baptism of the Prince.[50] On 22 November a copy of Adamson's poem appeared in the Commons when a motion was being made against "corrupt and wicked books" from overseas. It was espied by one James Dalton, who was thereby caused to make an intemperate speech.

James Dalton sat for Saltash Borough in Cornwall. An alumnus of Lincoln's Inn, he had probably been expelled from it for heresy during Mary's reign, but was subsequently readmitted.[51] From what we know of his speech of 22 November, it seems quite possible that Dalton was among those present at the disputation at Lincoln's Inn that found against Mary Stuart's claim. It also seems likely that Dalton supported Paul Wentworth when he asked his three questions.[52] He was obviously one of the hotheads among the Commons. The *Lewd Pasquil* called him "Dalton the denier," and we shall now see why.

On 24 November, Robert Melville, Mary Stuart's London representative, entered a formal complaint against Dalton's speech of the 22nd. Melville claimed that Dalton had used the following words: "God forbid, and I never trust to see the day that ever any Scot or stranger shall have any interest in the crown of this realm, for it is against the law that any person other than such as be born the Prince's subjects hold merit in this land."[53] Dalton was called before the Council, where he gave his own version of his doings of 22 November:

A motion being made against corrupt and wicked books that came from beyond the sea, and I happening to behold a slanderous libel in the House, in whose hands I remember not, touching the Prince of Scotland, titling him Prince of Scotland, England, and Ireland, and being very much moved therewith, commending the former motion wished provision against slanderous libels and such: How say you to a libel lately set forth in print, calling the infant of Scotland Prince of Scotland, England, and Ireland? Prince of Scotland, England, and Ireland? quoth I. What enemy to the peace and quietness of the realm of England, what traitor to the crown of this realm hath devised, set forth, and published this dishonor against the Queen's most excellent Majesty and the Crown of England? Prince of England; and Queen Elizabeth as yet having no child? Prince of England; and the Scottish Queen's child? Prince of Scotland and England; and Scotland before England? Who ever heard or read that before this time? What true English heart may sustain to hear of this villainy and reproach against the Queen's Highness and this her realm? It is so that it hath pleased her Highness at this time in part to bar our speech, but if our mouths shall be stopped, and in the meantime such despite shall happen and pass without revenge, it will make the heart of a true Englishman break within his breast. With the indignity of this matter being as it were set afire I was carried with the flame thereof, well I know not whither, but I suspect something escaped me unawares that made some doubt that I would have entered into some title of the crown; insomuch that Mr. Speaker said to me, "It were not well you enter into any title." But what I said I do not remember, but sure I am that I did not speak these words: "That no person might inherit the crown of this realm except he were a subject of the realm of England." For I answered Mr. Speaker that I did not mind to deal with any title of the crown. And thereupon making my conclusion, that it were good there were provision against such spreading of infamous libels, I did leave to speak further.[54]

Melville's charge or Dalton's denial, which is the more believable? Clearly that of Melville, who apparently was painfully aware of the unpopularity of the Stuart claim in the Lower House. He must have had more sense than to make a false charge that might provoke the Commons into a real demonstration of their feelings about the succession. On the other hand, a man of Dalton's background might be expected to make an attack on the Stuart title after being "set afire" by the sight of Adamson's poem. What he did admit saying is sufficiently reminiscent of Sadler's speech of 1563 to make it seem most likely that he went all the way in his anger. Moreover, he did confess his suspicion that something escaped him unawares. He denied speaking the words: "That no person might inherit the crown of this realm except he were a subject of the realm of England." Of course, there were other ways to express the same thought in the English language.

The Council evidently was not satisfied with Dalton's denial. On 26 November a message was drafted by Cecil in the name of the Queen to be sent to the House of Commons:

The Queen's Majesty hearing by some common report that one of this House named James Dalton would on Friday last, in declaring his misliking of a certain infamous book lately printed in Paris (being indeed very derogatory to the crown and dignity royal of her Majesty), enter into certain speeches and assertions concerning the right and title of succession to this crown, and therein to tax and abase the estate of the Queen of Scots with whom her Majesty is in amity: Forasmuch as her Majesty perceiveth it far unmeet and dangerous for any person of his own head to set forth or abase any particular title of this crown, the consideration whereof belongeth properly to her Majesty and the three estates of the realm; and that the said James Dalton hath been demanded whether he did in his said speech utter any such assertion; and hath answered that he did not either speak, or had any meaning to speak, to set out or abase any particular title to the succession of this crown; but did, being inflamed with a natural offense against the false entitling of the book, largely speak against the same, and did make sundry times mention of the Queen of Scots, and especially of the Prince of Scotland, whereby he suspected that some might mistake his speech: Wherefore her Majesty meaning herein, considering the case toucheth a Prince with whom her Majesty is in good amity, to have the question demanded of the House whether he did use any such assertion ... or no.[55]

This message is indicative of the Council's desire to please Elizabeth over what it expected her to consider a serious offense against the Queen of Scots. In fact, Mary was sufficiently angered by the affair to make a personal request through the Earl of Bedford that Dalton be punished for his words.[56] The message is also indicative of the Council's strong feelings about Adamson's poem. There was an implication in *"serenissimus princeps"* of Scotland, England, France, and Ireland that Mary's immediate claim to the crown was being reasserted. But the poem was only the work of a refugee Scot, and we may accept the claim that it was not written with Mary's consent.[57] The entire business was really being made too much of on all sides.

Elizabeth apparently realized this, and decided to call a halt on proceedings against Dalton before they provoked new troubles with the Commons. On 27 November Leicester informed Cecil that the Queen did not want Dalton's speech "to proceed to question or trial" in the House.[58] Her wishes put the Dalton affair to rest, and that in the nick of time.* If, as the Council intended, it had been brought to trial in the House, there is no telling what hostilities might have developed over the succession or over Parliamentary liberties.

---

* According to Silva, Elizabeth promised Melville that she would punish Dalton after supplies were voted. *CSP, Span., Eliz.,* I, 599. If she made such a promise, there is no evidence to indicate that it was ever fulfilled.

Elizabeth evidently decided that the only way to deal with her Commons was to appease them. Also on 27 November she followed up her revocation of the commandments for silence on the succession by remitting a third of the proposed subsidy. This produced "most hearty prayer and thanks," and an immediate reading of the subsidy bill.[59] Moreover, the idea of settling the succession during the present session was not brought up again. This was one time when appeasement worked.

Nonetheless, the Queen was once more to be vexed by her Commons. When the time came to compose a preamble to the subsidy bill, they hit upon the device of including the following bit of chicanery in it:

We cannot but... thankfully remember to your Majesty that it pleased the same to signify unto us that you did not mislike of us for our desire in this Parliament to have the succession of the crown declared. ... And signified further of your godly disposition and natural love toward us, to our great comfort, that rather than your realm should threat ruin for lack of declaration of succession—which you trusted Almighty God would shew of your own body in due time after your marriage—you would by God's help, though it should appear some peril to yourself (which God defend), declare the succession in such convenient time as your Highness, with the advice of your Council and assent of your realm, should think meet in such person as in whom the right thereof according to law and justice ought to be settled and remain.

The obvious purpose of the Commons was to make an official record of the Queen's words that would be circulated throughout England. This was an adroit way to try to bind an evasive promiser, but it was far from proper. Elizabeth saw the folio that we have quoted from, and wrote some appropriate comments at its foot:

I know no reason why my private answers to the realm should serve for prologue to a subsidies book. Neither yet do I understand why such audacity should be used to make without my license an act of my words. Are my words like lawyers' books, which nowadays go to the wiredrawers to make subtle doings more plain? Is there no hold of my speech without an act compel me to confirm? Shall my princely consent be turned to strengthen my words that be not of themselves substantives?[60]

Of course, in the end a substitute preamble was adopted, but the men of 1566 had gone down fighting.[61]

On 2 January 1567 Elizabeth was ready to dissolve Parliament. She had received her reduced subsidy. She could now speak her mind to those she had formerly had to appease. Before dissolving Parliament, the Queen delivered a prepared address, most of which was clearly a chiding for the Commons. Almost at the beginning she introduced the main issues: "Two visors have blinded the eyes of the lookers-on in this present session, so far forth as under the pretense of saving all, they have done none good. And these they be: succession and liberties." We need not dwell on the matter of liberties. In essence, the Queen told her Commons that the revocation of the orders for silence on the succession was purely an act of her own volition; any who thought she had recognized a freedom to speak on matters that she did not wish discussed were mistaken. On the succession she said:

The Prince's opinion and good will ought, in good order, have been felt in other sort than in so public a place be uttered. It had been convenient that so weighty a cause had had its original from a zealous Prince's consideration, not from so lip-labored orations out of such subjects' mouths. . . . Their handling of this doth well show (they being wholly ignorant) how fit my grant at this time should be to such a demand. In this one thing their imperfect dealings are to be excused, for I think this be the first time that so weighty a cause passed from so simple men's mouths, as began this cause.

Elizabeth had made similar remarks before, but it seems noteworthy that this time she did not see fit to accompany them with a promise to have the succession settled when convenient. Her surprise at the initiative of the Commons is understandable. She had experienced one of the earliest expressions of the political voice that would someday culminate in the Long Parliament.

The Queen concluded her chiding with a classification of the Parliament men:

You were sore seduced. You have met with a gentle Prince, else your needless scruple might perchance have bred your cause blame. And albeit the soothing [maintaining] of such be reprovable in all, yet I would not you should think my simplicity such as I cannot make distinctions among you—as of some that broached the vessel not well fined, and began these attempts, not foreseeing well the end; others that respected the necessary facies [appearances] of the matters, and no whit understood circumstances expedient not to have been forgotten therein; others whose ears were deluded by pleasing persuasions of common good, when the very yielding to their own inventions might have bred all your woes; others whose capacities, I suppose, yielded their judgment to their friends' wit; some other served an echo's place.[62]

Elizabeth did not choose to name names, but most of the members probably were able to fit themselves into one category or another. It is likely that most of the occupants of the leading categories were included among the forty-three radicals named in the *Lewd Pasquil* as the "choir." "As for the rest," that lampoon went on, "they be at devotion; and when they be pressed, they cry 'a good motion.' " Two sessions of insurgency had produced a coherent group that the Queen could not have been inclined to face again. This must have had much to do with her decision not to prorogue the Parliament, as evidently was expected in some quarters, but to dissolve it.[63]

The Parliament that met in 1563 and 1566 may well rate a unique place in the pages of Elizabethan Parliamentary history. Least of all was it an episode in the traditional love affair between Elizabeth and her subjects that culminated in the "Golden Speech" of 1601. If ever the Queen's scoldings of her Parliament may be said to "reek of the governess," it is in 1566.[64] If any Parliament markedly illustrates "the perennial conflict of radicalism and conservatism"—the conflict between Commons and Crown that Sir John Neale's great works have shown to be as characteristic of Elizabeth's reign as of James I's—it is this the Queen's second Parliament.[65] Here the conflict was not only hot, but definitely hostile.*

---

* None of what I have said or will say is meant to deny the basic loyalty of the Commons to their Queen. Indeed, the very Puritan lawyers whose novel tactics gave Elizabeth the most trouble in 1566 represented "the one element among her subjects which she could count on to the death." Read, *Tudors*, p. 135. I do respectfully doubt, as far as this Parliament is concerned, Neale's view that "the contest went on in a kind of romance," but not his conclusion that "any thought of divorce" was excluded. Neale, *Parliaments*, p. 29.

It was the issue of succession that made this so. To the Commons, feeling the pressure of public opinion and following the lead of the Puritan lawyers in their midst, an immediate settlement was urgent. To men still plagued by the memory of the Marian reaction, nothing was more important for the Protestant England they hoped to build than the identity of the next sovereign. Doubtless inspired to greater boldness by the rather unexpected victory of Elizabeth's first House of Commons, which in 1559 had forced on the Queen a religious settlement more Protestant than she had wanted, her second House, once it found a succession candidate it could agree on, pressed its suit with an uncommon inventiveness and even insolence.[66] To the Queen, on the other hand, an immediate succession settlement was out of the question. There were several reasons for this, some more legitimate than others: her desire to see no succession settlement at all; her objection to the claimant whose title the House was no doubt prepared to advance; the real danger that the international situation in 1563, and even more so in 1566, held for England if Parliament was permitted to make an anti-Stuart limitation of the crown; the fact that no successor who might be designated would be universally accepted in England; and very likely a feeling on Elizabeth's part that the succession was a problem exclusive to the crown, and should not be subject to Parliamentary jurisdiction. Clearly the House's determination to settle the succession was equaled by the Queen's determination not to yield to it on the matter.

What made Elizabeth's task all the more difficult was that she had to fight not only her Parliament, but, indirectly, her father. Henry VIII, whose wishes on the succession were never seriously opposed by his Parliaments, by thrice changing the succession in Parliament, had set precedents for a Parliamentary settlement; Elizabeth's second Parliament, whose wishes on the succession were not those of its Queen, expected her to follow those precedents. Moreover, Henry, as authorized by his last two Succession Acts, had designated in his will the very Suffolk succession that Elizabeth's Commons had come to favor. There were doubts about the authenticity of the will, but these might be resolved by an official investigation, which would be a logical

step in the making of a Parliamentary settlement. Henry's precedents and his will surely lay beneath the surface in the succession struggles between Elizabeth and her Commons. There is no
reason to believe that even the most hotheaded of the House
seriously thought Parliament could act without the Queen, but
there can be no doubt that the Commons thought Henry's precedents entitled them to have an important role in succession deliberations, if not actually to nominate successors, then certainly
to discuss and accept or reject nominations presented to them.
Surely when the Commons spoke of determining the succession
"according to law and justice," as in the proposed preamble to
the subsidy bill, Henry's will was foremost in their mind.

Henry's precedents and will in effect tied his daughter's hands,
if not in 1563, then certainly in 1566. His Succession Acts made
it almost impossible for Elizabeth, no matter what she felt her
authority should be, to settle the succession without Parliament,
especially since even Mary and Darnley, who claimed hereditary
right, demanded that their title be established by Act of Parliament. And a Parliamentary settlement could not very well ignore Henry's will, if it proved genuine, since its legal basis was
his Succession Acts. With her father's precedents pointing to
a determination of the succession in Parliament, and his will
pointing to Catherine Grey, the claimant preferred most by the
Commons and probably by the majority of the Lords but preferred least by Elizabeth, the only course open to the Queen was
negative. If she had wanted to disregard Parliament and dispose
of the succession as she pleased, the prospects would have been
little better than those of Parliament's attempting to settle the
succession without the Queen. All she could do was to try to
hold the line: she could not allow Parliament to discuss the succession; she could not even keep her royal word to the misguided
Queen of Scots to have Henry's will examined; she could only
make promises of future action that no one could have accepted
at face value.

Holding the line was by no means easy, at least in 1566. The
Tudors usually could depend upon the royal officials in both
Houses to keep their Parliaments from going too far. In the
Lower House in 1566, however, the royal officials clearly could

not control the Puritan lawyers, who had successfully assumed the leadership and even threatened to carry the reluctant Upper House along with them. The line was only held by the intervention of the Queen herself, and that by too narrow a margin for comfort. Nonetheless, time would prove this perhaps the most successful of the many holding operations that Elizabeth conducted in dealing with her Parliaments. About a half century later William Camden wrote: "Thus by a woman's wisdom she suppressed these commotions, which Time so qualified, shining ever clearer and clearer, that very few, but such as were seditious or timorous, were troubled with care about a successor."[67] The Parliament men who were sent back to their counties and boroughs on 2 January 1567, however, could hardly have dreamed of such a future. It must have seemed inevitable to them that the succession question would be raised anew whenever the next Parliament met, and that Parliament, benefiting from their experiences, might well succeed in breaking through the Queen's resistance.

II. *The Past Is Not Prologue*

In the year 1567 the prospects for a Suffolk succession were to reach their highest point. Of course, at first Catherine Grey's supporters must have been disappointed by the dissolution of Parliament on 2 January. A prorogation would have been encouraging; it would have promised another session soon and with the same experienced Parliamentary tacticians around to renew the succession fight. Nevertheless, the dissolution was not a crushing blow. The Queen's financial needs, which had only been satisfied in part by the recently granted subsidy, would almost certainly force her to call a new Parliament in due season. And the membership of the next Parliament would probably be much like that of the last one. The return of a considerable number of veterans of the previous Parliament could always be anticipated. Moreover, continued Protestant dominance in the Lower House was assured by the Act of 1563, which required all who would sit there to take the oath of supremacy.[1] Such a Parliament would not likely differ from its predecessor's succession sentiments. The Suffolk side could regard 1566 more as a delay than a defeat.

On the other hand, the friends of the Queen of Scots also apparently felt the situation was developing much to the Suffolk advantage. Maitland of Lethington complained of this to Cecil in his letter of 4 January 1567:

I pray you so counsel the Queen your Sovereign as some effectual reparation may follow without delay the many and sundry traverses and disfavorings committed against the Queen my Sovereign; as the publishing of so many exemplifications of King Henry's supposed will; the secret embracing of John Hales's book; the books printed but not avowed last summer, one of which the Queen my Mistress sent by Henry Killegrew to the Queen your Sovereign;* the disputes and proceedings of Lincoln's Inn, where the case was ruled against the Queen my Sovereign; the speeches by sundry in this last session of Parliament, tending all to my Sovereign's disherision, and nothing said to the contrary by any man, but the matter shut up with silence most to her prejudice,† and by so much the more as every man is gone home settled and confirmed in this error; and lastly the Queen your Sovereign's resolution to defend [stop] now by proclamations all books and writings containing any discussion of titles, where already the whole realm hath engendered by these former proceedings, and others' favored practices, a settled opinion against my Sovereign to the advancement of the Lady Catherine's title.²

Maitland's cries of woe were not exaggerated. The Stuart side was evidently faring badly in the battle for public opinion. At this time only two succession tracts advancing Mary's claim had been completed, namely, Sir Anthony Browne's tract, and the unimpressive *Answer to Allegations against Mary*. Besides these, there was *Allegations in behalf of Mary*, which attacked Catherine Grey but did not argue for Mary Stuart. There is no evidence that any of these manuscript tracts enjoyed a large circulation. Against them were *Gorboduc* and *Allegations against Mary*, both of which had been printed, and Hales's *Declaration*, with its many manuscript copies. Moreover, Catherine's backers had apparently devised another form of propaganda that may well have been more effective than any of the tracts, to wit, "the publishing of so many exemplifications of King Henry's supposed will." Earlier in his letter Maitland specifically protested "the many exemplifications and transcripts, which, being sealed with the great seal, do run abroad in England, and do carry away many men's minds as great presumptions of great verity and veracity."³ It is not difficult to imagine the weight carried by such copies of the will of the great King among the subjects

---

* Undoubtedly a reference to *Allegations against Mary*. See *CSP, Scot.*, II, 287, 308.

† Of course, the silencing of the Commons was probably more to Mary's advantage than to her prejudice.

of his daughter. If Elizabeth were going to stop any further succession literature, Mary's friends would have little chance of regaining lost ground.

If things did not look good for Mary in January 1567, in the coming months her position would hit rock-bottom. On 10 February the house at Kirk o' Field was blown up, and Darnley's body was found strangled nearby. It was quickly suspected that Mary was a party to the deed, and her lax efforts to discover her husband's murderer seemed to confirm this. Then on 15 May Mary reached the height of folly: she was married in a Calvinist ceremony to James Hepburn, Earl of Bothwell, the man who was generally held responsible for Darnley's murder. Of course, we need not go into the question of the actual guilt here; our main concern is with the political effects of the murder and its sequel.

Everywhere the immediate consequences were unfavorable to Mary. To the Scots, Darnley, considered contemptible in life, became a martyr in death. The Scottish nobility led a popular revolt against their Queen, which resulted in her capture at Carberry and her imprisonment at Loch Leven. On 24 July she was forced to abdicate and to nominate Lord James Stuart, now Earl of Moray, as Regent for James VI. In Catholic Europe friendship for Mary disintegrated with the news of the Bothwell marriage. Pius V's secretary sent the following communication to Scotland:

His Holiness has never hitherto dissembled about anything, and he will not begin to do so now, especially in this all important matter of religion. Therefore, in regard to the Queen of Scots in particular, it is not his intention to have any further communication with her, unless indeed, in times to come, he shall see some better sign of her life and religion than he has witnessed in the past.[4]

The development of the English Catholics' reactions can be seen from the dispatches of the Spanish ambassador. When the first news of Darnley's murder arrived, he wrote: "The case is a very strange one, and has greatly grieved the Catholics."[5] A month later Silva reported:

Nothing certain has been learned with regard to the conspiracy against her [Mary's] husband, nor has the Queen cleared herself, but rather have the accusations been pressed in consequence of the suspicions aroused by the bad terms upon which she was with her husband. She has, however, still many friends who cannot believe it if they had more proofs than they have.[6]

By 26 April, according to the Spaniard, certain Catholics had decided that the supporters of Catherine Grey were falsely trying to cast blame on Mary. Nonetheless, they were very much afraid that Mary would marry Bothwell.[7] And finally on 24 May Silva wrote: "Cecil sends to say that the Queen of Scots married the Earl of Bothwell. . . . The information comes from many quarters and is undoubted. It seems to have scandalized people here very much, and has caused sorrow to many who see the evils it will bring in its train."[8] Mary Stuart's stock had now reached a new low in England. The Catholics found themselves at a loss for an acceptable succession candidate.

The decline of the Queen of Scots was no doubt accompanied by a proportionate rise in the succession prospects of Catherine Grey. We get a significant indication of this in Silva's report of the Darnley murder:

On the night that the King of Scotland's death was known here Lord Robert [Leicester] sent his brother, the Earl of Warwick, to the Earl of Hertford, Catherine's husband, to offer him his services in the matter of succession, and Lord Robert himself went to see the Duchess of Somerset, the Earl's mother, with the same object, and has made friends with both of them, contrary to his former action as he has shown of a desire to help the Queen of Scotland.[9]

Though Leicester was an opportunist deserting a sinking ship, the swiftness of his shift to Catherine may mean he had become convinced that the triumph of her cause was now assured. And we may assume that a good many moderates who had been wavering between Mary and Catherine now definitely decided to favor the latter. Shortly after Darnley's murder, Silva advised Elizabeth "to be on the alert to prevent undue elation" among Catherine's supporters, "who were strong and might cause trouble."[10] By the end of 1567 the Queen herself seems to have become frightened at the way affairs were developing. On 29 December Silva wrote: "I am informed that they have again increased the strictness with which they have imprisoned the Earl of Hertford, Catherine's husband. They are possibly afraid of some movement in his interest, as I am assured that certain negotiations are afoot respecting the succession to the crown."[11]

A political forecaster living in England on 1 January 1568 might well have predicted that the end of the succession question was in sight. By 1566 the original confusion over the several candidates had cleared up, leaving Mary Queen of Scots and Lady Catherine Grey the only serious rivals, and by 1568 Mary seemed all but eliminated from the picture. One might have anticipated that whenever the next Parliament was summoned, it would be nearly one hundred per cent for an immediate settlement in favor of Catherine. Then Elizabeth would have found it difficult to argue for another delay. The old promise to marry was not likely to satisfy anyone; indeed, the Queen's earnestness for the match with Archduke Charles had apparently been cooled down by the new diplomatic balance that resulted from the Darnley murder.[12] Nor could it any longer be mantained that the recognition of Catherine's claim would be dangerous for England; Mary Stuart seemed helpless, and those in control of affairs in Scotland probably had little interest in pressing James VI's claim at this time.* Never had the chances for a Suffolk succession looked so good.

The succession situation, however, could change rapidly, since it depended upon particular individuals. On 27 January 1568 Lady Catherine Grey died.[13] This was a severe blow to the hopes of the Protestants. Six days later Silva reported: "She leaves two sons, aged six and four years. . . . The heretics mourn her loss, as they had fixed their eyes on her for the succession in any eventuality. The Catholics are pleased, and are already beginning to say that the children are not legitimate owing to Catherine's having married against the law."[14] The Catholics

---

* Moray was naturally more concerned with consolidating his own position in Scotland than with James VI's prospects in England. Indeed, later in the year, if we may believe Mary Stuart, Moray formed a league with the Earl of Hertford, apparently with the connivance of Cecil, whereby Moray would recognize the Suffolk claim, and Hertford would support Moray's claim to the Scottish succession. *CSP, Scot.,* II, 575.

had reason to be pleased about Catherine's passing. The Protestants now lacked a really suitable succession candidate to back.

The remaining Suffolk claimants were not an impressive lot. Catherine's sons, as Silva implied, were mere boys, and were legally bastards. Lady Mary Grey, Catherine's dwarfish younger sister, had made a rather bizarre marriage with one Thomas Keyes, a servant at the Court.* With such a consort she could hardly be considered an appropriate prospect for the succession. And Lady Margaret Strange, Catherine's cousin, had too many Catholic connections to be acceptable to the Protestants. Nor could they do better outside the House of Suffolk. The Earl of Huntingdon's claim was weak, and his relationship to the Earl of Leicester frightened many influential men. And very few English Protestants were yet ready to give serious consideration to James VI. He was an alien, and his religious upbringing depended too much upon the uncertain political situation in Scotland. In the course of the next few years, according to Silva's successors, the Protestants—or at least Cecil and his friends—decided that their best choice was Catherine's elder son.[15] But he, being legally illegitimate and a boy, would not be an easy candidate to push in Parliament.

Meanwhile, Mary Stuart reentered the picture. On 2 May 1568 Mary escaped from Loch Leven, and a fortnight later she was on English soil. Mary's presence in England quickly altered the succession situation. The woman was a magnetic personality; she could not help but attract people. Her side of the Scottish story came out: she was innocent; she had been wronged by evil subjects. Sympathies were aroused. The support of the Catholics was regained, both in England and on the Continent. By the end of 1568 Mary's succession stock had perhaps reached new heights.

This remarkable recovery, however, was dangerous. Mary's faction now consisted mainly of explosive elements. Discon-

---

* "Here is an unhappy chance and monstrous. The sergeant porter, being the biggest gentleman in this Court, hath married secretly the Lady Mary Grey, the least of all the Court. They are committed to several [separate] prisons. The offense is very great." Cecil to Sir Thomas Smith, 21 August 1565. Ellis, ser. ii. II, 299.

tended noblemen, both Catholic and Protestant, saw Mary as a means to bring about a feudal reaction and get rid of the Cecils and the Bacons. Humble folk in the North found espousing her cause a way to express religious, economic, and social grievances of long standing. And Guerau de Spes, the new Spanish ambassador, was a tactless zealot who had come to England intending to kindle a fire.[16] Here was a potent mixture that was almost bound to produce intrigues, and even worse. A plan for Mary to marry the Duke of Norfolk, and a plot to overthrow Cecil developed. Then in the last months of 1569, the Northern Rebellion broke out. Mary's claim to the succession, among other things, was put to test on the field of battle.

The failure of the Northern Rebellion did not lead, as it perhaps should have, to an immediate calling of a Parliament. Despite the need for legislation to deal with the leaders of the Rebellion, and for a subsidy to pay the cost of suppressing it, Elizabeth held out for over a year before summoning a Parliament. This delay was doubtless due to her fear that a new Parliament would insist more strongly than its predecessor on settling the succession. She probably expected the worst when her third Parliament opened on 2 April 1571; it contained about 115 veterans of her second Parliament, including nearly half of its so-called "choir" of 43.[17] Yet in the Parliament of 1571, the succession question was raised only once and negatively: Thomas Norton made a futile attempt to combine Elizabeth's treasons bill with a bill of his own that in effect would have eliminated both Mary Stuart and James VI from the succession.[18] The Queen's fears proved all but groundless.

Sir John Neale explains that Parliament did not reraise the succession question because, essentially, a more mature House of Commons was less inclined to defy and coerce its Sovereign at this critical time.[19] This is certainly true as far as it goes. The Parliament of 1571 doubtless represents a less adolescent stage of Parliamentary development than its predecessor. The crisis of the Northern Rebellion, followed by the Papal Bull of 1570, which deprived Elizabeth of her "pretended right" to the English throne and released her subjects from their allegiance, tended to bring the Queen and her Protestant Commons closer together. But another, and probably more important, reason why the succession question was not brought up positively in the Parliament of 1571 was that there was no suitable candidate whose title could be advanced.

That Norton's bill, which would have penalized the innocent James as well as the "guilty" Mary, very probably would have become law but for the Queen's disapproval indicates that Parliament was still basically anti-Stuart.[20] Though what had already been uncovered about the Ridolfi Plot was not known to Parliament, it must have been obvious that the situation was still fraught with constant danger that extended even to Elizabeth's very life, which would make it logical to demand an immediate declaration of the succession. Surely if there had been an appropriate Suffolk claimant available, if Catherine Grey had still been alive, Norton, of all the members, would have made a positive as well as a negative proposal. If Catherine were alive and were made the Queen's heir presumptive, the question of the legitimacy of her sons would eventually have been taken care of, even if Elizabeth's intransigence on the matter compelled awaiting her demise. Without Catherine, however, the bastardy of her sons, given the Queen's obvious disinclination to have the verdict against their mother's marriage reversed, presented a virtually insurmountable obstacle. With Catherine's sons unacceptable in law, and the remaining succession possibilities unacceptable for other reasons, there was no point to bringing up the succession settlement in the Parliament of 1571. Parliament had certainly matured enough not to start a pointless fight with Elizabeth at a time of crisis.

The Parliament of 1571 was really an early stage in an epilogue to our story. The failure of the Northern Rebellion and of the subsequent Ridolfi Plot, the full details of which were not discovered until some months after the Parliament's dissolution, were to have great ultimate consequences for the succession question. The Protestant gentlemen of the Parliaments to come would find it easier to deprive Mary Stuart of her head than of her "birthright." After Mary was eventually executed, the succession picture gradually assumed a completely new face. Protestants came around to the idea that Mary's royal son

—brought up as a Presbyterian—might make a more appropriate succession candidate than a legally illegitimate son of Lady Catherine Grey. And Catholics found it necessary to recall the Lancastrian descent of the Spanish royal family in their search for a claimant. A considerably different succession literature arose to replace our tracts. The idea of a Suffolk succession was on its way out.

Of course, we have gotten far ahead of our story and into the outlines of another story that does not come within the scope of this volume.[21] Our only purpose in doing this has been to suggest that the death of Catherine Grey and Mary Stuart's flight to England were genuine turning points. If so, the first decade of the reign of Elizabeth I was actually a distinct chapter in the history of the succession: a chapter in which men's concern over the succession question was probably at its highest, and one in which the ultimate outcome was by no means assured.

What if the turning points had not occurred and the chapter had not ended in 1568? Or what if Elizabeth had not lived on into the next century? In either case England might have experienced civil war and foreign intervention, or it might not have. But it might well have had a Suffolk succession. What would that have meant for the history of the next century? At least a Suffolk dynasty could not very well have been misled by notions of divine right: its title doubtless would have been basically a Parliamentary one. A royal line dependent upon Parliament for its existence might have been less prone to resist the forces that Parliament represented. The seventeenth-century development probably would not have been too different, but it might well have been more peaceful. But this was not to be. Thanks to the unpredictable—Catherine's early death, Mary's lot, and the length of Elizabeth's life—the road was comparatively clear for James VI of Scotland to become James I of England on 24 March 1603.

Appendix of Genealogical Charts

I. *The Descent of the Tudors from the Third and Fifth Sons of Edward III*

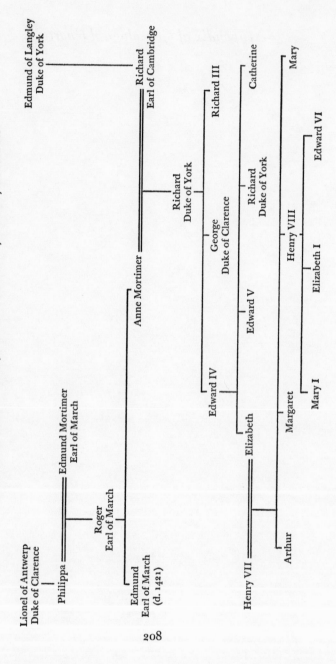

II. The Descent of the Tudors from the Fourth Son of Edward III

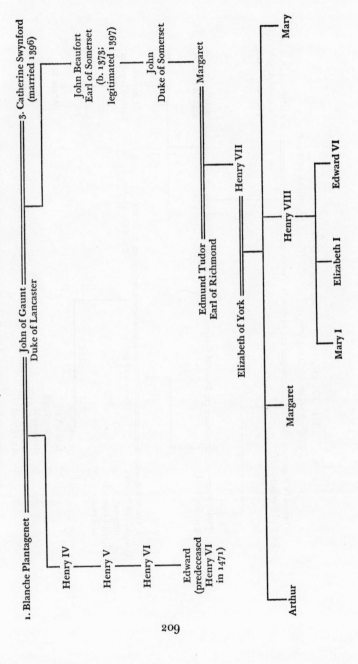

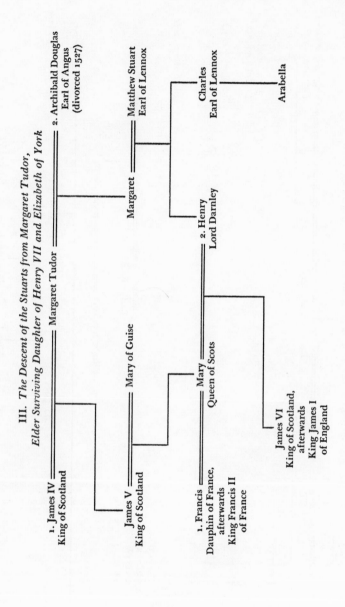

III. *The Descent of the Stuarts from Margaret Tudor,*
Elder Surviving Daughter of Henry VII and Elizabeth of York

IV. *The Descent of the Suffolks from Mary Tudor,*
Younger Surviving Daughter of Henry VII and Elizabeth of York

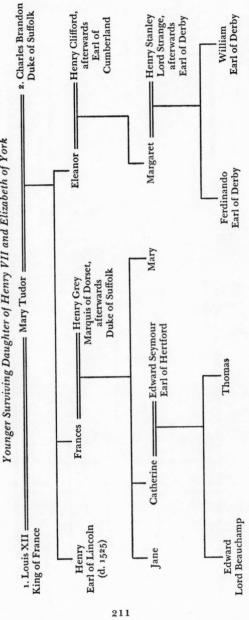

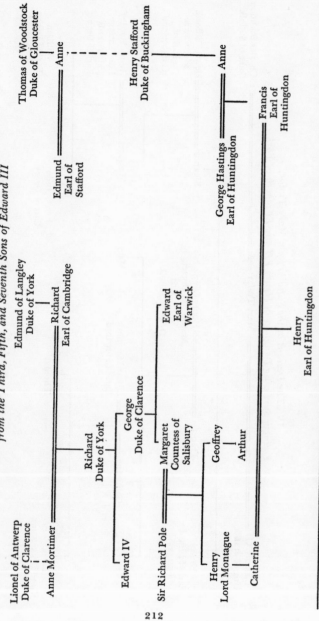

V. *The Descent of Henry Hastings, Earl of Huntingdon,*
from the Third, Fifth, and Seventh Sons of Edward III

Thomas of Woodstock
Duke of Gloucester

Anne

Edmund
Earl of
Stafford

Henry Stafford
Duke of Buckingham

Anne

George Hastings
Earl of Huntingdon

Francis
Earl of
Huntingdon

Edmund of Langley
Duke of York

Richard
Earl of Cambridge

Edward
Earl of
Warwick

Henry
Earl of Huntingdon

Richard
Duke of York

George
Duke of Clarence

Margaret
Countess of
Salisbury

Geoffrey

Arthur

Lionel of Antwerp
Duke of Clarence

Anne Mortimer

Edward IV

Sir Richard Pole

Henry
Lord Montague

Catherine

212

Broken vertical line means all generations not included.

Notes

Notes

Full citations for all references will be found in the Bibliography, pp. 231–38. The following abbreviations are used in the Notes and the Bibliography:

CMH—Cambridge Modern History.
CSM—Calendar of Salisbury Manuscripts.
CSP—Calendar of State Papers.
DNB—Dictionary of National Biography.
EB—Encyclopaedia Britannica.
HM—Harleian MSS.
JHC—Journals of the House of Commons.
LIBB—Records of Lincoln's Inn: Black Books.
PRO—Public Record Office.
SP—State Papers.
SR—Statutes of the Realm.

Chapter One

1. *CSP, For.,* ser. iii, I, 54–55.   2. *Burghley Papers,* I, 277–78.

3. Weiss, V, 463.   4. *CSP, For.,* ser. iii, I, 521–24.

5. See Klarwill.   6. Holinshed, IV, 179.

7. *CSP, Span., Eliz.,* I, 180.   8. Steuart, pp. 57–58, 64, 131.

9. For a list of claimants published in 1571, see Ellis, ser. ii, II, 141–42.

10. Lettenhove, II, 532.   11. *CSP, Span., Eliz.,* I, 176.

12. Knappen, pp. 194, 200, 296.   13. Neale, *Commons,* pp. 39–40.

14. *CSP, Span., Eliz.,* I, 192, 273, 297.

15. Lettenhove, III, 185.

16. *CSP, Span., Eliz.,* I, 296–97. In 1564 Lord John Grey testified that Huntingdon was favored by some M.P.'s. *Burghley Papers,* I, 412.

17. *CSP, For.,* ser. iii, V, 15.

18. *CSP, Span., Eliz.,* I, 137–38.

19. *Ibid.,* I, 262.

20. Lettenhove, III, 2–3, 6; *CSP, Span., Eliz.,* I, 297–347 *passim.*

21. *Ibid.*, I, 125, 244–45.
22. *CSP, Ven.*, VI, 1077.
23. *HM* 4627, no. 2, p. 14, and 849, fol. 7; Collier, p. 44; Leslie, pp. 60–61.
24. Rowse, pp. 164, 168–69, 252–54, 440–41, 446–49; Neale, *Commons*, pp. 154, 255–56.
25. Lord John Grey's testimony in *Burghley Papers*, I, 412.
26. *CSP, Span., Eliz.*, I, 433.

Chapter Two

1. *CSP, Span., Eliz.*, I, 45.
2. Lettenhove, II, 24–25.
3. *Ibid.*, II, 470, 486.
4. *Ibid.*, I, 612–13.
5. Antwerp, September 1559. *Ibid.*, II, 24–27.
6. *CSP, Span., Eliz.*, I, 114.
7. *CSM*, I, 197.
8. *CSP, Span., Eliz.*, I, 176.
9. Wright, I, 68–69.
10. *Burghley Papers*, I, 80.
11. 16 August, Lettenhove, II, 605.
12. *Burghley Papers*, I, 369–70.
13. Warner to Elizabeth, 21 August, *PRO, SP, Dom., Eliz.*, XIX, 32.
14. Chaloner had written of them. Lettenhove, I, 612–13.
15. *Ibid.*, II, 529–33.
16. 26 August 1561. Yorke, I, 177.
17. Lettenhove, II, 608*n*. My translation.
18. *Ibid.*, II, 619–20. My translation.
19. *CSP, Span., Eliz.*, I, 213–24.
20. Klarwill, pp. 88, 113.
21. Knappen, pp. 175, 207, 411; Rowse, pp. 408*n*, 409; Jewel, *Apologia Ecclesiae Anglicanae.*
22. Jewel to Peter Martyr, 7 February 1562. H. Robinson, p. 126.
23. *HM* 6286, pp. 36, 44.
24. Nichols, *Progresses*, I, 52.
25. Strickland, p. 126.
26. *HM* 6286, pp. 45, 79.
27. *Ibid.*, p. 46.
28. *Ibid.*, pp. 67–68.
29. *Ibid.*, p. 80.
30. *Ibid.*, pp. 33, 47–48.
31. Lettenhove, II, 625.
32. Pollen, *Papal Negotiations*, p. 69.
33. *CSM*, I, 272.
34. *Burghley Papers*, I, 378.
35. *HM* 6286, *passim.*
36. Tanner MS. 193, fol. 165.
37. Cotton MS. Vitellius C XVI, fol. 459.
38. *PRO, SP, Dom., Eliz.*, XXI, 55.
39. Nichols, *Progresses*, I, 37; Strickland, pp. 120–21.
40. *HM* 6286, pp. 42, 45, 81, 88.

37. *JHC*, I, 72.

38. Neale, *Parliaments*, pp. 126–27.

Chapter Five

1. Pollard, *Somerset*, pp. 200–237.
2. Whittingham, p. 113.
3. Printed in Foxe, VIII, 673–79.
4. Peck, X, 175.
5. See Lamond, p. xix*n*; Strype, *Sir Thomas Smith*, p. 122.
6. Peck, X, 159.
7. Garrett, p. 173. *Bulletin of the Institute of Historical Research,* I (1925), no. 2, 63–64.
8. *Return of Members,* p. 404.
9. *Lewd Pasquil,* fol. 826.
10. *Burghley Papers,* I, 412.
11. Printed in Hargrave, pp. xx–xliii.
12. Ellis, ser. ii, II, 285; Neale, *Parliaments,* p. 104.
13. On Beale see: *DNB*, II, 3–7; *Burghley Papers,* I, 413–15.
14. They are in Cambridge MS. Ii. v 3, fols. 1–96.
15. Camden, p. 386.
16. Tanner MS. 193, fol. 226.
17. Wright, I, 137.
18. Ashmolean MS. 826, fols. 5–6.
19. Pollock and Maitland, II, 370–71, 382.
20. Parsons, part ii, pp. 138–39.
21. Ellis, ser. ii, II, 285.
22. Wright, I, 179.
23. Strype, *Sir Thomas Smith*, p. 122.
24. *Burghley Papers,* I, 412; Hales, p. xli.
25. *Burghley Papers,* I, 416.   26. Hales, pp. xxxviii–xli.
27. *Burghley Papers,* I, 413.   28. Hales, pp. xxiv–xxv.
29. *Burghley Papers,* I, 412.   30. *Ibid.,* I, 414–15.
31. *Return of Members,* pp. 404, 406.
32. *CSM,* XIII, 66–67.
33. *Burghley Papers,* I, 413–14.
34. *Ibid.,* I, 414, 416.
35. On Dannett see Garrett, pp. 139–40.
36. *HM* 6990, fol. 29.
37. *Burghley Papers,* I, 416.
38. Cotton MS. Titus C VII, fol. 11.

39. Jackson, p. 153.
40. *PRO, SP, Dom., Eliz.,* XXVIII, 14.
41. *Burghley Papers,* I, 417.
42. Wright, I, 137.
43. Nichols, *Queen Jane,* pp. 53–54, 65, 71, 77.
44. Garrett, pp. 140–41, 165–67, 172–75, 325–27.

45. *Ibid.,* pp. 165–66.	46. *Ibid.,* p. 327.
47. Wright, I, 179.	48. *Ibid.,* I, 174.
49. Parsons, part ii, pp. 1–2.	50. *DNB,* I, 840, and VIII, 914.
51. Harington, *Tract,* pp. 33, 41.	52. *CSP, Span., Eliz.,* I, 378.
53. *Ibid.,* I, 365–79 *passim.*	54. *DNB,* I, 842.

55. Hales, pp. xxix–xxxvii.
56. The statement that Bacon later wrote a tract advocating the Stuart claim (*DNB,* I, 840) derives from the inaccurate title of the following work: Nathaniel Booth, *The Right of Succession to the Crown of England in the Family of the Stuarts . . . Asserted and Defended by Sir Nicholas Bacon . . . against Sir Anthony Browne* (London, 1723). A comparison of texts reveals that the tract attributed to Bacon is the second book of Leslie's *Defense of Mary* and that attributed to Browne is Hales's *Declaration.*

57. *HM* 1877, fol. 25.	58. Wright, I, 174.
59. *HM* 6990, fol. 28.	60. *Ibid.,* fol. 29.

61. *CSP, For.,* ser. iii, IV, 344, 363, 389, 418.
62. *HM* 6990, fol. 29.
63. Clapham, pp. 73–74.
64. *PRO, SP, Dom., Eliz.,* XVI, 52.
65. *CSP, Dom.,* I, 178, 182–83, 185.
66. Garrett, pp. 16, 165–66.

67. Ellis, ser. ii, II, 273–85.	68. Read, *Cecil,* p. 278.
69. *CSP, For.,* ser. iii, VI, 198.	70. Wright, I, 180.
71. Yorke, I, 174.	72. *Burghley Papers,* I, 444.
73. *PRO, SP, Dom., Eliz.,* XL, 91.	74. *CSP, Span., Eliz.,* I, 365–66.
75. *Ibid.,* I, 371–72.	76. Wright, I, 184–85.

Chapter Six

1. Hales, pp. xx, xlii.
2. One indication of its continued circulation would be the several answers to Hales's tract. Another would be the numerous manuscript copies of the *Declaration* extant, some of which are listed in the bibliography. It is likely that most of them belong to the period before Catherine Grey's death in January 1568.

3. Pollard and Redgrave, no. 18684.

4. This and the preceding paragraph owe much to Stone and to MacCaffrey.

5. Pollard and Redgrave, no. 17564.

6. *CSP, Scot.*, II, 287, 308.   7. *HM* 4627, no. 2, p. 4.

8. *Ibid.*, p. 26.   9. See Allen, p. 261.

10. *HM* 4627, no. 2, pp. 7–8.

11. The copy in Cambridge MS. Gg. iii 34, pp. 107–17, is entitled *An Answer to the Former Allegations against the Queen of Scots' Title to the Crown of England.* The other two copies are called *A Copy of an Answer to a Little Book Herein Mentioned.*

12. Ashmolean MS. 829, fol. 31.   13. *Ibid.*

14. *Ibid.*, fol. 36.   15. *HM* 849, fol. 1.

16. *Ibid.*, fol. 31.   17. Rawlinson MS. A 124, fol. 1.

18. *DNB*, XLV, 429.   19. *Ibid.*; Hale, I, 324.

20. The work is therefore listed under Plowden in the bibliography. See also chap. 7, p. 111, and the footnote thereto.

21. *HM* 555, fols. 11–16.   22. Neale, *Parliaments*, p. 130.

23. *DNB*, XI, 977.   24. Collier, pp. 41–49.

25. Pollard and Redgrave does not list the tract.

26. Atwood, Appendix, p. 3.

27. *Ibid.*, pp. 4, 5–17.

28. *Ibid.*, p. 5.

29. Levine, "Letter." The document is listed in the bibliography as *The Letter.*

30. Levine, "Letter," pp. 13–16, 28–36.

Chapter Seven

1. Hales, p. xxx.

2. 25 Edward III, st. 1; *SR*, I, 310.

3. Hales, p. xxx.

4. Leslie, pp. 62–63.

5. Hales, p. xxxii; *HM* 4627, no. 2, p. 17.

6. Hales, p. xxxii.   7. *Ibid.*

8. Leslie, p. 63.   9. *HM* 4627, no. 2, pp. 16–17.

10. Ashmolean MS. 829, fol. 33.   11. *HM* 4627, no. 2, p. 17.

12. Ashmolean MS. 829, fols. 33–34.

13. Painter, p. 4.   14. Maitland, *History*, p. 98.

15. *Ibid.*, p. 97; Painter, pp. 2–3.   16. Collier, p. 44.

17. Ashmolean MS. 829, fol. 34.   18. Hales, p. xxxii.

19. 42 Edward III, c. 10; *SR*, I, 389.

20. Holdsworth, IX, 76.

21. Cotton MS. Caligula B V, fol. 254.

22. Leslie, pp. 60–61.

23. *HM* 4627, no. 2, p. 14. A similar opinion had been given by the judges in 1485. Pickthorn, *Henry VII*, pp. 16, 151*n*.

24. See Holdsworth, II, 185.   25. Leslie, pp. 69–70.

26. *HM* 849, fol. 207.   27. Allen, pp. 256–62.

28. Quoted in Maitland, *Essays*, p. 104*n*.

29. See Maitland's introduction to Gierke, especially p. xi.

30. 24 Henry VIII, c. 12; *SR*, III, 427.

31. Neale, *Parliaments*, p. 85; Maitland, *Essays*, p. 106.

32. Pickthorn, *Henry VIII*, p. 283*n*.

33. 11 Henry VII, c. 1; *SR*, II, 568.

34. Pickthorn, *Henry VII*, pp. 139–40.

35. Maitland, *Essays*, p. 107.

36. Pollard, *Henry VIII*, p. 207.

37. Elton, *England*, pp. 166–67.

38. 25 Edward III, st. 1; *SR*, I, 310.

39. Collier, p. 44.   40. Leslie, p. 70.

41. Burgoyne, pp. 176–78.   42. *HM* 4627, no. 2, pp. 18–19.

43. *DNB*, VI, 516.

44. On Gaunt's strong position see Trevelyan, p. 9.

45. 25 Edward III, st. 1; *SR*, I, 310.

46. Hales, pp. xxx–xxxi.   47. Collier, p. 43.

48. *HM* 849, fols. 18–28.   49. Leslie, p. 85.

50. Collier, p. 43.   51. Leslie, p. 85.

52. *EB*, XXIV, 437, and XXVIII, 264.

53. Dyer, *Reports*, p. 304a.

54. Holdsworth, IX, 80–81; Tanner, *Conflicts*, pp. 268–69.

55. See McIlwain, p. 96*n*; Levine, "Rape," pp. 160–62.

56. 7 Henry VII, c. 6; *SR*, II, 553.

57. Forty-two from 1560 to 1568. *Cal. Patent Rolls, Eliz.*, II, 65, 101, 450–60; III, 165, 298–99, 328, 392, 443–55; IV, 31–33, 220–31.

58. *SR*, IV, liv, lv, lx, lxiii; *JHC*, I, 181, 213, 222, 224–25, 228, 236, 239, 241.

59. *HM* 849, fol. 28.

60. Pollard, *Henry VIII*, pp. 325, 327.

61. Tanner, *Documents*, pp. 415–16.

62. Elton, *England*, p. 161.

63. Maitland, "Settlement," p. 560.

Chapter Eight

1. Hales, pp. xxxviii–xl.
2. Atwood, Appendix, pp. 5–7.
3. *CSP, Ven.,* II, 618; *DNB,* XII, 1284; Brown, p. 150.
4. Strickland, p. 32.
5. *Ibid.,* pp. 6, 43; *Letters and Papers, Henry VIII,* II, no. 227.
6. Pollard, *Henry VIII,* p. 168; *Letters and Papers, Henry VIII,* IV, no. 4131.
7. M. A. E. Green, V, 1, 137.
8. *Ibid.,* V, 19n.
9. Hales, pp. xl–xli.
10. Pollard, *Henry VIII,* pp. 63–64.
11. Atwood, Appendix, p. 9.   12. *Burghley Papers,* I, 412.
13. Levine, "Letter," p. 35.   14. Atwood, Appendix, p. 10.
15. Pollard, *Henry VIII,* p. 152.
16. See *Letters and Papers, Henry VIII,* IV, no. 5859.
17. The bull in Latin is in M. A. E. Green, V, 576–78; English summary is in *Letters and Papers, Henry VIII,* IV, no. 5859.
18. The only other mention in our tracts was Maitland of Lethington's single reference to "the polygamy of Charles Brandon." Collier, p. 48.
19. Atwood, Appendix, p. 5.   20. *Ibid.,* p. 9.
21. Levine, "Letter," p. 32.   22. Beames, p. 181.
23. Levine, "Letter," p. 32.
24. *DNB,* VIII, 628; Strickland, pp. 105, 116.
25. Nicholas, pp. cxvi–cxviin.
26. Hales, p. xxxix.
27. *DNB,* VIII, 627; *Biographia Britannica,* IV, 2405–7; Craik, II, 265–66; Nicholas, pp. cvii–cxv.
28. *Ibid.,* pp. cxiv–cxv.
29. This was later alleged in an anonymous and unreliable tract. Burgoyne, pp. 169–70.
30. *PRO, SP, Dom., Eliz.,* XLVI, 23.
31. The author of *The Letter* referred to the marriage but did not discuss it. Levine, "Letter," pp. 32–33.
32. Atwood, Appendix, p. 12. On 17 February 1563 Lord Herbert married Lady Catherine Talbot. *DNB,* IX, 641.
33. Rutton, p. 121; *DNB,* IX, 640–41.
34. Rutton, p. 121.

35. Camden, p. 386.
36. Castelnau, p. 51; Naunton, pp. 25–26.
37. Quoted in Nicholas, p. cxviii*n*.
38. Powell, p. 3.
39. *CSP, Span., Eliz.*, I, 45.
40. *CSP, For.*, ser. iii, IV, 159.
41. Tanner MS. 193, fols. 224, 227.
42. *CSP, Dom.*, I, 174, 178, 182–83, 184.
43. See *HM* 6286.
44. *CSM*, II, 72–73.
45. Hallam, I, 273*n*.

Chapter Nine

1. Rymer, XV, 112–13.
2. 28 Henry VIII, c. 7, and 35 Henry VIII, c. 1; *SR*, III, 660, 956.
3. Pollard, *Henry VIII*, p. 279*n*.
4. 35 Henry VIII, c. 1; *SR*, III, 955.
5. Pollen, "Question," p. 528.
6. Pollard, *Henry VIII*, p. 210.
7. More, pp. 252–53.
8. Strype, *Thomas Cranmer*, II, 260.
9. Fuller, IV, 138.　　　　　　　　10. 1 Eliz., c. 3; *SR*, IV, 359.
11. Pollen, "Question," p. 518.　　12. Sir Thos. Smith, pp. 48–49.
13. *HM* 849, fols. 31–37; Collier, pp. 45–47; Leslie, pp. 87–89, 94–103, 107–8; Atwood, pp. 13–17.
14. *Ibid.*, p. 13.
15. Up to here this chapter is largely based on the fuller account in Levine, "Title."
16. Atwood, Appendix, pp. 14–16; *HM* 849, fols. 36–37.
17. Leslie, pp. 98–99.
18. *HM* 849, fol. 32.
19. *SP, Henry VIII*, I, 892, 897–98.
20. Hales, pp. xxiv–xxvii.　　　　21. Dasent, II, 11.
22. Collier, p. 47.　　　　　　　　23. Rymer, XV, 112–13.
24. *CSP, Span.*, XI, 310.　　　　　25. *CSP, For.*, ser. ii, p. 222.
26. Leslie, p. 99.　　　　　　　　27. Collier, pp. 46–47.
28. Leslie, p. 94.　　　　　　　　29. Collier, p. 47.
30. *HM* 849, fol. 32.　　　　　　31. Levine, "Letter," p. 33.
32. *PRO, Royal Wills*, E. 23, vol. IV.
33. Pollard, *Somerset*, p. 5; Hargrave, p. 206.

34. L. B. Smith, pp. 22–23.

35. Rapin, III, 483n; Bailey, p. 163.

36. Cf. Cotton MS. Vespian F XIII, fol. 71 (1518); Additional MS. 19,398, p. 644 (ca. 1519); Lansdowne MS. 1263, fol. 6 (1533), fol. 8 (1540); and *PRO, Royal Wills*, E. 23, vol. IV.

37. Pollard, *Somerset*, p. 7.   38. L. B. Smith, p. 25.

39. *Ibid.*, p. 19.   40. *SP, Henry VIII*, I, 897f.

41. *Letters and Papers, Henry VIII*, vol. XXI, part 2, p. 753; L. B. Smith, p. 24.

42. *PRO, Royal Wills*, E. 23, vol. IV; Bailey, p. 162.

43. Tytler, I, 15–16, 19; Dasent, II, 11.

44. Pollard, *Somerset*, pp. 6–8, 37–38.

45. Foxe, VI, 163.

46. Pollard, *Somerset*, pp. 21–22, 22n.

47. Foxe, VI, 126–27.   48. Hales, p. xxiv.

49. Leslie, p. 94.   50. See Henderson, I, 1–45.

51. Holinshed, III, 1066.   52. *CSP, Span.* XI, 134.

53. Dyer, p. 141a.   54. Rymer, XV, 111–12.

55. *PRO, SP, Dom., Eliz.*, V, 5, 9.

56. Labanoff, I, 390.

Chapter Ten

1. *Burgley Papers*, II, 757–58.

2. *CSP, Scot.*, II, 192–93.

3. *CSP, Span., Eliz.*, I, 574.

4. Garrett, pp. 279–81; Neale, *Parliaments*, p. 132.

5. Egerton MS. 2836, fols. 37–71 *passim.*

6. Klarwill, pp. 257–64, 300.   7. Neale, *Parliaments*, p. 129.

8. *LIBB*, I, 349.   9. Neale, *Parliaments*, p. 133.

10. *Burghley Papers*, II, 762.

11. Neale, *Parliaments*, pp. 151–52, 158–61, 162; *LIBB*, I, 323, 325, 335.

12. Neale, *Commons*, p. 302.

13. *Burghley Papers*, II, 762.

14. *CSP, Span., Eliz.*, I, 596.

15. *Ibid.*, I, 580, 586, 589, 597, 602.

16. Neale, *Parliaments*, p. 136.

17. Letter of La Forest; Disraeli, II, 182–83. Mr. Disraeli incorrectly identifies the French ambassador as La Mothe Fénelon, who did not come to England until 1568.

18. Neale, *Parliaments,* p. 137.
19. *JHC,* I, 74.
20. *Ibid.,* I, 75.
21. Disraeli, II, 184.
22. *JHC,* I, 75.
23. *CSP, Span., Eliz.,* I, 590.
24. Disraeli, II, 184–85.
25. Lansdowne MS. 9, no. 8, fol. 15.
26. Neale, *Catherine de Medici,* pp. 68–69.
27. *JHC,* I, 75.
28. *CSP, Span., Eliz.,* I, 591–92.
29. *Burghley Papers,* II, 762.
30. *CSP, Span., Eliz.,* I, 592.
31. *JHC,* I, 75–76.
32. Neale, *Parliaments,* p. 144.
33. *CSP, Span., Eliz.,* I, 592–93.
34. Neale, *Parliaments,* p. 144; Clifford, II, 553–55.
35. *CSP, Span., Eliz.,* I, 594.
36. *JHC,* I, 76.
37. Neale, *Parliaments,* p. 145.
38. *CSP, Span., Eliz.,* I, 590–91, 597.
39. Neale, *Parliaments,* pp. 146–50.
40. *CSP, Span., Eliz.,* I, 595.
41. *JHC,* I, 76.
42. *CSP, Span., Eliz.,* I, 595.
43. Neale, *Parliaments,* p. 152.
44. *JHC,* I, 76–77.
45. *CSP, Span., Eliz.,* I, 597–98.
46. *PRO, SP, Dom., Eliz.,* XLI, 22.
47. Neale, *Parliaments,* p. 157.
48. *JHC,* I, 78.
49. *DNB,* I, 112.
50. *Burghley Papers,* II, 726.
51. *Return of Members,* p. 402; *LIBB,* I, 323.
52. Neale, *Parliaments,* p. 152.
53. *PRO, SP, Dom., Eliz.,* XLI, 28.
54. *Ibid.,* XLI, 29.
55. *Burghley Papers,* I, 449.
56. *CSP, Scot.,* II, 310.
57. *CSP, Span., Eliz.,* I, 601.
58. *CSP, Dom.,* VI, 19.
59. *JHC,* I, 78.
60. Lansdowne MS. 1236, fol. 42.
61. Neale, *Parliaments,* p. 164.
62. *Ibid.,* pp. 174–75.
63. *CSP, Span., Eliz.,* I, 602, 607.
64. Elton, *Constitution,* p. 303n.
65. Neale, *Parliaments,* p. 28.
66. *Ibid.,* pp. 51–84.
67. Quoted in Black, p. 78.

Chapter Eleven

1. 5 Eliz., c. 1; *SR,* IV, 402–5.
2. Collier, pp. 48–49.
3. *Ibid.,* p. 47.
4. Pollen, *Catholics,* pp. 116–17.
5. *CSP, Span., Eliz.,* I, 617–18.
6. *Ibid.,* I, 626.
7. *Ibid.,* I, 638.
8. *Ibid.,* I, 641.
9. *Ibid.,* I, 618–19.
10. *Ibid.,* I, 620.

11. *Ibid.,* I, 690.   12. *Ibid.,* I, 626.

13. *CSP, Dom.,* I, 305.   14. *CSP, Span., Eliz.,* II, 4.

15. *Ibid.,* II, 85, 229, 325, 383, 490.

16. Black, pp. 97–98.   17. Neale, *Parliaments,* p. 181.

18. *Ibid.,* pp. 226–34.   19. *Ibid.,* pp. 178–79.

20. *Ibid.,* pp. 228–33.

21. On the late Elizabethan succession question, see Stafford; see also Hurstfield, "Succession," pp. 369–96.

Bibliography

Bibliography

For abbreviations, see p. 215.

Additional MSS., British Museum.

Allegations against Mary: Allegations against the Surmised Title of the Queen of Scots and the Favorers of the Same. Ashmolean MS. 829, fols. 23–31; Cambridge MS. Dd. ix 14, fols. 53–64; *HM* 4627, no. 2, pp. 1–32.

Allegations in behalf of Mary: Allegations in behalf of . . . the Lady Mary, Now Queen of Scots, against the Opinions . . . Touching the Succession. . . . Printed in a 19-page appendix to Atwood. Cotton MS. Caligula B IX, vol. II, fols. 233–43; Ashmolean MS. 829, fols. 12–23.

Allen, J. W. A History of Political Thought in the Sixteenth Century. London, 1928.

Answer to Allegations against Mary. Cambridge MSS. Gg. iii 34, pp. 107–17, and Dd. ix 14, fols. 64–70; Ashmolean MS. 829, fols. 31–36.

Ashmolean MSS., Bodleian Library.

Atwood, William. The Fundamental Constitution of the English Government Proving King William and Queen Mary Our Lawful and Rightful King and Queen. London, 1690.

Bailey, Alfred. The Succession to the English Crown. London, 1879.

Bain, Joseph. The Edwards in Scotland. Edinburgh, 1901.

Beames, John. A Translation of Glanville. London, 1812.

Biographia Britannica. London, 1757.

Black, J. B. The Reign of Elizabeth. Oxford, 1936.

Brown, M. C. Mary Tudor, Queen of France. London, 1911.

Burghley Papers, ed. Saml. Haynes and Wm. Murdin. London, 1740–59.

Burgoyne, F. J., ed. Leycester's Commonwealth. London, 1904.

Calendar of the Patent Rolls, Elizabeth. London, 1939–64.

Calendar of Salisbury Manuscripts. Historical Manuscripts Commission. London, 1883–1940.

Calendar of State Papers:

    Domestic. London, 1856–72.

    Foreign. London, 1861–1950.

    Relating to Scotland and Mary Queen of Scots. Edinburgh and Glasgow, 1898–1952.

    Spanish. London, 1862–1954.

    Spanish, Elizabeth. London, 1892–99.

    Venetian. London, 1864–1940.

Cambridge MSS., Cambridge University Library.

The Cambridge Modern History. Cambridge, 1903.

Camden, William. The History of Queen Elizabeth. Vol. II of Kennett.

Castelnau, Michael de. Memoirs of the Reigns of Francis II and Charles IX of France. London, 1724.

Clapham, John. Elizabeth of England. E. P. and Conyers Read, eds. Philadelphia, Pa., 1951.

Clifford, Arthur, ed. The State Papers and Letters of Sir Ralph Sadler. Edinburgh, 1809.

Collier, J. P., ed. The Egerton Papers. London, 1840.

The Complete Peerage. London, 1910–49.

Cooper, C. H. and Thompson. Athenae Cantabrigienses. Cambridge, 1858.

Cotton MSS., British Museum.

Courtney, L. H. "The Tragedy of 'Ferrex and Porrex,' " *Notes and Queries,* ser. ii, X(1860), 261–63.

Craik, G. L. The Romance of the Peerage. London, 1848.

Dasent, J. R., ed. Acts of the Privy Council. London, 1890–1907.

Dictionary of National Biography. London, 1908–9.

Disraeli, Isaac. Curiosities of Literature. London, 1866.

Dixon, R. W. History of the Church of England. Oxford, 1878–1902.

Dyer, Sir James. Reports. Trans. and ed. John Vaillant. London, 1794.

Egerton MSS., British Museum.

Ellis, Sir Henry. Original Letters, Illustrative of English History. London, 1824–46.

Elton, G. R. England Under the Tudors. London, 1955.

———. The Tudor Constitution. Cambridge, 1960.

Encyclopaedia Britannica. 13th ed. London, 1926.

Fabyan, Robert. The New Chronicles of England and France. Sir Henry Ellis, ed. London, 1811.

Fleming, D. H. Mary Queen of Scots, from her Birth to her Flight into England. London, 1898.

Forbes, Patrick. A Full View of the Public Transactions in the Reign of Queen Elizabeth. London, 1711–12.

Foxe, John. Acts and Monuments. Josiah Pratt, ed. London, 1870.

Froude, J. A. The Reign of Elizabeth. London, 1912.

Fuller, Thomas. The Church History of Britain. J. S. Brewer, ed. Oxford, 1845.

Gairdner, James. History of the Life and Reign of Richard the Third. Cambridge, 1898.

Garrett, C. H. The Marian Exiles. Cambridge, 1938.

Gierke, Otto. Political Theories of the Middle Age. Cambridge, 1900.

Green, A. W. The Inns of Court and Early English Drama. New Haven, Conn., 1931.

Green, M. A. E. Lives of the Princesses of England. London, 1849–55.

Hale, Sir Matthew. The History of the Pleas of the Crown. London, 1736.

Hales, John. A Declaration of the Succession of the Crown Imperial of England. Hargrave, pp. xx–xliii; *HM* 4666, fols. 1–19; Sloane MS. 827, fols. 1–17; Cambridge MS. Gg. iii 34, pp. 144–73; Rawlinson MS. B 7, fols. 1–14.

Hallam, Henry. Constitutional History of England. London, 1912.

Hargrave, Francis (under pseud. Geo. Harbin). The Hereditary Right of the Crown of England Asserted. London, 1713.

Harington, Sir John. Nugae Antiquae. Thos. Park, ed. London, 1804.

———. A Tract on the Succession to the Crown, A.D. 1602. London, 1880.

Harleian MSS., British Museum.

Henderson, T. F. Mary Queen of Scots. London, 1905.

Holdsworth, W. S. A History of English Law. London, 1903–26.

Holinshed, Raphael. Chronicles of England, Scotland, and Ireland. London, 1807–8.

Howard, G. E. A History of Matrimonial Institutions. Chicago, 1904.

Hurstfield, Joel. The Queen's Wards: Wardship and Marriage Under Elizabeth I. London, 1958.

———. "The Succession Struggle in Late Elizabethan England," in Elizabethan Government and Society: Essays Presented to Sir John Neale, ed. S. T. Bindoff, Joel Hurstfield, and C. H. Williams. London, 1961.

Jackson, J. E. "Wulfhall and the Seymours," *Wiltshire Archaeological and Natural History Magazine,* XV(1875), 140–207.

Jewel, John. Apologia Ecclesiae Anglicanae. London, 1562.

Journals of the House of Commons. London, 1803.

Kennett, White. A Complete History of England. London, 1706.

Klarwill, Victor von. Queen Elizabeth and Some Foreigners. Trans. T. H. Nash. London, 1928.

Knappen, M. M. Tudor Puritanism. Chicago, 1939.

Labanoff, Prince Alexandre, Lettres, instructions, et mémoires de Marie Stuart, Reine d'Écosse. London, 1844.

Lamond, Elizabeth, ed. A Discourse of the Common Weal of this Realm of England. Cambridge, 1893.

Lansdowne MSS., British Museum.

Lapsley, G. T. "The Parliamentary Title of Henry IV," *English Historical Review,* XLIX(1934), 423–49, 577–606.

Legg, J. W. "Notes on the Marriage Service in the Book of Common Prayer of 1549," in Ecclesiological Essays. London, 1905.

Leslie, John. A Defense of the Honor of . . . Mary, Queen of Scotland . . . , with a Declaration as well of Her Right, Title, and Interest to the Succession of the Crown of England. . . . London, 1569. Also Liège, 1571; Rheims, 1580 and 1584; Rouen, 1587. Citations are to the London edition.

Lettenhove, Kervyn de. Relations politiques de Pays-Bas et de l'Angleterre sous le règne de Philippe II. Brussels, 1882–1900.

The Letter. Ashmolean MS. 829, fols. 36–40; Cambridge MS. Dd. ix 14, fols. 70–74.

Letters and Papers, Foreign and Domestic, of the Reign of Henry VIII. London, 1862–1932.

Levine, Mortimer. "A 'Letter' on the Elizabethan Succession Question, 1566," *Huntington Library Quarterly*, XIX(1955), 13–38.

————. "A More Than Ordinary Case of 'Rape,' 13 and 14 Elizabeth I," *American Journal of Legal History*, VII(1963), 159–63.

————. "A Parliamentary Title to the Crown in Tudor England," *Huntington Library Quarterly*, XXV(1962), 121–27.

————. "Richard III—Usurper or Lawful King?" *Speculum*, XXXIV (1959), 391–401.

A Lewd Pasquil Set Forth by Certain of the Parliament Men, 8 Elizabeth. Cambridge MS. Ff. v 14, fol. 826.

MacCaffrey, W. T. "England: The Crown and the Aristocracy," *Past and Present*, no. 30 (1965), pp. 52–64.

Machyn, Henry. The Diary of . . . J. G. Nichols, ed. London, 1848.

Maitland, F. W. "The Anglican Settlement and the Scottish Reformation," in *CMH*, vol. II.

————. The Constitutional History of England. Cambridge, 1920.

————. Selected Essays, ed. H. D. Hazeltine, G. T. Lapsley, and P. H. Winfield. Cambridge, 1936.

McIlwain, C. H. The American Revolution: A Constitutional Interpretation. New York, 1923.

More, Cressacre. The Life of Sir Thomas More. Jos. Hunter, ed. London, 1828.

Mullinger, J. B. "Philip and Mary," in *CMH*, vol. II.

Mumby, F. A. Elizabeth and Mary Stuart. London, 1914.

————. The Fall of Mary Stuart. London, 1921.

Naunton, Sir Robert. Fragmenta Regalia. London, 1870.

Neale, Sir J. E. The Age of Catherine de Medici. London, 1943.

————. Elizabeth I and Her Parliaments, 1559–1581. London, 1953.

————. The Elizabethan House of Commons. London, 1949.

————. "Parliament and the Succession Question in 1562/3 and 1566," *English Historical Review*, XXXVI(1921), 497–520.

————. Queen Elizabeth. London, 1938.

Nicholas, Sir Harris. Memoirs and Literary Remains of Lady Jane Grey. London, 1832.

Nichols, J. G. The Chronicle of Queen Jane. London, 1850.

————. The Progresses and Public Processions of Queen Elizabeth. London, 1823.

Norton, Thomas, and Thomas Sackville. The Tragedy of Gorboduc, in A Supplement to Dodsley's Old Plays, III, 90–160. London, 1853.

Painter, Sidney. The Reign of King John. Baltimore, 1949.

Parsons, Robert. A Conference About the Next Succession to the Crown of England. Antwerp(?), 1594.

Peck, G. T. "John Hales and the Puritans During the Marian Exile," in Church History. Berne, 1941.

Philippson, Martin. Histoire du règne de Marie Stuart. Paris, 1891–92.

Pickthorn, Kenneth. Early Tudor Government: Henry VII. Cambridge, 1934.

———. Early Tudor Government: Henry VIII. Cambridge, 1934.

Plowden, Edmund. Commentaries. Dublin, 1792.

———. A Treatise Proving ... the Queen of Scots ... Not Disabled ... to Receive the Crown of England ... ; A Brief Declaration of the Invalidity of the Last Will of ... Henry VIII. Rawlinson MS. A 124, fols. 1–47; HM 849, fols. 1–38.

Pollard, A. F. England Under Protector Somerset. London, 1900.

———. Henry VIII. London, 1905.

———. The Political History of England, 1547–1603. London, 1910.

———. "The Reformation Under Edward VI," in CMH, vol. II.

Pollard, A. W., and G. R. Redgrave. A Short-Title Catalogue of Books Printed in England, Scotland, and Ireland, and of English Books Printed Abroad, 1547–1640. London, 1926.

Pollen, J. H. The English Catholics in the Reign of Queen Elizabeth. London, 1920.

———. A Letter from Mary Queen of Scots to the Duke of Guise, January 1562. Edinburgh, 1904.

———. Papal Negotiations with Mary Queen of Scots During her Reign in Scotland, 1561–67. Edinburgh, 1901.

———. "The Question of Queen Elizabeth's Successor," The Month, CI(1903), 517–32.

Pollock, Sir Frederick, and F. W. Maitland. The History of English Law Before Edward I. Cambridge, 1895.

Powell, C. L. English Domestic Relations, 1487–1653. New York, 1917.

Proctor, Francis, and W. H. Frere. A New History of the Book of Common Prayer. London, 1905.

Public Record Office. State Papers, Domestic, Elizabeth.

Rait, R. S. Relations Between England and Scotland. London, 1901.

Rapin, W. Acta Regia. London, 1727.

Rawlinson MSS., Bodleian Library.

Read, Conyers. Mr. Secretary Cecil and Queen Elizabeth. New York, 1955.

———. The Tudors. New York, 1936.

The Records of the Honorable Society of Lincoln's Inn: The Black Books. London, 1897.

Return of Members of the House of Commons, 1213–1874. Accounts and Papers, vol. XVII(1878), part 1.

Robinson, A. M. F. "Queen Elizabeth and the Valois Princes," *English Historical Review,* II(1887), 40–77.

Robinson, Hastings, ed. The Zurich Letters. Cambridge, 1846.

Rotuli Parliamentorum. London, 1767–77.

Rowse, A. L. The England of Elizabeth. London, 1951.

Russell, E. Maitland of Lethington. London, 1912.

Rutton, W. L. *Notes and Queries,* ser. viii (1895), VI, 121–22.

Rymer, Thos., ed. Foedera. London, 1726–35.

Sackville, Thomas. The Complaint of Henry Duke of Buckingham. Marguerite Hearsey, ed. New Haven, Conn., 1936.

Salzman, L. F., ed. The Victoria History of the County of Warwick. London, 1951.

Sayles, G. O. The Medieval Foundations of England. London, 1948.

Sloane MSS., British Museum.

Smith, L. B. "The Last Will and Testament of Henry VIII: A Question of Perspective," *Journal of British Studies,* II(1962), no. 1, 14–27.

Smith, Sir Thomas. De Republica Anglorum. Leonard Alston, ed. Cambridge, 1906.

Stafford, H. G. James VI of Scotland and the Throne of England. New York, 1940.

State Papers, Henry VIII. London, 1830–52.

Statutes of the Realm, London, 1810–28.

Steuart, A. F., ed. Memoirs of Sir James Melville of Halhill. New York, 1930.

Stone, Laurence. "The Educational Revolution in England, 1560–1640," *Past and Present,* no. 28 (1964), pp. 41–80.

Strickland, Agnes. Lives of the Tudor and Stuart Princesses. London, 1868.

Strype, John. The Life of the Learned Sir Thomas Smith. London, 1689.

———. Memorials of . . . Thomas Cranmer. . . . 3d ed. London, 1853.

Symonds, J. A. Shakespeare's Predecessors in the English Drama. London, 1900.

Tanner, J. R. English Constitutional Conflicts of the Seventeenth Century. Cambridge, 1928.

———. Tudor Constitutional Documents. Cambridge, 1940.

Tanner MSS., Bodleian Library.

Taswell-Langmead, T. P. English Constitutional History from the Teutonic Conquest to the Present Time. 10th ed. T. F. T. Plucknett. Boston, 1946.

Teulet, Alexandre. Relations politiques de la France et l'Espagne avec l'Écosse au XVIe siècle. Paris, 1862.

Trevelyan, G. M. England in the Age of Wycliffe. London, 1909.

Tytler, P. F. England Under the Reigns of Edward VI and Mary. London, 1839.

Vergil, Polydore. Urbinatis Anglicae historiae libri vigintisex. Basel, 1546.

Watt, H. A. Gorboduc; or Ferrex and Porrex. Madison, Wis., 1910.

Weiss, Chas., ed. Papiers d'État du Cardinal de Granvelle. Paris, 1841–52.

Whittingham, William. A Brief Discourse of the Troubles at Frankfort, 1554–1558 A.D. Edward Arber, ed. London, 1908.

Wright, Thomas. Queen Elizabeth and her Times. London, 1838.

Wycoff, W. T. Feudal Relations Between the Kings of England and Scotland Under the Early Plantagenets. Chicago, 1897.

Yorke, Philip, second Earl of Hardwicke, ed. Miscellaneous State Papers. London, 1778.

Index